daddy's girl

ARMINLEAR

Library of Congress Control Number: 2022947997

ISBN (hardback): 978-1-956450-35-4
(paperback): 978-1-956450-36-1
(eBook): 978-1-956450-37-8

Armin Lear Press Inc
215 W Riverside Drive, #4362
Estes Park, CO 80517

daddy's girl

A Father, His Daughter,
and the Deadly Battle She Won

Michael A. Schnabel

ARMINLEAR

Dedicated to:
Stephanie, our warrior and the bravest person I have ever known.
Colleen, Mark, and Caden who championed her quest.
Scott, who helps others deal with life.

Those in crisis, I pray you find hope and help.

A blessing takes place in the woods as a doe gives birth to her fawn. Instincts take over as the deer cleans and feeds her offspring. Her maternal drive is so powerful she would risk her life to protect the newborn from danger. Yet that ultimate offering would seal the newborn's fate, so the mother must also save herself.

chapter 1

PARENTING IS A SIDE EFFECT OF SEX. That doesn't sound right.

Parenting is the art of raising a child. That's too fluffy and nondescript.

Parenting needs to be experienced to be fully understood, and each experience is different. Let's go with that.

My daughter Stephanie has always been drawn to children and started babysitting at age ten. That helped motivate her to become a teacher – no, check that – a caring teacher devoted to helping her students. You remember teachers like that, don't you?

Stephanie is pregnant with her first child. She and her husband Mark couldn't be happier or more excited. Into her second trimester, new emotions of anxiety and fear enter their lives as pain and bleeding force her to the hospital. The doctors can't do the testing needed because it could place the baby at risk. Stephanie makes it clear they can't do anything that puts her child in danger.

The pain and bleeding get worse leading to more hospital stays. Mark is asleep when Stephanie makes her decision. She confides to her unborn child, sharing her deep dark secret. Steph believes she has cancer. Knowing how crazy it sounds, she hasn't told anyone else. Steph then writes in the child's baby journal: *My top priority is to have a healthy baby, so I keep telling myself to tough it out and keep my eye on the prize. You are that prize, little one. I love you and pray you are all right.* Stephanie is becoming a parent.

I can't sleep the night before my daughter's C-section. For the first time in Stephanie's pregnancy, I am terrified. Worry about the delivery and fear of the unknown blocks out everything else. As I sit in our kitchen, she smiles at me from pictures on our refrigerator as if to say everything will be all right. My eyes well up as I wonder if I take her love for granted, and memories of Steph as a child flood my mind.

The first time I accept full responsibility for my daughter is when my wife Colleen, getting a much-deserved break, goes to dinner with girlfriends. It leaves a lasting impression. We are doing great and then an hour into our adventure Steph begins to cry. No problem, I've been changing diapers, burping, and rocking her to sleep for weeks, so what could go wrong? The diaper is dry, she doesn't want a bottle, and the faster I rock, the louder she cries. I lay her on a blanket and bring out the toys. She senses I'm not getting it and believes if she screams louder, I might understand. I start to sweat and become more flushed than she is. As I promise her anything, the phone rings, and it's Colleen asking. "Is everything alright?"

"Yeah, I think so."

"You think so?"

"Well, your daughter won't quit crying, but I'm handling it," I lied. "Why did you call?"

"We just finished dinner, and my milk let down. Sometimes

that happens when the baby cries, so I thought I would check in with you."

What is this, some alert system that goes off when I fail at being a good father? I come clean and tell her I don't know what else to do. My wife laughs and says she is on her way home. Stephanie melts into Colleen's arms, nurses, and falls asleep. She just wanted her mom. Thankfully, I will improve, and soon she becomes a Daddy's Girl. Over the next sixteen years Steph grows into her five-foot-two-inch trim frame, topped off with long brown curly locks.

We remain a tight-knit family even as Steph and her brother Scott become adults. Our home is a refuge where they can escape, remember simpler times, and get advice. It's great to help each other deal with life's business, and Steph hasn't run out of questions to ask. We try to provide honest if not wise answers.

"Daddy, can I live in the Disney Castle?"

"No sweetheart, no one really lives there."

"Daddy, will I ever fall in love and get married?"

"Yes, honey, I'm sure of it."

"Dad, how do I know if he's the right one?"

"Because you won't be able to live without him in your life."

"Dad, do you think we will ever have kids?"

"You are so loving and patient with children that I'm sure you will have your own."

The questions become more challenging as the children grow older.

"Dad, am I going to die?"

The day after answering that question, I begin writing a journal to our grandchild.

In each person's life, some events forever change their course.

Stephanie experiences two in as many weeks. The birth of her first child and news she has an eight percent chance of living. At twenty-seven she is haunted by one question: Will my baby only know me through videos and pictures?

This story is about love, hope, and survival as three generations of a family respond to a crisis. The newborn's deep brown eyes and unconditional love fuel Stephanie's courage. Her faith comes from the belief that something greater than ourselves provides us with what we need, when we need it. Her maternal instincts tell her she must survive to raise her child, and that above everything else defines her quest. Love is the bond that holds us together in hard times and helps us celebrate good times. Hope keeps us moving forward.

My purpose in writing this is to document Stephanie's strength and bravery, in case she's not here for her child to experience first-hand. How does a father capture the soul and essence of his daughter to pass on to her newborn? That is my challenge and gift to my grandchild. By the time the child is old enough to read this, he will already know his mother's fate. I don't know that outcome, and am more frightened than I have ever been. There is nothing more important than her survival. Nothing.

Stephanie is undergoing her second surgery in two weeks. First, she had a cesarean to bring her child into this world early and begin a new life. Now three surgeons are working to save hers. But her story begins before that. In college, she meets Mark, and they are married in our back yard. Two years later, they learn she is pregnant.

chapter 2

I NEEDED TO EXPERIENCE PARENTING to understand it because I had no idea what I was getting into. It's easy to judge others on their parental skills and overlook the strength of the emotions hidden inside. When it's your emotions, everything changes. A crying baby inflates fear and uncertainty, replacing logic with self-doubt and anxiety. What do I do now, why don't I know these things, why aren't babies born with an owner's manual on their butt, guiding us in the right direction and providing updates with each diaper change? That would be so cool. Instead, Colleen, the five-foot brunette fireball I was smart enough to marry, teaches me to simply love and nurture the child, and let the rest come naturally.

As the delivery team preps Colleen, my anxiety grows. Everything that can go wrong runs through my mind. That's the price of being so analytical. When I am about to panic, a nurse leads me into the delivery room. My mind settles as I see my wife is all right. Uncomfortable, but all right. She shares her experience by digging fingernails into my hand as I count through the contractions. Colleen is determined to have a natural childbirth – a 70s thing to lessen the baby's exposure to drugs – no matter how much mom suffers. But we are together, and that helps us both. I am relieved that the graphic sights and antiseptic smells haven't put me on the floor, since real men don't faint. Well, at least not until a few years later, but that's another story.

Then it happens. My heart beats like a kettledrum as I hold my brand-new daughter. She is beautiful, soft, helpless, and did I say beautiful? Her perfect life flashes before me until I realize I don't have a clue what to do with this stranger in my arms. I have never taken care of a baby before. Is this the way to hold her, what if she slips out of my hands? With my anxiety returning, I look across the room, seeing Colleen's face glow with love and relief after twenty-four hours of labor. Then I become aware of the doctor still helping her. Is that a look of concern on his face? What am I doing? I need to be with the love of my life, and I'm stuck holding this little person I just met. The first issue I interpret as a crisis, and I'm ready to hand off our baby. I guess that will count against me as the father of the year. The birthing team finishes their work quickly as both mother and daughter are doing fine. Half an hour later, my all-knowing wife formally introduces me to our daughter Stephanie, starting one of the most important and rewarding relationships of my life. Slowly I begin to understand. Colleen has been the center of my world for seven years. I don't want to take any love away from her to give to someone else. Then this gift from God snuck into my heart and taught me a lesson. Love is not something finite; it's a bottomless source that only requires me to share it. I'm amazed by how much I still have to learn about life.

Later that night, I write a love letter to Colleen, then sleep through nine inches of rain that fills our neighborhood. Lawns and streets disappear in water from door to door, and four feet in our basement. I'm not an expert about parenting, but I don't think it's supposed to start with a flood.

On July 4, 2005 Steph and Mark announce her pregnancy. Colleen and I are thrilled that our first grandchild is on the way. Colleen wants to be called Nana, and I like Papa. Grandparenting should be easier than parenting based on several things. First, you've been through this before and hopefully learned something. Second, if you didn't, you can just give the child back when you've had enough of them. Third, you can spoil the child to gain their affection and only receive minor aftershocks from the parents.

Steph and Mark share the news, shop for the nursery, and hear the baby's heartbeat, which energizes their emotions. As the reality sets in, they start a Baby Journal with a simple entry: *'I write this for you, little one, so you know how excited your Mommy and Daddy are to meet you. We can't wait to hold you and share our lives with you. Love, Mommy.'* Afterward, they talk about how much their lives are going to change. The magnitude of the change thundering into their lives is beyond their imagination.

At the beginning of Stephanie's second trimester, a sonogram shows the first pictures of their little angel, who is the size of a peanut. Not wanting to know the gender, they embrace *Peanut* as a perfect pre-birth name. They read to Peanut every night, hoping the baby will recognize their voices at birth. Mark reads as Steph rubs her growing baby bump and dreams about what it will be like to be a mom. Nana and I help the kids paint the nursery, but soon the walls scream BIG BIRD YELLOW, leading to a second coat with a less traumatic color for anyone in the room. Most nights Steph wakes up craving bagels and chocolate milk, so she sneaks down to the kitchen and stuffs herself. To offset this habit, she walks with Mark most mornings. After the walks, Peanut stretches and pokes around, but never wants to sleep. The exception is when Steph sits in the rocking chair, where its rhythm always settles the little one down.

The first four months of pregnancy pass smoothly. Then in late October, Steph begins to have abdominal pain and some bleeding. She doesn't panic, but what pregnant woman wouldn't be concerned? Dr. Christopher Lynch, Steph's OB/GYN examines her, saying everything appears to be okay. Afterward, Steph and Mark drive to visit his family for Thanksgiving. The five-hour trip becomes difficult as cramps double her over, and her stools turn dark with blood. They know this isn't good and hope it will stop soon. Peanut continues to be very active, practicing soccer kicks, which they believe is a positive sign. Thanksgiving Day is a struggle, and their fears increase as the bleeding continues. Steph calls her mom, who usually knows what to do. Nurse Nana tells her to get to a doctor as soon as possible. It's late in the evening, so they leave for home early the next morning.

An on-call doctor directs them to the Maternity Ward where Colleen and I meet them. Our concern is very high since Steph is only twenty-six weeks along, has abdominal spasms and her hemoglobin has dropped significantly from the blood loss. She needs fluids and knows what that means.

Steph hates needles. When she was seven, she spent time at a children's hospital where needles were plentiful. I told her, "Sweetheart, I'm sorry, but we have to do this. The easy way is you sit here, take my hand and let the nurse give the shot. Or, I can hold you down and you still get the shot." One of the larger nurses said, "I like your dad's style, and he's telling you the truth." Steph didn't like it, but knew I was right. Most times, she shut her eyes, crushed my hand, and took it, but she never got used to needles.

Stephanie's veins are small and have always been tough to

access. The nurse finds a vein on the third stick and hangs an IV bag filled with fluids. After several hours the pain and cramping slow down, but Steph remains afraid and prays that her baby is all right. Colleen and I give her a little stuffed lamb, which Steph names Lambie. Lambie is kitten-soft and Steph snuggles her, imagining what it will be like to cuddle her baby. Mark never leaves his wife's side, holding her hand from a chair as she catches up on her rest. His six-foot-five-inch solid frame is too much for the chair, but he never complains as he tries to sleep in it. He escapes his increasing concern by seeing to his wife's every need, which helps him deal with the helplessness of the situation. This gentle giant is Steph's rock, and she loves him so much. They are fortunate to have each other.

The doctor keeps our patient for observation and tests, so her sixth graders need a substitute teacher. Being protective of her kids, Steph talks the doctor into letting her leave for two hours to complete lesson plans for the sub. Steph takes her teaching responsibilities seriously and knows first-hand the impact one teacher can have on a child.

Long before, one of Steph's middle school teachers had told Colleen and me that our daughter wasn't college material because she didn't get it. We had disagreed and sought outside help, who uncovered a learning disorder and taught Steph how to overcome it. Steph not only got it, but she also worked hard earning straight As her last two years in college. Her grades weren't that good the first year, possibly because she shared a house with two boys and a cat. It reminded me of the television show *Three's Company*, only the gender mix was reversed. Steph had had the support of Colleen and even Grandma Agnes, who thought it was a good idea for her to stay with the boys. But I had been unconvinced. Steph had told me, "Dad, it's okay. Nothing is going on and living with two guy friends, I couldn't be safer." Eventually I believed her, and she didn't disappoint us.

Now, after completing her lesson plans, our daughter is being prepped for a procedure to examine the lower portion of her colon. More informative procedures are ruled out, as they could induce labor or harm Peanut. Steph makes it boot camp clear they cannot do anything to risk the baby's health.

The doctor finds two polyps and a bleeding ulcer. This is based on a minimal entry to prevent the start of contractions. He believes the ulcer is causing the bleeding and pain but plans a full colonoscopy after birth. He prescribes medicine to heal the ulcer and releases Steph. We are relieved and happy it's nothing serious.

Over the next month, the pain and blood return and grow in severity. We try everything the doctor and Nurse Nana suggest but nothing helps. Christmas comes with relatives and festivities, and Stephanie tries to stay in the spirit of things, but the now sharp, knife-like pain and fear make it difficult. Steph's OB/GYN admits her to the hospital and brings in a GI specialist.

The GI Doc runs tests and says there is nothing else that can be done. Mark sees his wife's suffering and insists there must be something that can help her with the pain. The doctor tries to reassure them by saying, "This isn't anything catastrophic, and if it were, I would be treating her differently. You need to be patient." Stephanie asks him if it could be colon cancer. He smiles and tells her, "There's no way it could be, because we don't see colon cancer in twenty-seven-year-olds." Steph is released from the hospital even though she is still in pain. Her physician Dr. Lynch is now planning a C-section to take the baby early.

Mark reads to the child with a hand on his wife's tummy, smiling each time the baby kicks it. After he falls asleep, Steph confides in her unborn child, sharing her deep dark secret:

Throughout the pregnancy, she has believed she has cancer. Knowing how crazy it sounds, she hasn't told anyone, but believes it's true. The pain and bleeding have confirmed her fears. Steph writes in the Baby Journal to let Peanut know how committed she is to having a healthy baby–her priority and the "prize" she longs for, loves, and prays for.

Soon Stephanie is back in the hospital getting fluids, which consistently help with the pain. The GI doctor prescribes three drugs and releases her. At a follow-up visit, she tells him the pain is increasing and that the new meds aren't helping, only adding side effects. The steroids make her feet swell up so much, she can only fit into her Crocks. The doctor again tells her to be patient and give the drugs more time to work. He smiles, but is in a rush and doesn't seem to hear any of Steph's concerns.

That night she shares her frustration with Mark, Nana, and me, looking for advice. Nana and I have experience in the medical world, each having spent over thirty years in it, Nana as a registered nurse and me in pharmaceuticals. I offer to go along for support on her next GI visit, and she likes that idea.

There are baby showers celebrating Steph and Mark's good fortune thrown by her sixth graders, neighbors, and friends. The Grandma's shower has pink and blue cookies revealing the baby names, Caden if a boy and Ashlynn if a girl.

Stephanie's pain and bleeding continue to increase. She calls the GI doctor's office from school at 8:00 a.m., noon, and 3:30 p.m. without any calls returned. Nana takes her to an OB appointment since Steph doesn't feel safe driving with the intense pain. Mark meets them there. Dr. Lynch monitors for contractions and checks the baby's heartbeat. Peanut looks wonderful on the equipment's screen without any signs of distress. The OB sees Steph's discomfort and admits her to the hospital when he also can't reach the GI doctor. After multiple needle sticks, two bags of fluids begin to ease the pain. Steph is comforted by the sound of the baby's heartbeat on the monitor and laughs when she feels and hears Peanut hiccup. By the time the GI doctor arrives, the discomfort is gone, and he releases her saying there is nothing else they can do until the baby is born.

Four days later, Steph and I meet with the GI doctors. She tells him the treatment doesn't seem to be helping, and the only thing that brings relief is the IV fluid. He dismisses the idea and tells her the fluids are just giving her a placebo effect and nothing more. When we ask additional questions, he seems annoyed and abruptly says there is nothing else that can be done until the baby is born.

Steph and I leave the appointment frustrated and wonder why the doctor is so condescending and short with us. We have been professional in the way we shared our concern over the increasing pain, and nothing was said in a demanding or inappropriate way. We are simply worried that something is very wrong and Steph needs help. Each time we check out the GI doctor with other health professionals, we consistently hear he is a good physician and a nice person. We decide to trust him and stay the course, even though we agree he isn't the best fit for Stephanie. His indifference prompts me to write a life lesson to her unborn child.

✤

life lesson #1

It's important to realize that everyone has bad days. Having spent all of my adult life around physicians, I understand some of the difficulties they face. When you see them, you don't know

what's weighing on their mind. They may have
just shared great news with a patient, or have had
to tell someone they have an incurable disease. A
friend may have died, or the doctor may have just
spent the last 36 hours saving a life. It's easy to put
physicians on a pedestal because of their education
and skill, but they are human and susceptible to
misjudgment, mistakes, and moods like all of us.
Be careful not to judge too quickly. Give others the
benefit of the doubt you would want them to give
you. Also, realize that sometimes in life things just
don't fit, but that doesn't mean you don't learn
something from the experience. Keep looking for
the good, and you will find it. The passing of time
will often help you see things clearly and understand that they happened for a reason.

It's a sunny day, and Steph's pain is tolerable, so we go out for
lunch after the appointment. We talk about how exciting it will
be to have a baby in the house, while we walk into the restaurant
holding hands and laughing about who is going to spoil the baby
more. I kiss my daughter on the cheek and notice a couple staring
at us. I smile telling Stephanie, "They are thinking, there is one of
those old men who had to marry his pregnant secretary." We both
laugh. I am really with my little girl, who held onto me when she
was scared and jumped into my arms when I came home from
work. Steph tells me, "I love you, Daddio." I feel special just having
her in my life.

My daughter is admitted three more times before the end
of January as her discomfort and worry increase. When she is
well enough to teach, she sits in a chair because standing doesn't

work. Dr. Lynch moves up the birth date twice, and it's evident his concern for Stephanie is increasing as he tries to balance the risks for her and her unborn child. The baby is always active, and Steph loves feeling the movement, wondering if she will miss it after birth. She feels excited, anxious, and scared at the same time.

The pain forces Steph to leave church this morning for her seventh hospital admission. Fluids are administered, and the procedure to check the baby's lung development is set for tomorrow. Mark is asleep next to Steph's bed. She watches him, thinking, "He is always there for me and she loves him so much." She sees the worry on his face and prays that everything will be fine.

The next morning the baby plays with the physician throughout the amniocentesis. The doctor is careful and gentle with the long scary needle, but every time she finds a pocket of fluid to sample, Peanut kicks and puts a foot in her way. The fourth try she finds a spot the baby can't reach. The test determines Peanut's lungs are ready for birth. With a big smile on his face, Mark tells the doctor he and Steph are so excited to meet their baby and feel like the luckiest people in the world. The hospital is settling down, and Mark wraps up in a blanket, making the best of the chair next to Steph's bed. As he leans over and kisses her goodnight, they cannot contain their love for each other and the excitement of their future family.

Congratulations, Peanut! Today is your Birth Day! Steph wakes up excited and feels great until a migraine begins to pound in her head. The anesthesiologist is concerned the bright lights in surgery could increase the pain, forcing them to postpone the caesarian. Steph doesn't like that option and starts to get upset.

Thinking I can help, I turn down all the lights and close the window curtain. I tell Steph to close her eyes, breathe deeply, and go to her happy place: Steph is ten years old and we're walking along Ka'anapali Beach in Maui. I tell her we are going to make a memory. She asks what that means, and I tell her to close her eyes and then ask her four questions.

"What can you hear?" She answers, "The waves and seagulls."

"What can you smell?" "The ocean."

"What can you feel?" "I feel the wind, sand, and sun."

"How do you feel?" "Happy!" She giggled.

I laugh and tell her to keep her eyes closed, and while she experiences all these things, picture them in her mind to strengthen the memory. Anytime you want to be at the beach you can close your eyes, bring back this memory, and feel good because you've returned to your happy place.

In the hospital, I gently stroke her hair like petting a kitten. and whisper that I will move the pain right out of your body. All you have to do is relax and go to your happy place. I hum a tune that I sang to Steph as a child, and minutes later, the migraine is gone. She asks me how I did it, and I tell her she just needed to let go and relax. Steph smiles and tells me, "Dad, no one knows me as well as you do."

Things move quickly to the operating room, and the procedure begins. Everything is progressing well, but as they remove the baby, Steph feels empty like part of her is missing. The nurse drops the drape, and Mark announces that Peanut is a boy. Surprised, Steph questions him saying, "We have a what? Are you sure it's a boy?" Dr. Lynch laughs, saying he will check again as he holds the baby up to his nurse for a second opinion. "Yep, he's still a boy!" Mom and Dad look at each other still surprised. For no particular reason, they just believed Peanut was a girl. They name him Caden Marcus.

A nurse quickly cleans the baby up and lays him beside his mother. Steph can't remember anything so beautiful as she strokes his black curly hair while both of them cry. Dr. Sheri Martin, Caden's new pediatrician, checks the baby out, agreeing that he is perfect. Minutes later, Mark, Steph, and Caden are left alone as a family. All the pain and anxiety are gone as Steph starts nursing. She is filled with wonder and thankfulness and excitement and love, knowing this new life is worth all the challenges faced during her pregnancy.

Later Caden is introduced to the rest of our family, and we each agree he is the most extraordinary child in the world. Colleen and I go home late, but I write Steph a note before turning in.

My Dearest Stephanie,

Mom and I are so proud of you. I cannot believe how brave you have been these last few months. You are stronger than I would have ever thought, enduring so much pain and difficulty with this pregnancy, yet most people would never know it. You never complained or stopped being a great wife, daughter, and teacher. And on top of that, somehow you learned to become a great mom.

This afternoon you looked and acted like you had been a mother for years instead of just hours. You were so natural with Caden and at peace with the world, no one would have known the ordeal you've endured before his birth. Your love, patience, and gentleness were incredible to watch.

The night before Caden was born, I couldn't sleep. For the first time in your pregnancy, I was really worried about you. I sat in the kitchen and saw your face smiling at me from the pictures on the refrigerator. I worried about the delivery and wondered if I took your love, spirit, and friendship for granted in my life. So many memories rushed through my mind. The

beach in Maui, the backyard sandbox at our first home, picnics
at Sand Lake, and so many other special times with my little
girl. I prayed everything would be all right and thank God it
is. Now my little girl is a mom.

Please remember that you are in my mind and heart
and will always be my little girl. Life is a journey with many
highs and lows. Caden will be one of the highest points in your
life, just as you have been in mine. Nothing is more important
than that. I love you and feel blessed to have you in my life!

— Papa

The first week home is a dream full of family bonding and new routines. Caden falls into a three-hour sleep schedule, nursing and pooping just like a newborn should. Steph is doing great and Mark helps with everything. He can't believe how much fun it is merely holding his son and watching him sleep.

Nana and I enter Baby World, which exists in the same orbit as Puppy World. Our demeanor changes as we try to be noticed. Expressions become exaggerated. Our voice finds highs and lows and fasts and slows not usually used, to draw the baby's attention. Speech becomes repetitive. We imitate the child and lose ourselves in blissful silliness. The second week everything changes.

chapter 3

STEPHANIE IS HEALING QUICKLY and off her pain meds, but her mind is only focused on fear. The pain and bleeding are back, and now that she has Caden to take care of, she can't get sick. She doesn't fear a painful death or life after death. Her fear is cancer will steal her away from her family with so many things unfinished in her life. As she shares this with us, we remind her not to think the worst because the GI doctor has insisted she is too young for that.

As the week progresses, the pain grows until Steph can't eat or drink anything, then she is directed to the hospital and admitted. Caden and Mark never leave her side, which helps her stay brave. The kindhearted nurses place a newborn bassinet next to her hospital bed, so Caden is always within reach of his mother. Steph balances Lambie on the edge of it. She is mesmerized as Caden reaches out for the stuffed animal and tells him, "Caden, have I told you how precious you are? There is so much I want to tell you, but don't know if I will have enough time."

Stephanie is scheduled for a CT and told she should consider discontinuing nursing since the prep and pain meds will cross over to her milk. She is committed to breastfeeding Caden for its health benefits and wants to put his needs before her own, but makes the difficult decision to stop since pain keeps her from eating or drinking. She feels guilty, but realizes she doesn't really have a choice. The procedure goes smoothly, and the physician stops by the next day with the results. There is a mass in the colon and several spots on the liver, but he won't speculate what they are. A colonoscopy is scheduled in two days to get a closer look and harvest tissue samples. This is not welcome news. We try to stay positive while Steph wonders to herself if this is confirmation of her deep dark fear.

Colleen began her nursing career in a hospital Intensive Care Unit, an opportunity earned by graduating top of her class. She knows how doctors talk and act when things are severe and understands how cancer presents on film. We leave Steph's room late that night, and as we enter the elevator, Nana is overcome with tears and struggles to catch her breath. As I hold her up, she tells me our daughter has cancer. I try to comfort her by saying we need to wait until it's confirmed, but there is no doubt in her mind. I deny the facts, but as I drive home, panic overtakes my mind and then my body. I can't breathe as I realize my wife's nursing instincts are always on target. Pulling off the road, we cry in each other's arms as thoughts race through our heads. We can't let our little girl die ... it has always been our job to protect her ... what if this time we can't ... oh my God, this can't be happening! We are overcome with grief by the time we arrive home and soon find ourselves walking room to room aimlessly. In bed, we hold each other close, as our sleepless night fills with misery.

Colleen and I return to the hospital early the next morning. Stephanie is full of questions for Nurse Nana, but most answers have to wait until we know more. Colleen doesn't share the diagnosis she believes to be true. We hold Caden and focus on his needs to set our worry aside.

Later I sneak out to buy a second Lambie but find none. The clerk sees me struggling and asks if she can help. I explain that we gave the stuffed animal to my newborn grandson, but now his mother's life is at risk. I want a second lamb to be placed with my daughter if we lose her. With trembling lips and damp eyes, the clerk calls to locate the stuffed animal and then arranges for overnight delivery. It's strange what you think of in a crisis. If we lose Steph, I want her and Caden to each have a lamb and in some small way stay linked forever. I am clearly grasping at straws. Would this really help or had I simply bought into the illusion that it would? I couldn't think of anything else to do, and at least this made me feel like I was doing something.

The next day Mark and Colleen accompany Stephanie to the colonoscopy while I stay in her room with Caden. As they leave, my daughter teases me about not remembering what to do with a baby, and says he'd better be in clean diapers with she gets back. We exchange hugs and kisses as we try to be brave, but it's easy to see the fear in each other's eyes.

Stephanie wakes up in recovery with Mark and Nana by her side. When the GI doctor finally comes in, his face is pale and serious. He looks his patient in the eye and tells her she has cancer. Immediately the family starts to cry. Steph is horrified as her mind fills with unanswered questions. Am I going to die ... how long do I have ... will I live to help Caden grow up ... will I even see his first day of school?

The doctor explains this cancer is so unusual that it's only discussed in textbooks. The interior of the colon is covered with thousands of carpet polyps, which look like the top of shag carpeting, and tumors too large for the scope to squeeze past. He has spoken with a surgeon who will meet with us later to discuss an operation already scheduled for the next morning. Our world is turned upside down and shaken hard. Steph tells the doctor she needs to get back to her room, to be with her newborn child.

Mark tells Stephanie it's going to be all right, but her mind is stuck on the horror of never seeing their baby grow up. Two nurses push the bed back to Steph's room while Nana walks alongside holding her daughter's hand. Mark walks behind because he doesn't want his wife to see him crying. His heart is in his stomach as he wonders, "How can my young wife can have cancer? Our dreams have just come true, but now everything is falling apart. I can't go on without my best friend and the love of my life."

I love taking care of Caden, and it brings back memories of my daughter's first year.

After dinner, I take Steph upstairs for a bath while Colleen finishes in the kitchen. Steph is squeaky clean as we return to play. I place her blanket on the floor and throw her binky in the middle of it. She looks at me with excitement in her eyes, and quickly crawls onto her velvety soft pink blanket where she shoves the binky in her mouth and turns onto her back. Her sucking mixes with giggles as I crawl up to her. I wrap her up in the blanket and sit in the rocker. She watches me, waiting for me to smile, then immediately smiles back at me. I rock her, and she falls to sleep quickly. She absolutely owns me, and I love it. I lay her down, and Colleen reminds me it's her turn for a back rub. I guess they both own me.

Now it is Caden smiling at me, making me feel special, until I realize he is just filling his diaper. Oh well, take the smiles when you can get them.

I'm getting anxious waiting for everyone to return, as the

two-hour procedure has turned into four. A nurse opens the door, and I can see it's bad news. Stephanie looks at me with her sad clown face and bursts into tears while Colleen quickly tells me everything. The nurses wipe away tears, telling Steph how sorry they are. And then we are alone. Four adults in the room looking at each other, not knowing what to do or say. It seems impossible to help each other, as each of us is drowning in our own emotions. We are numb with disbelief. We want off this runaway roller-coaster that thrilled us two weeks ago with the miracle of birth and now horrifies us with the possibility of death. In the midst of this is a baby, who remains untouched by the crisis. Like a ray of sunshine, his calm and serenity draw us in, while his smile helps settle us down. Two weeks old and he is accomplishing what no one else can. Nana would tell me later that babies usually don't smile until their first month, but maybe he understands we need it early.

The GI doctor joins us and repeats what he said in recovery, then addresses our questions. Before leaving, he tells us how sorry he is and that the surgeon is on his way to talk to us. Debi, one of the nurses we have grown close to, checks in on us. I think how hard it must be for her to step into this room knowing what we have just learned. She expresses her sorrow and tells us she is here to help with anything we need; the other nurses will cover her additional patients. Debi is compassionate and gentle with us. I ask her to stay when the doctor arrives.

Dr. Bruce Graham, the Colorectal Surgeon, introduces himself and tells us he has reviewed the results of the CT and Colonoscopy and talked to the GI doctor. He is straightforward, as most of the surgeons I have worked with in the past. He draws a picture of the colon, points out locations of the major tumors, and shows the proximity of the surrounding organs to help us understand. He suggests we move quickly to remove the cancer and provide Stephanie relief from the pain and obstructions saying, "This is what I do, I know what I am doing, and perform this type of surgery often."

The doctor explains that the colon absorbs water and nutrients, then forms and eliminates waste. By surgically removing the five feet of colon, waste will pass more frequently. He strongly suggests we proceed the next day to remove the cancerous colon and then presents three surgical options. If things go well, he will leave a few inches of the colon nearest the rectum to reattach her digestive system. That will be decided in surgery where he can examine the damage, see if lymph nodes or other organs are involved, and determine what he has to work with. If the cancer is too advanced or other organs are involved, he may just have to close Steph back up. The room is silent as we process his last sentence.

I look at my family to get their thoughts, but realize they are in shock. The bad news has settled into their minds, and they are struggling to get a grasp on it. I am still numb to it and start asking the surgeon questions. What other organs could be involved … how aggressive is the cancer … what about the three spots on her liver … what risks are associated with the operation … what would you do if it were your daughter? Some questions I just can't ask because I don't want to know the answers.

The discussion continues for an hour as we try to understand the options and how best to move forward. It's overwhelming, but we don't have time for indecision. All the while, Dr. Graham is incredibly patient. He has to repeat himself often, so we fully understand, but he never bats an eye over it. I am afraid of missing something important, but he assures me we covered everything. I ask him if we can talk about it as a family for a few minutes and then give him our decision. He agrees and leaves the room. As Debi starts to follow him out, I ask her to stay.

I've learned that when you don't have experience but have to make a difficult decision quickly, you try to find experienced people you trust to guide you. I tell Debi I want to ask her something, but she doesn't have to answer if she is uncomfortable with it. "We just met this surgeon, and he seems very professional and experienced. You've worked this floor for years and observed his surgical skill, bedside manner, and patient recovery rate. If this were your child, would you choose him?" She thinks about it and answers, "I would. His follow-up is great, and his patients consistently do well." I thank her and ask her to leave for a few minutes.

Colleen thinks to call Dr. Robert Jackson, one of the doctors she has worked with for years and a good friend. Having been the Medical Director at this hospital a few years earlier, he will also have an informed opinion. Colleen quickly explains our situation. Dr. Jackson tells her he wouldn't hesitate using Dr. Graham to operate on anyone in his family and believes him to be an outstanding surgeon. When the doctor and nurse rejoin us, we agree to his plan and thank him for his patience.

After spending nearly two hours with us, the surgeon leaves, saying he is sorry for Stephanie's diagnosis but confident the surgery will put her on track for recovery. The good doctor is exactly what we need. He fills in gaps of knowledge and helps us make critical decisions quickly. His confidence and experience rekindle our hope, and we believe he is a good fit for the surgery.

Steph is still in shock and for a short time doesn't want to be comforted or even hold her child. Afraid she won't survive the surgery, she asks me point blank, "Dad, am I going to die?" What should a father say? With tears spilling from my eyes and my voice failing, I tell her the truth, "Sweetheart, I don't know." Stephanie always trusts me, and right or wrong, I believe she deserves the truth no matter how hard it is to hear. We cry and hold on to each other as tight as we can like somehow that will stop time from moving forward. I want to pretend everything is going to be all right, but I'm not sure, and we both know it. This won't be the last time my little girl asks me that question, and it's true, the questions do get harder as the children grow older.

Looking at my family, it is easy to see that we are just barely hanging on. The cancer news has brought with it additional enemies in the forms of fear, apprehension, and dread. I realize Steph needs to be filled with hope, and instead we are all suffering beside her. This crisis touches each of us in a very personal way, but it's happening to Stephanie. It's her life and future on the line as she stands in the epicenter of this crisis. At this moment, she needs to be infused with hope, the essential element to never giving up.

I stand up and tell my family that we are going to beat this thing. I promise to take Stephanie to the best doctors and hospitals in the world to do it. Nana and I will take care of the bills, even if we have to sell our home to do it, to allow Steph and Mark to focus on the fight and not worry about expense. I look my daughter in the eye and say, "Tonight you can feel sorry for yourself. You can get angry, throw things, and complain that this isn't fair, because it isn't. Anything you want to do or say is okay because you have the right to. But beginning tomorrow, you need to own this disease by taking charge of your attitude and fighting for your life. We will help you get well, but you have to do your part. Is that a deal?" She smiles through her tears and simply whispers, "Yes." We all hug and begin to reconnect, which makes us feel a little better.

I have learned from my business experience that when you

face a big challenge, you shouldn't waste time reacting to it. You need to define it and create a plan of action to overcome it. It's incredible how developing a good plan begins to nurture hope, belief, and self-confidence. And sometimes you have to put on your bravest face and believe in miracles.

Our family commits to a pact that together we are going to beat this thing. Failure won't be considered because our end goal is for Stephanie to survive and lead a healthy life. She will never be alone, one of us will always be with her, and we vow to fight beside her. To celebrate Steph's victories, we discuss rewards like special dinners, margaritas by the pool, and picnics in the tree house yet to be built. Steph sets goals of helping Caden learn to walk and taking him to his first day of school. Slowly our emotions soften, and this becomes a turning point as we band together. We form a Team of Five: the teacher, architect, nurse, sales manager, and two-week-old baby. Not your average team, but one to be reckoned with. Tonight I have been the leader of this team, but each member will take their turn as we start sowing the seeds of hope.

✤

life lesson #2

Sometimes life can be frightening and make you feel like you're alone in the world. Then someone stands beside you with love and support, making you feel stronger than you ever thought was possible. It's an incredible feeling to have somebody there for you, boosting your strength and courage and hope. Remember that when you see a soul in need. It's one thing to act friendly, but so much more to be a true friend. True friends stay with you through the difficult times as well as the good. This attribute is a must to find in anyone you plan to spend your life with.

Stephanie asks me to make sure her baby understands something important about her cancer. It's not his fault in any way; in fact, the opposite may be true. The pregnancy hormones accelerated her cancer's growth, warning us something was wrong. If it had grown slower, we might not have noticed the warning signs until it had spread further. The pregnancy may have provided Steph with her only chance to fight this disease, which started from a single cell and is now destroying her body and life. The baby may have been born just in time to save his mother's life.

My daughter's natural warm smile helps her make new friends quickly. She is trusting and generously opens up her life, allowing herself to be vulnerable. Some people take advantage of this, others may think it a ruse, but most respond by opening up themselves. There is an innocence about her that draws people in, especially children, and much of this comes from her beliefs. She has her flaws as we all do, but she is a student of life and tries to learn from her mistakes.

Stephanie connected with hospital staff on each of her stays, because that's who she is. She knows their children's names, things they have in common, and truly takes an interest in them. Her story spreads quickly through the hospital staff. This is apparent when these new friends begin to stop by to share their sympathy and concern. They seek her out in the hope of somehow helping. Most are moms and can imagine the horror Steph is facing.

The team calls family and friends to let them know what has developed. Scott leaves college to join us. Hearing her cancer may have spread to Steph's liver, he offers part of his. Everyone wants to help, but for now there is little to do but pray and wait. Colleen requests a larger hospital room so we can have the space needed to help care for Steph and her newborn after surgery. The nurses, quickly becoming Steph's guardian angels, find a tuberculosis room with an entry area that provides extra space for baby supplies and two fold-up beds.

Different emotions are surfacing now as Steph feels anger, frustration, and disbelief. Colleen rocks her daughter as she releases these emotions and the tension they bring with them. I drive Mark home to pack what he needs to stay in the hospital with his family. The drive is quiet. I tell him I don't know what to say. He understands.

Mark walks inside his home while I wait in the car. My mind is spinning around the diagnosis and decisions we have made. I jump hearing a knock at my window and turn to see Page, a neighbor and close friend of Steph and Mark's. Page tells me, she doesn't want to intrude but wants us to know how sorry they are. If there is anything they can do, just call, and it will get done. She leans through the window and gives me a hug. This simple gesture will be repeated often and grow in its importance to our family. This is more than just physical contact. It feels like the energy of two souls merging and synergistically expanding, leaving both with more than we had before it happened. It's uplifting, and we become addicted to it.

Mark stays at the hospital with his wife and son tonight just as he did throughout her pregnancy. This is his family. He needs to be with them and watch over them. Colleen and I drive home to our own bed and then lay awake unable to sleep. Sometimes you don't have control of your thoughts as they take you to dark places like funerals, eulogies, and life without a child. Does she want to buried or cremated? We've never discussed it. I try unsuccessfully to block out the dark thoughts, but over and over, I hear her ask, 'Dad, am I going to die?' I'm haunted by the question and that I answered the wrong way. Colleen and I hold each other and eventually doze off to find our dreams reflecting the state of our minds – filled with nightmares and situations out of our control.

Everything around me is dark and cold and damp. In the distance, I see Stephanie's silhouette, and she is calling for me. I try to cry out, but no sound escapes my mouth. I try to run to her, but cannot move. Something is wrapped around my body, holding me in place. She calls again pleading for me to help her. My heart pounds and it's hard to breathe as I struggle. My daughter starts sinking into the ground, screaming, "Dad, please save me." Panic overcomes me as I fight the restraints and watch her disappear into the earth. There is a hand on my shoulder, as I wake up in a cold sweat and out of breath. My legs are tangled in the sheets. Colleen tells me I was thrashing about and moaning. I get up on shaky legs, change into dry pajamas, and walk the house to settle my mind before coming back to bed. Colleen's hands caress my face as she tells me that we will save our daughter. I pray she is right.

chapter 4

STEPHANIE'S GRANDMOTHER WAS BORN on February 14th. Agnes was everything a grandmother should be: patient, loving, an excellent cook and a little plump, which increased her hug-ability. She was the family's peacemaker and accomplished this with little notice or fanfare. She was also Steph's favorite grandparent, and they enjoyed time together. Most days, Agnes baked, and let her grandkids help when they were around. When Stephanie helped, Grandma Aggie made her a special batch of cinnamon toast with brown and white sugar before they started. This reward wasn't because she had earned it; the toast was a diversion to keep her from eating all of the raw baking dough. Agnes swore Steph to secrecy, as she knew Colleen and I wouldn't approve of her eating so much sugar. After baking they would sit down to watch *Days of our Lives* and Agnes would sort out the drama for her grand-daughter while they enjoyed warm sticky caramel rolls and milk.

Steph spent much of the time at Grandma's with her cousin Heather. They had sleepovers and were usually good together. Grandma Aggie let the girls play in the basement where they enjoyed adventures and exercised their freedom away from parents. Sometimes slept down there. At one sleepover while telling scary stories, they jumped when the noisy old furnace kicked in, creaking and moaning as the metal warmed, boosting the girl's imagination and fear. They decided this furnace was the real home of Darth Vader. Between the giggling and fear, both girls soon needed to pee, but Vader's home was centrally placed between the bedroom and stairway and blocked their way. The girls decided it was too dangerous to sneak past it and their five-year-old minds decided that the trashcan would work just fine. Thus began a tradition that took several sleepovers for Grandma to figure out. She scolded them for peeing in the trashcan, while struggling not to laugh at the same time. Agnes has a beautiful soul. We lost her eight years ago after her battle with ALS.

Today is Agnes's birthday and Valentine's Day, which both represent love to Stephanie. She doesn't think it is a coincidence that her operation is also today. Steph believes that Grandma Aggie will be watching over her as three surgeons work to help her. Steph can't sleep and takes a moment to write a note to her son. *Caden, I love you so much. I am terrified and honestly don't know if I will make it off the operating table alive today. I'm not sure if I will see you again and can't imagine you growing up without a mother. You have such an amazing Dad and family around you that you will be fine, but I can't think about us being separated. Every time I worry about the cancer, I look at you and have my reason to keep on fighting. I am determined to live for you, my baby boy. I made a deal with you and the rest of our team that I will never give up. Whatever happens, know that I love you and that I never, ever gave up. Love, Mommy.*

The morning activity begins early, when a nurse arrives to insert a PICC line – a long, thin, hollow tube used to deliver fluids and medicine. The good news is that it can be left in for more extended periods, meaning fewer sticks. The bad news is that the nurse unsuccessfully tries multiple sticks in four locations. Mark and I watch horrified as she then uses a scalpel to locate and enter a vein without anesthesia. Steph is exhausted and feels like a pin cushion, but tries to console the nurse, who feels terrible and leaves in tears after the two-hour ordeal.

The mood settles as Steph and Mark's pastor stops by. He is so positive, and his prayer provides new hope and calms us down. The nurses come to take Steph to surgery, but she won't let go of Caden and says she needs to talk to her mother first. As Nana leans over the bed, her daughter asks, "Mom, will you please take care of my baby boy, if I don't make it?" Nana nods as they both struggle to contain their emotions. Our young mother hands her child to Nana, and the nurses wheel the bed down the hallway. Nana holds Caden tight and stays in the room while the rest of us follow Steph's bed in silence.

Colleen is horrified at Steph's request. It both validates the fear of her death and makes it feel imminent. Is this the last time to kiss her daughter, to touch her warm skin, or to make a wish come true? Colleen's mind can't process everything happening around her. It becomes numb to protect her. The rest of us leave the room without realizing that Colleen is barely hanging on, but mercifully Caden keeps her grounded.

Baby Caden sleeps contently without a care in the world. Two weeks old and he's already brought so much excitement and happiness to our lives. He is so precious and innocent. As his mother fights for her life, I pray Caden continues to be protected from the nightmare that everyone around him is living.

His parents and I walk to the waiting room while Mark stays with Steph as they prep her for surgery. He thinks about the seven hospital visits during her pregnancy and how she found a place in the hearts of so many of the nurses and doctors. Steph has a unique way of touching those around her. She puts others first, and Mark hopes his son will also stay strong in times of trial. Last night his wife asked him to be her rock, but it's so difficult. He told her she has to live and help him raise Caden. He needs her to be healthy and happy and smiling again. That's not too much to ask, is it? As the staff sets up an epidural, Mark stands in the hallway alone. Without his wife, he will be lost.

Dr. Graham visits Steph to discuss the procedure and finds her weeping. The colorectal surgeon takes the time to comfort her and tells her that everything will be okay; she will go to sleep while they remove her cancer and she'll wake up to her new baby. She believes he truly cares and that helps to reassure her.

When the doctor leaves, Mark and I join Stephanie. We try to stay positive and strong and say all the right things; but nothing seems to help and nothing seems real. I feel trapped in an hourglass that has only a little sand left, and I don't know what happens when it runs out. As the sand drops faster, my mind freezes up and my anxiety increases. I fear that I am wasting the last few minutes I may ever have with my little girl, and I have absolutely no idea what to do about it.

It's time for surgery, and the nurse asks us to go to the waiting room. Stephanie starts sobbing and cries, "NO!" grabbing our arms tightly and not letting go. The nurse firmly tells us we have to leave. She promises Steph will settle down after we are gone. We don't want to pull away from her – we don't know if we will ever see her alive again. Gently, slowly, we loosen her grip and walk away although it goes against everything we believe in. I feel like I am betraying my daughter at her greatest time of need.

The nurse escorts us to the door, and we turn to see the operating team wheel Steph away, still sobbing. The windowless metal door leads to a short gray hallway which is empty and cold. When the heavy door shuts, it echoes like we have entered a tomb. My son-in-law and I hold each other as we weep, and all of our emotions pour out. Mark and I have always been close, but at this precise point in time, we share a moment. A moment filled with panic, and pain, and fear, and guilt that overtakes us. We need each other to survive that moment as our suffering forges a permanent bond between us and places a lasting imprint on our souls.

✛

life lesson #3

Remember that even the darkest clouds can have
a silver lining. You will share many experiences
with other people in life. Sometimes the experience
will include strong emotions of love or fear. In rare
instances, the impact of that emotion will be so
great that everything else ceases to exist and you will
create a connection with another soul that remains
throughout the rest of your life. This can happen in
life and death situations. Live in the present moment
to enjoy the most that life has to offer.

As they wheel Stephanie into the operating room, she is terrified and can't stop thinking of Caden deprived of his mother. Then a thought fills her mind, *Let Go and Let God*. Everything fades away as she answers, "God, I can't handle this anymore, you have to take over." The transition is instantaneous as her body relaxes and her mind finds peace. This feeling is so welcome and natural that she doesn't question it. Minutes later, they lift her onto the operating table, deliver the anesthesia, and she slips into a peaceful, deep sleep.

Mark and I walk back to Steph's hospital room. He says he feels hollow inside and wants to be with his son, the closest thing he has to being with Stephanie. The child radiates hope and comfort each time we hold him. Mark believes this is because God tells Caden not to worry, that everything will be all right. I like the idea that children have a direct line to God. Maybe we should all be more aware of what we can learn from the little ones.

chapter 5

WAITING ROOMS ARE FILLED WITH MAGAZINES and televisions to provide some escape for those caught in the limbo of waiting and worrying about loved ones. These diversions fail to keep my mind off what is happening in surgery and do little to quiet my fear. I want to be in the operating room to know Steph is all right and to hold her hand. I believe strongly in the power of touch. The communication that takes place when skin touches skin is incredible. A mother bathing her child, a teenager's first kiss, or holding a loved one fearing you will lose them. When rocking Caden to sleep, I place my pinky finger in his little hand, and he responds by tightening his grip, which I absolutely love. This is one of my favorite things, and I hope it provides him the same feeling of comfort and connection. Colleen tells me she feels adrift without Caden. I take her hand, and she leans into me, snuggling her head between my shoulder and chest. My mind jumps from one thing to the next until it settles on Steph's first surgical experience when she was nine and had a cyst removed from her arm.

As the nurse prepped Stephanie, the surgeon explained they

would open the lump to determine the cause and proceed based on what they found. He tells us that one parent can join her in surgery. With Colleen's nursing and surgical background, it's a no brainer until Steph chimes in saying, "I want Daddy with me." She doesn't see the disappointment in her mother's face or the terror in mine at her request. The nurse takes my arm as I ask Steph if she is sure and before I know it, I'm dressed in scrubs and ushered into the surgical suite. Stephanie grimaces with pain as they inject local anesthesia multiple times around the nodule. The doctor shows me where to stand and jokes that I should grab a nurse if I feel faint. My impromptu plan is to stare at the floor or walls and think about anything other than what is going on. That approach works until the surgeon says there doesn't seem to be anything in the cyst except these strings of tissue. "Dad, see what I mean?" I look up to see him lifting out what looks like angel hair pasta in a marinara sauce from the gaping slit in my daughter's arm. I feel flushed and sweat runs down my back. The room seems to be moving around me. I hear the nurse next to me announce, "We're losing Dad. Someone help me get him to the floor." No problem – I find the floor all by myself.

I never fully lose consciousness, but embarrassment quickly replaces other emotions as the nurse places under my head the pillow that Steph had been using. I apologize and the surgical team says it's okay. They begin sharing stories of others who've knocked over instrument carts, vomited on the nurses or broken bones when they hit the floor. They tell me I crumbled gracefully like a dancer. The surgeon adds that he passed out while watching his son's surgery, telling me it's different when it's a family member. I realize that they might just be making it all up to make me feel better, but it works. The whole time my daughter just laughs and can't believe her Daddy is lying on the floor and has stolen her pillow.

Mark sits on the ledge under a large window outside the waiting room with a distant look on his face. A passing observer may be reminded of a young boy filled with wonder and innocence marveling at the sunshine streaking through the dripping trees after the quick cloud burst. But a closer look would reveal the intensity of emotions overwhelming him. Mark is in an unfamiliar place where the warmth of his love and faith collides with fear's ice-cold gloom and dread. He helplessly waits for fate to deliver either catastrophe or ecstasy. And he prays for the latter.

Halfway through the operation, a surgical nurse gives us an update. The doctor has removed the colon, and from the initial inspection, he doesn't think other organs are involved. We react loudly and embrace each other as some of our fear gives way to hope and joy.

After six hours of surgery, Stephanie is placed into postoperative care. Dr. Graham tells us that the surgery couldn't have gone better and briefs us on the procedure. Assisted by two surgeons he has removed the colon, containing numerous enlarged polyps and tumors, one blocking 95 percent of the transverse colon. He said Stephanie must have been in tremendous pain and asked, "How long has this been going on?"

Mark answers, "For over three months."

The doctor shakes his head, saying, "I don't know how she was able to sustain her own life, let alone grow a child inside of her." This confirms just how tough and determined Steph is.

The surgeons have removed lymph nodes, including some that were enlarged and wrapped around the aorta. Surrounding tissue has also been taken to create a clear margin and increase the chance of eliminating hidden cancer. All accessible organs have been checked and appear to be absent of lumps, hard spots or cancer. Spots seen on the liver are similar to cysts the doctor often sees and don't appear to be unusual, but should be evaluated by an oncologist. Stephanie needs to heal up and then be treated by an oncologist with chemotherapy to kill any leftover microscopic cancer cells.

This kind man is our hero and we thank him profusely. Last night he provided us hope, and today he has extended Steph's life. A weight has been lifted off our shoulders. We can smile again. For the first time in days, we feel hungry and want something to eat, but not before we see our patient.

Stephanie slowly wakes up from surgery and realizes, I'm still alive! What an incredible feeling. She slides in and out of sleep, so things are hazy, but she remembers the surgeon telling her everything went very well, and he believes they removed all of her cancer. She can't wait to hold Caden and be with her family. Mark is so excited to see her that he waits by the elevator for two hours. When the doors open, Steph sees his face from the gurney and they are overjoyed to hold each other tightly. Mark is overcome with emotion when Caden is placed in Steph's arms. It feels like she is seeing her son for the first time and she tells him, "You are my little boy and motivation to survive. I need to raise you and watch you go to your first day of school and help you grow up and have a family of your own. Little one, you and Daddy are the ones I am fighting for."

It's like the bell has rung and it's time for recess! All of our serious activities and worries are put on hold and replaced with smiles and laughter and joy. We are high on life – Steph's life – and appreciate being able to see and touch and help each other through it.

When my son Scott arrives, we update him on everything the doctor has told us. I start typing notes on my computer. I include the next steps we need to plan for, and then put down some of the feelings I have experienced. By merely parking these issues into a Word document, my brain feels less cluttered and some of them are no longer spinning around in my mind. This process is both liberating and calming. I start documenting anything relevant to Steph's journey and thus begins my journal to Caden. I feel driven to capture my daughter's spirit and devotion to her son, in case he can't experience it himself. As I record the moment Mark and I shared, I add a life lesson to pass onto Caden. I' always wished for a grandparent who would take me aside and teach me about life; perhaps I can be that grandparent for my grandson.

Mark's parents say their goodbyes and drive home while the team starts making phone calls to share the great news. Over the last week, more of our family and friends have contacted us for updates on what is happening. We want to speak with them, but it's difficult to relive the facts repeatedly. Often we have to stop talking to gather ourselves to fight back emotion and regain our voices. Then listeners struggle for words to give us support. These exchanges drain our energy and it becomes clear we need a better way to communicate. Steph has won her first battle, but we understand there is a long, challenging road ahead of us.

Mark stays at the hospital with his family, and during the night, Steph's pain increases dramatically. The epidural slips out for the third time since surgery and can't be reconnected since the night shift isn't trained to do so. Neither Steph nor Mark sleep much because of her pain, but fortunately, Caden seems oblivious to it. Colleen and I drive home and collapse in bed, and soon my thoughts again drift back to Stephanie's childhood.

Since she was a toddler, we had a running joke where I asked her, "Who's your Daddy?" and she would always laugh and answer, "You're my Daddy!" Then one day her answer to my question was "Mark" and it broke my heart a little. We laughed it off, but I could see her concern. It was a silly thing, but I had been the most important man in her life for so long. I understood she would always be my little girl and I would still be her father, even when she had a family of her own and two new men in her life who get top billing. Everything changes with time, so we are wise to look for the best in every reincarnation. It also helps to keep your knees bent and roll with the punches.

⚙

life lesson #4

A beautiful thing about love is that it grows when someone special comes into our life. If you light one candle from another, the second adds its own light instead of robbing from the first. When new love enters your life, it doesn't diminish the love you already have for others, it merely adds to it. In my experience, the more love you give away, the more you get back in return. Don't be afraid to love, embrace it, and be thankful. There will never be too much love in the world.

chapter 6

COLLEEN AND I ARRIVE AT THE HOSPITAL finding Caden refreshed, Mark tired, and Steph completely wiped out. She smiles in the mirror and says the NG tube sticking out of her nose makes her look like Gonzo from the Muppets. Six IV lines run in delivering fluids, antibiotics, and medication, while draining tubes and a catheter run out. Steph is in pain, but grateful to be alive. Midmorning a nurse arrives to help the patient sit up, get out of bed, and walk to a chair. This slow, painful ordeal is rewarded with a gentle sponge bath and massage from Nurse Nana. We find comfort in doing anything to help our little girl and take responsibility for most of her personal care. Scott tells Steph the pain will peak on day three. He recommends the breathing exercises and music which helped him move beyond the pain of three knee surgeries he endured after soccer injuries.

The surgeon stops by to check Stephanie's incision and stresses the importance of chemotherapy after she heals. He reminds us this cancer is very aggressive and needs to be treated at a cancer center with experience in unusual cases. He names three high profile research centers and suggests specific drug combinations to consider for the chemo regimen before he leaves. We appreciate his ability to provide us with information and still keep us part of the decision-making process.

Mark tells his wife that her two incisions – a curved horizontal smile line that brought Caden into the world and a vertical one above it that saved his mother – form an anchor shape. He declares that an anchor secures a vessel in place, therefore Stephanie is not leaving us. Steph smiles at his comment and gives him a big hug. It has become easy to believe in anything that supports her survival.

The GI doctor joins us and says the cancer is most likely a variant type of Familial Polyp Syndrome or a mutant gene that began developing in her teens. Twenty-five of the thirty-six lymph nodes removed during surgery were cancerous, positioning Steph's cancer at Stage 3. As cancer progresses from Stage 1 through Stage 4, it spreads, becomes more challenging to treat, and lowers the chance of survival.

Simplified definitions: Stage 1 - cancer appears in the mucosa lining of the colon. Stage 2 - cancer moves through the muscle layer of the colon. Stage 3 - cancer spreads into surrounding lymph nodes. Stage 4 - cancer migrates to additional organs.

As the doctor leaves, he advises that all of Steph's immediate family should have colonoscopies to rule out anyone else at risk.

Mid-afternoon I slip out and pick up the second stuffed lamb, hiding it in the trunk of my car. I want to keep it a secret. I'm worried that the team may think it morbid or that I was giving up. There was no reason for anyone else to know about it. The truth is I am embarrassed about my grasping at straws.

Mark writes in Caden's Journal: *We survived another day, and Mommy is slowly getting stronger. Everything she does is to survive so she can be your mother. We are blessed to have so much support from our family and friends. At night things quiet down and even though you sleep in a bassinet, Mommy in a hospital bed, and me in a chair, we are together as a family, and that's what is important. Good night little one, I love you.*

The next morning Steph glides out of bed and walks down the hall, which greatly surprises the nurses based on the difficulty she had the previous day. Steph stops at Caden's bassinet when she returns. His little yawn makes her laugh and she insists on changing his diaper. Once she is back in bed, the pain begins to grow. Nana lays Caden next to his mother and this diversion helps Steph fall asleep. What would she do without him?

Choosing the right baby bottle and nipple proves somewhat challenging with too many cooks in the kitchen, each having an opinion, and all of us strong-willed. Caden ignores the discussion, rejects all the binkies, and chose the nipple on the most complicated bottle system. Check and mate! He continues to excel at his job of eating, sleeping, pooping, and providing ongoing entertainment.

A physical therapist asks our daughter to walk to the nurse's station to observe her progress. Steph scoots out of bed and walks four laps around the unit. The therapist remarks that it appears she's working with an overachiever. As Steph walks, I push her two IV poles, hold her output bags, and make sure she is steady on her feet. Staff members stop to talk, and it seems everyone knows Steph's story. We pass some patient rooms filled with activity; others are quietly still. We realize that each room represents a story that has disrupted people's lives. Each patient is challenged and in need of hope, love, and help. The weight of these facts settles in our minds as we quietly walk down the hall.

In the aftermath of an assault such as surgery, the body

rejoices in the small comforts of a warm blanket, an ice chip, or the touch of a loved one. Steph can now have small sips of water, gum, and hard candy. Her face lights up as she says, "Oh my God, it tastes SOO GOOOD!" I'm reminded we take so much for granted. Afterward, Stephanie decides it's time to give her son a bath.

Nana sets a basin on the hospital bed and helps get Caden ready. Steph kneels on the floor beside the lowered bed, tubes running everywhere, yet unaware of anything except her son. She tenderly washes her child while singing to him. He gets excited and kicks his feet while she sings, laughs, and covers him with kisses. A fresh diaper, then Caden takes his bottle. He sucks it down and falls asleep in his mother's arms, while she contentedly smiles, lost in her thoughts.

The team is exhausted by evening and asks Scott to take the night shift. We prep the bottles, but don't realize that he has never changed a diaper before. At 2:00 a.m. he is valiantly struggling with the task. Steph wakes up and laughs at her brother's desperate attempts to not to cover himself or the baby with poo. Big sister comes to his aid and points out that she still knows some things he doesn't. The next morning Scott makes it clear that he is not qualified or interested in serving time on the night shift.

The NG tube and catheter are pulled, dramatically increasing our patient's mobility and comfort. Steph is healing quickly and remains positive. She has taken ownership of her disease and fights it by exceeding every expectation set for her by the staff. Nana walks ahead of Steph using Caden as bait enticing her to walk further. When they return, more flowers have been delivered. The hospital room is beginning to look and smell like a flower shop.

At last our patient can eat anything she wants in small

quantities. She is up to the challenge and gobbles down two Oreo's, then mashed potatoes, quiche, pudding, and a roll. With a full mouth, Steph asks if her mother thinks she is spoiling Caden by holding him too much. Nana laughs and says that is impossible. "The love you share while holding Caden helps you in ways the medicine can't." Steph's smile indicates that it was the right answer. Tonight, Mark covers the night shift, and Scott is relieved by the decision.

The team is laughing more, but still carry concern about the future. We keep busy to offset our fears, but long days and nights take their toll. We find it difficult to sleep as worry, anxiety, and depression stalk us. The only one of us not losing weight is Caden. To our surprise, the hospital room has become our safe haven, because that's where our loved ones are. It's where we see can Steph's strength and positive attitude; it's where we can play with Caden and hold each other for comfort.

That night at home, I wander into Steph's childhood bedroom. Sitting on the dresser is the small pink fuzzy elephant she had as a baby. I wind the key of a music box hidden inside, and it plays *You are my Sunshine*. When it comes to "Please, don't take my sunshine away," my emotions sweep over me. Lately, when I dress and place my wallet and keys in my pockets, I also find room for tissues and Visine®. Tears just come too quickly and too often. I'm reminded of a friend of mine whose tough exterior never showed emotion, but all of that changed after his heart attack. The trauma knocked down the walls that contained his emotion and now they surface quickly, which he doesn't care for. I am not embarrassed by my emotion, but being unable to control its timing can be challenging. Still, it's better to have a safety valve to release the building pressure than to blow up.

This morning's challenge for our patient is stair climbing.

Standing at the bottom looking up, I ask Steph if she is ready. She replies, "Don't know, but let's do it before I chicken out." She walks up one flight and back down without additional pain. She smiles and tells me it's easier than after her C-section. The doctors coax Steph to eat more and prescribe medicine to slow down what's left of her gut because the nutrients are passing too quickly to be absorbed.

As a family, we sit down and discuss plans to help us move forward. When Stephanie is released, she, Mark, and Caden will move into our home. The house is large enough to keep the team together and provide a healing environment. In some ways is still home for Steph. We have gelled into a team now and find strength in staying together. I call Dr. Teresa Varanka, a family friend and psychiatrist, to discuss potential issues Steph may encounter with postpartum depression or anxiety from her cancer. She is very gracious and offers to come to our home for an evaluation once we are settled. Another close friend tells me that his son can set up a webpage for us to post our updates. I didn't expect a fifteen-year-old to know how to do that, but it could solve many of our communication challenges, so I thankfully agree.

Colleen is on the night shift when Steph becomes nauseated, and the medication given to help causes an allergic reaction. Her legs and arms become restless; she itches and feels like she is crawling out of her skin. Steph is jittery and frustrated, then becomes angry and starts throwing things across the room. She has a full meltdown. A second drug counteracts the first and puts her to sleep. Caden is restless all night while Nana rocks, feeds, and basically tries everything to settle him. The next morning continues to challenge our patient.

Steph wakes up nauseated and starts vomiting. A sharp pain shoots through her gut at the incision line as the abdominal muscles cut during surgery try to empty her stomach. She cries as she fights the pain and tries to regain control. The surgeon has planned to release her today, but after his patient's difficult night and morning, he wants to observe her another day. Stephanie decides that's not going to happen. She tells the surgeon she needs a different environment to get well. She wants to sleep in her own bed, eat better food, and not be awakened so often. The doctor agrees to monitor her progress through the day before making a decision. My daughter counters with a compromise. If she can keep her lunch down, she can go home. He looks at her for a minute and agrees. We all want her home but know if she isn't ready, it could turn into a nightmare.

Stephanie is still nauseated but puts a smile on her face and starts walking the halls to support her argument. Meanwhile, our team begins moving out all the stuff we have accumulated. Steph eats some soup, applesauce, and crackers for lunch and keeps it down. Nana takes a bite or two to help empty the tray. Stephanie talks to the surgeon, and he agrees to let her go home. It seems my daughter is quite the salesperson. A nurse walks in and removes the PICC line, and magically, her nausea disappears. There is a discussion as to why, but Steph doesn't care, she's just happy it's gone.

Nana and I gather up radiology scans and pathology slides, while Mark retrieves the medical records needed for the next battle in this war. This leaves Stephanie alone with her baby. Caden throws up while lying on his back in the bassinet. Steph slides out of bed and picks up her son in one quick movement fearing he will choke. She takes off his jammies, cleans him up, and crawls back in bed with him resting on her chest. Mark returns and smiles, finding mother and child sound asleep. He turns on the video camera and enjoys the quiet moment.

After 11 days in the hospital, the team moves into our home. Steph eases out of the car, looks around, and closes her eyes, feeling the sun on her face. She is grinning ear to ear and says, "I feel absolutely fantastic and am so glad to be home." It may be my imagination, but I think she clicks her heels adding, "There's no place like home!" That seems appropriate since we live in the Land of Oz.

Our home sits on twenty-six acres of trees crisscrossed with trails we have carved out for walking and leisurely drives on the golf cart. We don't golf, but the electric vehicle allows us to approach the wildlife living on the property quietly. We built the house we built fifteen years ago, adjacent to a peninsula that projects into a five-acre bass pond in the back yard. Colleen thought I was crazy dragging our family into the country, but I always dreamed of having some land with trees and water. Soon we all fell in love with the peace, quiet, and escape we find here. Many nights Colleen and I drive the trails listening to birds, sneaking up on deer, and enjoying the sunset.

Stephanie's attitude is terrific, and she is free of pain and nausea. Colleen makes homemade chicken dumpling soup, and her daughter devours an entire bowl. It's her first full meal in over a week, and she tells Nana her cooking can make anyone feel good. The team agrees. Tonight everyone sleeps soundly for the first time in a while. There really isn't any place like home.

⚘

life lesson #5

Find joy in simple things. This world we live in
has so much to offer. It's easy to become used to
everyday things and only notice the extraordinary.

Today Steph found delight and so much happiness from the blessings of feeling well, being at home with her family, and a bowl of chicken soup. Caden's world is small, and he is just starting to notice things. Soon it will expand quickly, and we will remind him that sometimes the simplest things bring us the most enjoyment.

chapter 7

NANA IS IN HER ELEMENT, cooking, cleaning, and mothering a full house. If she isn't holding Caden, she is helping his mother or doing laundry. Colleen gives until everything is completed and only then does she rest. She tells me these are things within her control, and it feels good to get things done. Lately, so many things have been out of our control. I understand. Nothing is being taken for granted by any of us.

Stephanie's pain eases as her body heals, but she's challenged by fatigue and a compromised digestive system. She works to stay positive and is strong most of the time, but occasionally she breaks down. Fear starts to grow as focus shifts from the crisis of surgery to chemotherapy and an uncertain future. Dr. Teresa Varanka stops by to assess Steph and emphasizes the importance of staying positive and nurturing a belief that things will work out. An hour later Teresa switches roles from psychiatrist to friend and brings out baby gifts and fusses over Caden. This warm, gentle woman is quickly becoming one of Steph's angels, our description of the people who touch her life in a special way.

Our family is recharging but understands the importance of quickly finding the right medical team to help Steph move forward. It's vital for us to stay positive and have faith that she will beat this disease; we must believe it and display that belief. As a team, we decide not to ask the doctors about Steph's chances of survival or search the Internet. We are simply afraid of what we might find. Nurturing a peaceful atmosphere for Steph, we try to filter out the world's unrelenting noise that seems to be everywhere these days.

Our country home, surrounded by woods, water, and memories, creates a healing environment outside while inside, we provide our patient with love, humor, and her favorite music. I don't get all my daughter's music, which recalls memories of my own parents' opinion of music I liked. But come on! Who doesn't like classic rock and roll? The team continues to implement Steph's action plan for survival.

I contact the Oncology Division of the pharmaceutical company I work for to gain perspective on selecting cancer centers, oncologists, and chemotherapy. A Regional Director gives me an overview and provides contacts for each area we discuss. She becomes emotional as I share Steph's story, and then I learn she is also a new mother. The story of Steph's fight begins to spread through the company. A young mother in crisis tugs on everyone's heartstrings. A Director from our Nutrition Division sends us baby formula. Cards and well wishes pour in. Everyone wants to help.

Today we visit a large oncology group the GI doctor has suggested. Caden, Mark, Nana, and I join Steph as we promised. The oncologist reviews her scans and doesn't believe the spots on the liver warrant concern. We ask about chemotherapy options, and he tells us to not worry about it because he knows what to do. I politely explain we just want to gain a clearer understanding of the choices. Looking annoyed, he discusses a three-drug combination supported by studies in the New England Journal, then talks about drug side effects and the need for a surgically implanted port to deliver the drugs.

Chemo will be given every two weeks and take 1-2 hours. We tell him Stephanie will be visiting a cancer research center for a full evaluation. He is okay with that, but admits he may not follow their recommendations, since he already knows what to do. I ask him about a new drug the FDA has just approved for colon cancer. The doctor appears upset and shifts in his chair. He sounds aggressive and condescending in telling me the drug is only approved for Stage 4. I reply that we understand the guidelines and ask if the uniqueness of Steph's cancer and her age makes her an exception. He tells us it really doesn't matter; his job is treating cancer, and he uses the same algorithm for every colon cancer patient. This leaves us cold. Other specialists have told us we have to be very aggressive with treatment and not follow the guidelines for a seventy-five-year-old.

We thank this doctor for seeing us and ask if he or his staff can suggest reading material to help us stay positive and hopeful – perhaps a guide to fight cancer, deal with the stress or provide success stories. The doctor and staff can't think of anything to recommend. His nurse hands us a brochure on colon cancer, its warning signs, and the importance of getting colonoscopies after age 50. Not at all what we need. I am stunned that this large group of oncologists doesn't have resources or even suggestions on how to positively build the mental outlook of the cancer patient.

We need to keep searching.

The Team sits down afterward to discuss the appointment. We agree Steph needs an oncologist with cutting edge knowledge, experience treating rare cancers, and can connect with and become her champion. The selection of this champion may be one of the most important decisions of her life. We decide that the doctor we have just consulted isn't the right fit and we need to keep searching. We also learn the value of discussing everything we heard. Because our appointment moved so quickly and contained a mixture of medical information and emotions, we discover that not everyone heard or understood the same things. By discussing it, we all achieve the same level of understanding This strengthens the teams' ability to make an informed decision. We are disappointed not to have found our oncologist, but will try to learn from the experience. This appointment becomes a turning point for Stephanie; she now views the chemotherapy as a tool to keep her alive, rather than something to fear.

We return home and update our employers. House payments, other bills and life continue even when your world is turned upside down. Nana takes an indefinite leave of absence. My boss has assigned someone to manage my district's daily activities, and I will handle the rest from the office in my home. Mark's firm assures him that family comes first, and they will work something out with his vacation. By the time Mark returns to his desk, one of the principles has gifted him a week of his personal vacation. We couldn't ask for better people to work for and support us in this time of need. The importance of having good people in our lives reminds me of a long-ago conversation with my family.

As I drive, Colleen and our young children discuss what they would ask for if a genie granted them a wish. Money, more wishes, a new bike, and the usual things kids wish for are weighed and debated. Then Steph asks me what I would wish for. After a moment I say I would want for them to find a mate that will make them as happy as Colleen has made me. Someone to share dreams with and help them come true. The kids think that's a perfect wish. Colleen smiles at me and agrees.

Colleen and I first met Mark when he and Steph were dating in college. We found him to be a gentle giant. He is smart, easy to get along with, and consistently does the right thing, but I tease him that we really want him in the family to add height to our gene pool. Our daughter did an excellent job finding us a wonderful son-in-law and granting the wish I made so many years before. Mark works a full day, then comes home to help us, and takes Caden at bedtime. It drains him physically and mentally, but he never complains. He's always so excited to see Steph and Caden each night. Nana and I periodically take Caden at night so Mark can catch up on his sleep. Tonight is my turn.

Caden's cry and movement wakes me but quickly softens when I pick him up. We lock eyes and smile. I feel loved and my joy immediately follows. Having a baby in the house is magical. We understand how lucky we are to have him healthy and happy. That said, getting up with a newborn is a lot tougher in our fifties than our twenties. I'm amazed how Caden can wake us from a sound sleep and yet melt our hearts when we pick him up.

The next morning Colleen thanks me for taking Caden during the night. "I watched you turn on the lantern to keep the light soft and whisper to him as you changed and wrapped him all up. After his bottle you cuddled him to your chest, patted lightly on his back, all the while humming and slow dancing him to sleep. I don't know that I have ever been more in love with you than at that moment when I watched my silver-haired husband dance with his grandson at three in the morning."

That afternoon Colleen calls a cancer research center for an appointment and learns Steph's insurance is "out of plan" and won't pay. Without coverage, the center requires $13,000 paid upfront before starting the evaluation and suggests we plan to stay for five to ten days. They have specialized equipment for better testing, clinical trials using unapproved drugs, and some of the top cancer specialists in the world. They also confirm what we already believed – with Steph's age and aggressive cancer, she can't afford any margin of error. We discuss this as a family and agree that traveling to this Research Center is the next step. A cancelation provides an appointment in two weeks. Colleen contacts the GI doctor and asks if he would write the insurance company requesting an exception to their coverage based on Steph's unique disease. He agrees to write the letter.

Planning for transportation reveals several issues to solve. Driving will take multiple days and be complicated since Stephanie is still healing and needs quick access to a restroom. The flu strain is deadly this year, placing our premature baby and post-surgical patient in the highest-risk category. Traveling by commercial airplane with contained space could increase their exposure, and Steph's physicians strongly advise against it. We search for other options. A friend of a friend involved with Angel Flights offers to contact them for help.

The crisis has consumed us and overshadowed everything else in our lives. We are overwhelmed by caring for Steph and Caden, searching for a treatment team, and communicating with everyone involved. Colleen and I spend hours on phone each day moving the process forward. Colleen also manages our home, while I organize the data we gather into a computer for easy retrieval. The team is exhausted. Time we require for exercise and play to replenish our energy has evaporated. I find some relief writing in my journal. Tonight I place the first update on Stephanie's new website, which dramatically streamlines the communication process to keep friends informed. The web counter quickly climbs as people visit the site.

It's Saturday and everyone takes the day off. Steph, Mark, and Caden spend time as a family catching up on their rest. Colleen and I stock up on groceries. For no particular reason, anxiety catches up with me by late afternoon. My emotions build, and as I hold them back the muscles in my shoulders and jaw tighten until I feel like I'm going to burst. I close the bathroom door, put my face in a towel and sob so hard I can hardly breathe. My fear, worry, and feelings of helplessness pour out until I'm an empty shell sitting on the floor. My body and mind are numb, and time stands still while I catch my breath. In business, I am used to organizing a plan, attacking an issue, and gaining control of the situation. None of us are in control of our current situation, and we try everything we can to move forward. I get anxious when the phone rings, hoping it isn't bad news. I remind myself to keep watch for signs of depression. It doesn't worry me. I just need to be on guard so that it doesn't get the best of me, because the best of me is currently reserved for my daughter.

As long as I can remember, I have loved to watch television. Early in my life it was my babysitter. *Father Knows Best*, *The Andy Griffith Show* and others taught me right from wrong and reinforced many values I still believe in today. Television has always provided me with an escape. Even as an adult, I can "check out" and shed everyday stress by watching a comedy show. Steph's cancer has changed that. Now everything I see on TV seems connected to her illness. My escape now escapes me. I'm confident this will wear off over time, but just as sure, some things will never be the same.

chapter 8

STEPHANIE AND I COMPOSE A LETTER to her insurance company requesting they cover the assessment at the Research Center. Colleen has talked to them several times on the phone, without making any progress, and they find no record of any request from the GI doctor. I uncover the name of their local Medical Director, so we address the letter directly to her attention and summarize Stephanie's situation. The letter is professional but also includes an emotional plea from a mother needing help. We highlight the uniqueness of her disease, her age, and that each of her specialists said she needs to be assessed at a top cancer research center. I fax my letter directly to the Medical Director's office.

Afterward, Steph and I talk about how refreshing it is having a newborn around. The baby smell and softness, their innocence and delight in experiencing new sounds, tastes and touch. Only wanting the basics of food, sleep, and comfort. We laugh and agree that from our perspective, that sounds like the good life.

Colleen and I drive two hours to visit Scott at his university the next morning. The three of us meet with the Associate Dean to discuss the classes he missed due to Steph's illness. Some of his teachers aren't as understanding as others about making up tests and assignments, as it seems some students actually fabricate similar reasons to skip class. Imagine that! We develop a plan for Scott to complete his work. The Associate Dean offers to organize it with his teachers.

College kids are always hungry, so we take our son out to lunch before heading home. Scott and Steph were best friends growing up, and we understand it's difficult for him not to help us protect his sister. Protecting others has always been second nature to Scott, whether it was confronting bullies at school or asking his father to stop scolding his crying sister. Once I joked that he was the man of the house when I traveled. That night Colleen noticed him locking the doors and he told her it was his job to protect the house. As an adult, I have seen him walk into volatile situations and quietly defuse them while I just stood and watched. He doesn't have the opportunity we have to be with Steph and get support from the other team members. Nana and I agree to check in with him more often.

While we are away, Stephanie has a girlfriend over to assist. The two women take full advantage of the warm day by taking Caden out in his stroller for a walk around the pond. When we return, Steph tells us it was so peaceful strolling through the trees with the sun glimmering off the water. She felt God was all around her. She thanks us for all we are doing and says our home has always been a place of love, healing, and sanctuary for her.

Our family believes in God and that things happen for a reason. That said, none of us are sure what it is we're supposed to learn from this experience. Colleen and I have begged God to save Stephanie's life and take from us anything he wanted in return, including our lives. I'm not sure bargaining with our Creator is the right thing to do, but I am a little surprised that none of us has ever became angry with God. Steph has never asked, "Why is this happening to me and not someone else? What did I do wrong? Why is God punishing me?" She's never even proposed a bargain with God as we have. We tell her how proud we are of her. She responds that she is following Grandma Aggie's example.

Agnes had suffered from ALS for two years, eventually losing all muscle control. Even with constant pain, she seldom showed that she was suffering. She never questioned why it was happening to her and simply accepted it was part of God's plan. Towards the end, she couldn't speak, but Steph asked her, "Grandma are you in a lot of pain?" Aggie nodded, yes. "On a scale of one to five, how much pain do you feel?" She held up five frail wrinkled fingers. The answer stunned Steph and filled her with heartache. We hadn't known it was that bad because Agnes never complained.

Today is full of appointments. Colleen takes Steph and Caden to see a surgeon about implanting a port. This device permits repeated access to the venous system for the delivery of various fluids or blood withdrawal. It's sewn into a small pocket under the skin and rests between the shoulder and breast. The port provides quick, easy access to the vein and reduces the pain of sticks to improve patient comfort. Surgery is set for the end of the week.

While they are with the surgeon, I meet with both our tax accountant and financial planner to better understand my options to liquefy assets to cash if needed. Afterward, I set up time with a realtor to get the current value of our home. We have savings available, but I am uncertain what expenses might be in our future. I'm happy we started saving sixteen percent of my income in our twenties for a rainy day. Lately, it's been pouring.

As I ponder our transportation challenge, I think of my

longtime barber who may know someone with a jet. His job brings him in contact with a variety of professional people, and he is excellent at networking. I stop by his shop and explain our situation. He is sorry to hear about Steph's cancer and tells me he will check with a client whom he believes has access to a Lear Jet.

Colleen has been relentless in her follow-up with the insurance company. Today, after reviewing Steph's case and the letter we faxed to their Medical Director, they agree to cover the cost of the assessment at the Research Center. They will not pay for treatment there, which is fine as we hope to do that locally. Colleen calls the Research Center with the insurance information and receives the name of the oncologist Steph will meet with. My corporate colleagues tell me she is highly respected, but more clinical than warm and fuzzy. Now we can focus on transportation and lodging.

We are ecstatic at the great news from the insurance company! That night we celebrate with a toast to Colleen's hard work and Steph's future. We hope that this Research Center will assess Stephanie's illness and develop a specific plan of attack to overcome it, building our hope, confidence, and Steph's chances of survival. We desperately need someone we can trust to take our hand and lead us down the road to recovery, because we feel so much on our own and unsure what direction to take. I worry about making a mistake or not moving quick enough. There is no room for error with Steph's life on the line. My anxiety grows just thinking about it, and I carry its increasing weight on my shoulders. It would be nice to have a filter to trap unwanted thoughts. Without such a device, I depend on faith, hope, and the love of my family.

While Nana takes care of Caden and makes appointments, I take Steph to an outpatient center for her port surgery. The nurses allows me to stay while they prep her. When asked why she needs the port, Steph tears up as she shares her story. The nurses are visibly moved and ask if there is anything they can help with. They don't know us and they see people in need every day, but they genuinely want to help. Being married to a nurse, I understand they have an exceptional mothering gene that lets them assist people in the worst situations of their lives and do it with love and patience. They're expected to deal with crises and conditions that would make most of us want to turn and run. But something allows them to do what needs to be done while telling you it's no big deal. Nurses are consistently listed among the most trusted professions. Unfortunately they are often taken for granted, like the teachers, police, firefighters and members of our armed services who give so much of themselves.

To keep busy, I call Colleen and Mark to let them know the surgery has begun. Colleen has spoken with Angel Flights and learned they require a client to be in their system for five days before scheduling a flight. Steph's information hasn't been put in, and now there aren't enough days to set it up. Angel Flights will try to overcome this obstacle, but it's complicated since the trip will be made in two legs. We'll have to change pilots and planes halfway to our destination because volunteer pilots are limited in the miles they can fly. Everything is understandably set up to protect the pilots and passengers associated with this life saving non-profit organization.

My barber lets me know his client is sorry, but he can't fly non-company personnel in their jet because of insurance reasons. I understand and thank him for trying. Then I realize my own company might have transportation. Everyone I work with keeps offering to help, so why not ask. I call my Director and he in turn talks to our Vice President. Five minutes later, I am asked to send a summary of Stephanie's current situation, and upper management will review it over the weekend. Again, I am reminded of what great people I work with. I join Steph in the recovery room where she gives me a big hug and tells me the surgery was a piece of cake. I update her on the transportation issues, and she tells me she isn't worried, she has great people working on it.

I travel with my work, and one benefit of frequent hotel stays is earning points for future visits. Elite status with one chain guarantees me rooms at any location with 24-hour notice. They have a hotel a few blocks from the Research Center, but it's booked up. I use my elite status only to find out it expired two days before. Timing is everything. They tell me several unusually large national events overlap the same dates we need and all the rooms in the city are booked. After an hour of phone calls, I can't find a room within two hours of the hospital. I contact Tommy Tullo, a friend I work with lives near the Research Center. He suggests we stay with him, but warns that they are in the process of moving in while builders finish their new home. Maybe Tommy is not the best option, but at least we have something.

Colleen drives to the gym to work off some stress. The owner asks how Steph is doing, and the conversation leads to the complications we have with travel and lodging. A woman walking by overhears and asks, "Do you need a place to stay while you are there? I have a townhouse you can use." Colleen can't believe it and shares Steph's story with this person she has never seen before. This kind-hearted woman says her husband uses the townhouse when he is there for business, but it will be empty the dates we are there. She would love to help us, insists we use it, and won't even let us pay for it. Colleen is overwhelmed and can't believe this stranger's generosity and the series of unrelated events that fell together to make this happen. She accepts this angel's offer and hurries home to tell us.

Whatever treatment is prescribed by the Research Center,

we understand it will be administered close to home. I talk to people in our oncology division who interact with all the cancer centers and oncologists in Kansas City. I tell them we need a specialist who is excellent at what they do and understands the latest developments in cancer research and treatments. Someone who recognizes Steph's circumstance and adjusts treatment accordingly instead of using a set algorithm. We also need someone with empathy that realizes this is the scariest thing we have ever faced. What I really want to say is that we must quickly find someone who will save Steph's life. One female oncologist at The University of Kansas Cancer Center stands out, so Colleen calls and sets up an appointment with her.

It's Friday night, and everyone is ready for the weekend. At dinner we talk about everything we accomplished in the last week. Quickly the conversation moves to how overwhelmed and exhausted we are. We need more sleep and less stress, but there is so much to be done and we worry we aren't moving fast enough. Nana suggests we just need to keep moving forward and things will work out. As we talk, two things become apparent: we need to take one day at a time and we need focus on what we can control. We agree to break things down into simple steps and do our best. We will live in the moment and make the best of it. This simple decision makes an incredible difference in our lives. It reduces our stress and lets us appreciate everything we have right now, precious time with Stephanie.

Stephanie places an update on the web page:

> *I want to thank everyone for your prayers in this time of challenge in my life. The outpouring of love and support has really touched my heart. I am very thankful for everything our family and friends have done for us. I know I can count on*

your continued support and love during this time of recovery. I am overwhelmed by the number of people who have placed us on their prayer chains. I thank God for each and every one of you and truly feel blessed to have all of you in my life.

Thank you for the flowers, cards, gifts, and phone calls. They have all been so helpful on my road to recovery. Everywhere I look, someone is asking what they can do to help out. Your prayers are enough, and I can feel them working. The power of prayer is absolutely amazing! I would like to thank all the doctors, nurses, and everyone at the hospital for their excellent care and genuine concern for my recovery.

—All my love, Stephanie

chapter 9

TODAY IS A MILESTONE DAY IN CADEN'S SPIRITUAL LIFE as
Steph and Mark's pastor is coming over to baptize Caden in our
home. Steph dresses Caden in the baptism gown that Grandma
Aggie made for her as a baby. Caden stays wide-awake for the
ceremony. Afterward we talk about the magic of motherhood.
Mothers accept the lack of sleep and dirty diapers in stride,
remembering the good and trying to grow through the challenges.
Mothers not only recover quickly from giving birth, but they also
get supernatural strength to lift the child, car seat, diaper bag,
and a sack of groceries without a problem. They simply rise to the
occasion. Well, most of the time.

Two days later, our home wakes up in a bad mood, and our
daughter is no exception. Caden has been fussy the last two nights
while Colleen and I watched him. After a disagreement, Steph
gets angry and yells, "I'm just going to take my baby and go home!"
It's so out of character that Colleen and I burst out laughing.
Steph doesn't really mean it – well, check that – she definitely
meant it in that moment. It's just a reaction, and Colleen and I

are the only ones here to react to. Mark is the smart one – he is at work. We give Steph some space, and she calms down. Next Colleen and I start to argue and quickly realize we need space, too. During that time of quiet reflection, the drama in our minds clears, and we all regain perspective and appreciate our blessings.

The team is physically and mentally exhausted. We know better than to get angry at each other, but somehow the stress just takes over. Fear, anger and the unknown keep building on us, and there is so much to do. Each of us is overloaded and needs someone to help us. But when you are struggling, it's a challenge to assist others. When you are drowning, it's impossible. On top of that, as much as Colleen and I try not to interfere, it's difficult for Steph and Mark not to have the privacy and intimacy they deserve with their newborn.

The trigger today was what we commonly referred to as, 'the damn baby bottles.' The nursing system has many parts and it seems that all we do is clean them, yet we never have time to do it. With other bottles, Caden swallows too much air and gets fussy, or he simply won't take the nipple at all. The team is split on what to do, but when emotions finally subside, we agree to try multiple nipples on a simpler system.

Later I am driving in traffic when someone cuts me off and I have to slam on the breaks. I still carry some stress with me and yell through the windshield, "Damn It! Don't you know understand what I am going through?" Of course, he doesn't. Then I realize that I don't know what he is going through either. Just because I'm struggling doesn't mean my life is any more difficult than it is for others who cross my path. I love these *ah-ha* moments for what they teach me, but feel a little dense having to learn them over and over again.

A local pilot with Angel Flights calls to inform us they can't get Steph a flight, but he is willing to do it on his own. He will have to refuel at least once but will fly the entire way. I thank him and offer to pay for the fuel, but he can't accept the money due to the rules of this nonprofit organization. I don't want to take advantage of him, but I know this may be our only option because we have to leave in two days. We will be limited to a total of 50 pounds of luggage based on the weight limits of the plane. Hopefully, Steph will be in their system for the return flight. This gentleman is very kind and willing to help any way he can. We agree to talk the next day.

I call Tommy, and he offers to shuttle us around when we arrive. We can also mail him anything we can't load on the plane. It looks like our transportation is now covered, but one thing is still unresolved. Stephanie is using the bathroom more than a dozen times a day and has little control of timing the events. I don't know how we are going to manage the hours on a plane without a bathroom.

The next day Nana takes her daughter to get stitches removed. Afterward the girls go to lunch and shop for baby clothes. These are events most mothers experience often, but Steph hasn't so far. When they return home, Dr. Varanka stops by to check on her patient. Teresa has so much compassion for Stephanie. Medications are adjusted, strategies discussed, and relaxation CDs are presented. When business concludes, the ladies talk about babies and laugh for the better part of an hour. It's easy to see something is developing beyond a doctor/patient relationship. They are becoming friends.

Our Angel Flights pilot calls and tells me everything is set to leave at 8:00 a.m. the next morning, but suggests we make reservations on a commercial flight as a backup plan. The weather forecast is cold, with a 90 percent chance of thunderstorms, and we won't be able to take off if there is ice or lightning. With the likelihood of rough weather, a second pilot will join us to provide a second set of hands on the controls for safety. This addition of the second pilot to the six-seat prop plane means we won't be able to take Caden's car seat. We'll have to hold him instead of strapping him in. My anxiety grows, but I thank the pilot for his concern and precautions.

One hour later, my Director calls and tells me a corporate jet is approved for our trip. Neither of us can believe it. I tell him I will never say anything negative about our company and he laughs, telling me I shouldn't change because I obviously made some friends in the organization over the last 30 years. The jet is flying in from Europe to pick us up tomorrow and will return us home a week later. I hang up the phone and shout, "We have a jet!"

The team has a quick family meeting before heading to our next appointment. We are reenergized but still in disbelief about our good fortune. Everything keeps working out for us! Each step of this nightmare has started with a black cloud that gives way to a rainbow. Steph's diagnosis led to surgery that went smoothly. No room at the inn led to a townhouse from someone we didn't even know. The Angel Flight that wasn't in the system led to the corporate jet with a bathroom. Everything has progressed from a long, drawn-out process with one problem after another, to the best possible outcome. We are on a roll now. As long as we achieve our goal of keeping Stephanie alive and becoming a cancer survivor, we are willing to deal with all the difficulty. In fact, we are eager to do anything.

At 4:00, our team meets with Dr. Joaquina Baranda, an oncologist at The University of Kansas Cancer Center. She walks into the room looking trim and athletic while her focus immediately turns to Caden. She tells us she has little ones of her own, and you can sense a bond growing among the mothers in the room. The doctor is warm, professional, and welcoming. Stephanie shares her background and story. Dr. Baranda listens intently and then tells her, "Young patients can have a more aggressive type of cancer, and with the pregnancy hormones driving it we need to be just as aggressive by starting chemotherapy quickly." The doctor recognizes the uniqueness of Stephanie's crisis.

The oncologist spends two hours with us completing a physical, then reviewing Steph's history, pregnancy, cesarian and cancer surgeries. She discusses the disease and potential treatment options telling us the standard multiple drug treatment carries a 50 percent chance of the cancer returning. Adding the newly approved drug could move that up to 88 percent, but it's only approved for use in Stage 4 patients. Another new drug could be used, but she wants to keep that in reserve in case the first drugs fail. Chemotherapy will start with an all-day treatment at the clinic and continue via a portable pump for an additional two days at home. By spreading out the chemo over time and mixing in additional medications, this cancer center has been successful in reducing side effects. The doctor is innovative and understands the latest developments in research and treatment.

The plan puts together a specialized treatment therapy in high doses that is very aggressive and yet delivered in a way to make it more comfortable for Stephanie. Moving on from the drug discussion, the doctor reviews the potentially life-threatening side effects of blood clots and increased potential for infections associated with chemotherapy.

We discuss our trip to the Cancer Research Center and find she knows the oncologist we will be seeing. Dr. Baranda reviews the CT scan with us and says because of their shape, she believes the spots on Steph's liver are in fact cancer tumors. She will contact the Research Center oncologist and suggest a liver biopsy be done to confirm. Clearly this doctor is connected. If the spots are cancerous, Steph's diagnosis will move to Stage 4. Then the plan will change to complete six rounds of multiple drug chemotherapy cocktails to shrink the tumors in the liver, followed by surgery to remove them. The doctor schedules Steph's first round of chemo for the day after the jet brings us home. She is taking us by the hand and leading us down the road to recovery.

Dr. Baranda has an excellent bedside manner, is compassionate, and committed to saving Steph's life. She cares about both Steph and Caden and understands the uniqueness of her disease and age, telling us they will do everything possible to save her life. Steph is young and strong, so they can get more aggressive than with older frail patients. "We will take you as close to death as possible to kill your cancer with the chemo and then bring you back again. A very aggressive therapy for a very aggressive cancer." Dr. Baranda then tells Steph she cannot get pregnant under any circumstances.

After the appointment, a nurse practitioner takes us on a tour of the chemotherapy delivery area to meet the staff and get an overview of what to expect. When we get home we have a family meeting, and it's unanimous: Dr. Baranda and KU are a great fit. Stephanie has found the right doctor, the right staff, and the right place to fight her battle. We appreciate everything about the meeting, except the news of possible tumors in the liver. If there is cancer we need to know about it, but if there isn't we don't want to worry. So, of course, we worry. What a remarkable day, we found the oncologist, the chemotherapy delivery center, and a jet. Now we need to pack for tomorrow's flight.

Caden is fussy most of the night. Steph makes a "mom decision" by switching back to the complicated bottle system and later tells us, "That is that, no more discussion, done deal!" After she rocks Caden back to sleep, she isn't able to do the same for herself. All the new information shared at the appointment and concern surrounding the liver spots keeps cycling through her mind. In the middle of the night, she joins Colleen and me in bed. We hug, and there are tears. We tell her everything will be all right; we just need to keep the faith. No matter how old you are, sometimes nothing is better than holding on to Mom and Dad.

✛

life lesson #6

I believe God gives us what we need. We often don't see it when it happens, but looking back can provide perspective to see clearly. I also believe we must be responsible for doing everything we can to help ourselves. In the last six days, we worked relentlessly and received the rewards of insurance, port surgery, lodging, transportation, a great oncologist, and an aggressive chemotherapy plan. On the seventh day, we will fly instead of rest. Faith is a magical feeling that is often strongest in the young and old. The young are filled with trust and belief that nourishes their faith. The old extract faith from their experience that things happen for a reason and usually work out.

chapter 10

AT NOON WE LIFT OFF THE RUNWAY, and the Gulfstream G500
Rolls-Royce engines propel us quickly to 41,000 feet. None of us
have ever flown on a private jet, and in any other circumstances we
would be overjoyed. Instead, we feel conflicted between the surreal
luxurious setting we are in and the unknown we are heading to
at 510 mph. We share Steph's story with the pilots and atten-
dant, then snap a quick picture of the pilot holding Caden in the
cockpit. It's his first flight, after all. The crew is gracious, treats us
like royalty, and serves up a gourmet lunch for us.

It's quiet in the spacious plane for most of the trip. Each of
us is lost in thought. We understand that no matter how hard it is
or how tired we are, our priority is clearly defined; we have a baby
and his sick mom to take care of. We hope our destination will
provide us new strength and confidence through their leadership.

The jet taxies to a private terminal rolling up next to Tommy
Tullo's Suburban with its blacked-out windows. The G5 attracts
attention. Anyone watching could think we are rock stars or celeb-
rities. Nope, just a family in the fight of our lives. The pilots transfer

our luggage while Tommy focuses on Steph and her needs. He treats her like antique bone china and lights up if there is anything he can do to help. Steph continues to be weepy. Anything can set it off, but mostly it's just fear of her cancer, the unknown, and her future. As the worry grows, so does her nausea and disdain for food. Colleen watches her daughter's nutrition closely, knowing it's critical to keep up her strength.

Tommy brings a car for our use and then helps us settle into the townhouse with groceries he brought with him. The home has two bedrooms and baths with plenty of extra room for privacy if needed. Before Tommy departs, he hands me an envelope from home. It holds a card signed by everyone in my sales team and a gift card to offset some of our trip expenses. It's incredibly generous, and I am touched by the support we continue to get from friends.

Tommy picks us up and delivers us to the cancer center early the next morning. I am excited to meet the clinicians who will help us achieve Steph's goals. We didn't receive the pre-appointment packet they tell us was sent, so Steph fills out numerous forms at multiple departments before getting her busy schedule for the day. At the first appointment, a medical oncology fellow completes a preliminary check up on Steph and then discusses the diagnosis, numerous polyps, and locations of the tumors. Usually colon cancer fits into one of two categories, but Steph's doesn't fall neatly into either one. It's unusual, and the doctor hasn't known of another patient that fits Steph's profile.

The oncologist joins us. She introduces herself and confirms that Steph is the patient without a word to the rest of the team. She discusses treatment options and mentions they don't have any clinical trials appropriate for Steph's case. Striking some keys on the computer, she reviews the original CT scan with us and then focuses on the largest of the three liver spots. She wants an updated CT with more slices to see if anything has changed. She also wishes to complete a biopsy of the liver spot to determine if it's malignant. The researcher and scientist in her are clearly present as she interprets the facts of Stephanie's illness. The data leads her to direct decisions and comments. There is an impersonal, clinical presence about the doctor. Spending a career dealing with disease and patients in crisis may have dulled the empathy she shows to patients. Or maybe the social skills aren't as polished as the physician's medical expertise, but it's the latter that's most important to us. The oncologist seems oblivious to the baby in the room, which strikes us as odd.

The biopsy can take place in five business days, with results three days later. I share our timetable and the fact it's driven by the constraints of a flight plan and lodging arrangement which are not in our control. The doctor seems annoyed and says she will call in some favors and try to schedule the biopsy within our timeframe We thank her. The communication has been mostly one direction, from the doctor. That is fine until she rejects our travel issues, and instead tells us we have to figure it out. "You can either stay longer or come back later to get the results. My other patients do it all the time, so you can too." She doesn't understand how many strings we had to pull just to get here. The oncologist is intelligent, confident, clinical, very busy, and indifferent. Eight days to perform a biopsy and get results seems a long wait for an institution that must require it often. The estimated time the center asked us to plan for initially has now doubled. The appointment is over quickly, and we leave feeling uncertain and unsettled. Blood work is next on Steph's schedule.

The laboratory waiting room reminds me of a busy airport as we see hundreds of people waiting for their turn. Many patients are thin, balding, and dressed in hospital gowns. Some are connected to IV stands and look despondent as they are at various stages of their battle. Some look emaciated like victims of concentration camps. This is something we haven't encountered before, and it fills us with compassion as well as trepidation. The patients sitting alone and children have the most significant impact on our souls. Steph wonders if this is what her future looks like, if so for how long?

Colleen joins Steph as she is called to the back along with twenty others. The tech tells them she can't use the port without an order from a staff doctor. Colleen asks if the oncologist can be called and is told, "That's not my job," and there is nothing she can do. This is the third time we received the 'that's not my job' answer since we arrived two hours ago. On the third stick, the blood is drawn.

This cancer research center has a large campus composed of numerous buildings with volunteers to help direct patients to their appointments. We use our schedule and wall maps, but it's usually Mark who finds our way through the maze. Sometimes one department helpfully calls another to let them know we are on the way since we have ten minutes to cover twenty minutes of ground. Steph is still recovering and regaining her strength, so Mark pushes her in a wheelchair. We are a sight to see, moving quickly down the halls pushing Caden and Lambie in the stroller, with bags and jackets hanging off our shoulders, and the wheelchair leading the way.

When we arrive at radiology, Stephanie asks her mom to help her change for the chest X-ray. As Steph undresses, she laughs, noticing her underwear is on inside out. Anything that makes us laugh is welcome. Colleen watches Steph in the mirror as she pulls a gown over her scarred body and wonders how much more her daughter can take. We want to find hope here, but concerns about the liver spots have Colleen's head spinning. She has successfully blocked out dark thoughts until now and grows quiet as her mind drifts to a future where Stephanie is not part of our life. Colleen and Steph fight back the tears until their eyes meet in the mirror and they both give in. After regaining their composure, Colleen pulls back the curtain and notices a woman sitting on a bench across the room. She is impeccably dressed and stays focused directly on them. There is a calm about her, which contrasts with the busy activity throughout the room. A moment later, Stephanie is taken for her X-ray, and afterward we move on.

A Physician Assistant at Interventional Radiology briefs us on the liver biopsy. A surgeon will insert a long thin tube through Steph's side to the liver and harvest tissue from the targeted spot. Due to the location, it may be tricky to get around her lungs. If necessary, he will move the instrument through a lung, puncturing it on both sides, to get the sample. It's easy to read the concern on our faces. I tell her the lung involvement sounds dangerous and she says, "Not really, as long as you aren't planning on flying in an airplane for twenty-four hours, due to air pressure issues." I tell her we will be flying in less than twenty-four hours and explain our situation. She is kind and compassionate and tells us they will do everything they can to avoid puncturing the lung.

After the biopsy consultation, Caden is hungry. Actually he is always hungry and seems to be in a growth spurt. We all enjoy giving him bottles, but none more than his mother. She cares for him as much as she can, because it's good medicine for both mother and child.

Radiology allows Mark to go back with Steph for her CT scan while we wait. The tech sees all the bruises and scars from previous sticks and asks Steph, "My goodness child, what has happened to your arms? Have you already started chemo?" They talk while the tech places the needle on her first try, but the large needle generates a lot of pain.

Colleen and I sit outside the waiting room in a small quiet seating area that creates an oasis in the crowd. It's close to the elevators and as people walk by, most smile at our five-week-old grandson. In the two hours we sit there, one person stops to talk to us. The same tall impeccably dressed woman Colleen had noticed in X-Ray. She remarks, "What a beautiful baby boy. I hope everything is all right with him." Colleen shares Steph's story, and the woman listens intently. Then she informs us the same thing happened to her forty years ago. She had a Caesarian, but there were complications. A cancerous obstruction was uncovered during the procedure, and they removed her colon. The doctors told her she would likely die, and shortly after surgery, she lapsed into a month-long coma, while the nurses cared for her baby girl in a bassinet next to her bed. She spent four months recovering in the hospital, but never received chemotherapy or other treatment. She smiles and says her baby is now forty years old. Colleen tells the woman Steph needs to hear this story, but she's been taken back for a CT. A beeper goes off, and this gentle soul is called for her procedure. As she walks away, she turns back, smiles, and tells us, "Your daughter is going to be all right; I am certain of it." No one has ever told us that before. She looks so knowing and sure of herself when she says it. She finds Steph with Mark and shares her story, then tells our little girl not to worry; she will be fine. This person doesn't know us but is so compassionate and caring. Again, we were reminded that everyone has a story.

Later the mystery lady returns to our oasis and tells Colleen she has spoken with Stephanie. She confidently tells us, "Your daughter is going to be fine, and everything will work out." She smiles, walks over to her own daughter, and they disappear into the elevator. It's surreal. Of the hundreds of people that walked by, she is the only one that stopped to talk to us. She is the first person we have ever met that experienced exactly what Stephanie is going through. Most importantly, she survived. I keep wondering, what are the odds of this happening? I don't believe in coincidence. I believe there is a grand plan.

This soul just seemed unusual, but I am not sure why. She appeared wise and heavenly, but I can't explain how. There was a peaceful, loving aura around her and her clothing flowed as she walked with the grace of a dancer. It seems incredible, but I find myself wondering if she is a messenger from God. I keep this to myself and then ask Nana if she thinks anything was different about the woman. Her eyes light up, and she immediately says, "Yes, but I can't put my finger on why. Her skin didn't look normal, it glistened." I realize that we didn't even ask her name. Whoever she is, this soul provides us with a message of hope at a difficult time in our journey. She had the baby, colon cancer, and survived for forty years. That is amazing, and it boosts both our faith and optimism. I believe things happen for a reason. I also believe that God gives us what we need when we need it.

Throughout the day, we ask each department about books to help us understand how to battle cancer, stay positive, motivated, and win our fight. Something with success stories about people who beat cancer and how they did it. Again, we are disappointed not to find anything. Either we aren't looking in the right places, asking the right questions, or this is a need yet to be filled.

The day is full of activity and challenges as we look for the bright side of things and keep our sense of humor. We stay strong for Steph, but each of us wavers during the day. As a team, we meet the obstacles head-on, stay positive, and focus on solutions. When one of the team isn't sure what to do, another picks up the lead.

✤

life lesson #7

> There is much to learn by observing nature. A flock of geese can fly 70 percent further than a single goose. The first goose leading the V cuts the wind creating a small updraft from its wings, which makes it easier for the bird next to them to fly. This effect continues down the line. As the lead bird gets tired, it drops back in the formation to replenish its strength; another takes the lead, allowing all the birds to continue. The flock is stronger than the individual, and the same is true for our team.

Steph is emotionally drained and freezing when we get back to the townhouse. We wrap her in blankets and add a heating pad, but she is cold to the bone. After a little dinner, a hot bath finally warms her up. It's the first time since Caden's birth that Steph's incisions are healed enough to be submerged in water. Caden joins her in the tub, and I can't tell which of them is more excited. For a time, Steph is lost in Caden's innocence, splashing, and joy. He giggles as she kisses the souls of his feet. The child is the most essential part of her team. Between the food, a short nap, and a warm bath Steph looks and feels better.

Before bed, Steph and I talk about the day and the fear that has grown since we left home. We are entirely open to each other. After listening to her concerns, it's obvious she is overwhelmed with emotion. She tells me things happen so fast, and everything we encounter seems to be the most important to her survival. There is no margin for error, and any mistake could cost her life. After feeling sorry for ourselves, we discuss the positive things that have happened and remember to focus on what we can control. We must overcome this disease, instead of letting fear control us. Easily said, but challenging to accomplish. Steph joins Mark in bed where he cuddles her until they fall asleep.

chapter 11

OUR TEAM SPENDS THREE DAYS trying to rest and recharge while waiting for the liver biopsy. Nausea keeps Stephanie from eating, and she is losing weight. She tells Mark the only thing that sounds good to eat is *Peanut Butter Cap'n Crunch*. Mark and I jump in the car and stop at four stores before we find it, then bring back two large boxes for her. She takes one bite and is all smiles until the bowl is empty. Not much of a balanced diet, but it's something.

Worry and stress create muscle pain, raw nerves, and trouble sleeping for our team. After being so busy, this downtime should be a blessing, but instead we feel stuck in limbo waiting for time to pass. I make a call and find out the jet schedule can't be changed to accommodate the oncologist's request to stay longer. The team weighs options and decides to leave things the way they are, hoping all will work out. We are disappointed that we won't return home with the test results or the new leadership we had hoped would boost our strength and confidence. Maybe our expectations are unrealistic, but we're not ready to settle for less.

Steph catches me alone in the kitchen and asks, "Dad, do you really believe I'm going to live?" I walk her into the living room and we sit down. "Sweetheart, in the beginning, we only knew you had cancer and understood we could lose you. Now I believe with all my heart that you will live. It's going to be difficult for a while, but you are young and tough and will overcome anything that happens, even if the cancer is in your liver. With Dr. Baranda joining our team, there isn't anything we can't overcome." Steph needs to be reassured and yet hear the truth. She still seeks her dad's guidance, and I'm so grateful for our ability to connect.

"Dad, I love you so much." After a hug, Steph sits down to update her game plan. She organizes each day starting with her appointments and then schedules time to play with Caden, write in her journal, and get additional rest. After setting tomorrow's schedule, she feels better. Planning and action reduce worry.

In the late afternoon we head out to dinner hoping to awaken Stephanie's appetite. Nausea and the smell of food overwhelm her halfway through her soup, so she waits outside the restaurant while we quickly finish our meal. Steph watches people outside the restaurant waiting for seats as they laugh and enjoy the warm sunshine on a Friday night out. She wonders if her life will ever be carefree again. She carries a burden of fear and anxiety, and I don't know how to remove it. That night as Colleen holds her daughter, it stirs up memories of Steph as a baby. They talk about how quickly time passes and Steph tells her mother how guilty she feels, not having the strength to take care of Caden. All she really wants to be is a good mom. Colleen tells her she already is.

This cancer has altered the adults on our team. It's a mental challenge. Simple sights and sounds that had little impact on us before now trigger emotion as we see them through the lens of Steph's illness. A mother and her newborn prompt the question, are they healthy? A father alone with his child makes us wonder if the mother is alive. A sad song coaxes emotion too quickly.

I experienced the same thing after Steph was born. In the movie theater, Colleen and I watched a car chase in which one car jumps the curb and barely misses a mother pushing a baby stroller on the sidewalk. The only reason for the close call was to elicit emotion in the audience, and as a new parent, it struck home. I felt manipulated and so angry I wanted to walk out of the theater. My wife told me I was overreacting as she shoveled popcorn into her mouth. She was so happy just to have a sitter and be out of the house, she didn't care about the car chase. Looking back on it, she had the right perspective.

Stephanie isn't eating or sleeping and is becoming more fragile. She talks to Teresa Varanka frequently as their relationship grows. Dr. Varanka has a big heart, which is one reason she is a great psychiatrist. She cares and tries to find solutions that make a difference in people's lives when they need help. Steph needs others outside the family to talk to, and when Teresa listens, it helps more than she realizes.

Nana remains the silent hero through much of this ordeal. Her nursing background helps us navigate the medical systems and find solutions to our ills. She helps Steph with ailments and offers strategies to improve her daughter's comfort. Colleen's motherly instincts know if her patient needs rest or food or just to be comforted. Nana cooks, watches over us, and gives until there is nothing left to give. We are so lucky to have her. She is a loving soul, and I don't know what I would do without her. I'm glad I was smart enough to pursue her after we met.

In high school, a friend of mine who knew Colleen thought we should meet. A few nights later, he points her out to me at a back yard party. Her petite five-foot frame topped off with long brown pigtails, brown eyes, and a cute smiling face immediately piques my interest. Colleen is fifteen, and I am sixteen. We live in a small town but never met because we attend different schools. I am nervous and not sure how to approach her, so I just stand there watching kids kick a soccer ball around the yard. When the ball rolls to me, I think maybe I can get her attention by kicking it hard. The ball explodes off the side of my foot, quickly traveling the twenty feet between us and hitting her square in the face. That face immediately turns red, reminding me of a cartoon character right before steam blows out its ears and the top lifts off its head. She thinks I did it on purpose and doesn't want anything to do with me. After trying to apologize several times without any luck, I try a different approach, stealing her scarf and telling her I will return it on our first date. She tells me, "You can keep the fuchsia scarf!" (She may have used another term unrelated to color). She walks away and before I know it, leaves the party.

Later that night, I call her. "Oh, it's you." She says after answering.

"I want to return your scarf."

"I told you what you could do with the scarf."

"Is your face okay?"

"It's fine. I have to go."

"Wait, you need to know that I only kicked that ball to impress you."

"Well, you definitely made an impression."

"I had no idea it would hit you, and I feel terrible about it. Please give me another chance." After an hour of banter and begging, I wear her down, and she finally agrees to go out with me. To my disappointment, the next night our conversation feels forced and we don't seem to have much in common. The date doesn't go well. Colleen is still mad at me and has a headache, so I take her home early. On the quiet drive home, she says, "I'm sorry." When I ask about what, she tells me, "I didn't really give you much of a chance and think we should try again." Reluctantly she adds, "On top of that I'm having my period." This isn't a subject any girl has ever discussed with me, and I am taken aback by her honesty. No girl has ever been this straight-forward with me.

The next night we laugh at a movie, drag Main Street with every other teenager in town, and begin to enjoy each other's company. When I drop her off at home, Colleen tells me I'm a good kisser, something else no girl has ever told me. I find myself drawn to her differences. She is spontaneous, bold, and tests boundaries while I tend to be cautious, analyze options, and follow the rules. She's a tomboy and enjoys the outdoors as I do. In addition to everything else, there is a double uniform bonus; she wears both Cheerleader and Catholic School Girl. Soon we spend all our free time together. With youthful curiosity we discuss and define our principles, beliefs, and ideology together, which then becomes the foundation of our relationship and our lives. We become best friends, never break up, and are married five years later. That foundation built together in our teens, blended with love, communication, and hard work, makes our dreams come true. Colleen becomes the exclamation point in my life. She is confident and draws me out of my sensitive, introverted comfort zone. Over time we realize that the only people who can build or destroy our life together, is us.

At breakfast, Stephanie's head is pounding from a migraine. She lies down in the dark bedroom to rest but wakes up to Caden crying. He hasn't slept well for Mark the last few nights and has a lot of gas. We notice an abundance of bubbles in his formula when it's mixed up fresh, so we try mixing up six bottles at a time, hoping the bubbles settle out in the fridge. We also discover that stirring the formula instead of shaking it, creates fewer bubbles. Caden does better on his next feeding and doesn't seem to care that he counters James Bond's preference of 'shaken, not stirred.'

Stephanie gets weaker as the days pass. She's nauseated and only gets so far on Cap'n Crunch. Steph needs her strength for the biopsy the next day and the chemo when we return home. Nana tries to combat Steph's nausea with over-the-counter remedies and prescriptions, but nothing helps. As a last resort, Colleen tries Benadryl®, which settles Steph's stomach and helps her sleep. Nurse Nana figures it out again. She is a fixer, always trying to solve issues to make things better.

That afternoon we clean the house and pick up gift cards for Tommy and the owners of the townhouse. These small tokens can't begin to thank them for all they have done for us, but we want to show them our appreciation.

When the kids go to bed, Mark cuddles his struggling wife. Steph's held her tears all day, not wanting to burden Colleen and me, but now they pour out, revealing her fear about the liver biopsy. Mark tells her everything will go smoothly tomorrow and comforts her until she drifts to sleep.

Tommy picks us up early, and we drive to the cancer center. Nana stays at the townhouse to let Caden sleep in a less stressful environment. A nurse calls Steph back to prep her for the biopsy. Only one person can go along, so Mark joins her. It's tough being the parent sometimes. You help a child grow up and deal with every challenge impacting their lives, then all of a sudden you have to step back and let someone else take your place. Even with that shared history, I understand her husband needs to come first in her life. She is lucky to have him. We are all lucky to have him.

Steph is awake during the procedure with her attention fixed on the overhead monitor. She finds it both fascinating and unsettling as she watches the long needle-like instrument eased toward its target on her liver. She can't feel a thing. The surgeon harvests a tissue sample and sends it to pathology. A nurse takes Steph to join Mark in recovery. He calls me with an update on her progress, and then I pass the information onto Colleen. Mark asks one nurse after another if I can come back and join them until the fifth one finally says yes. He looks out for me. Our team always looks out for each other, because that's what families do.

Steph's face lights up when I walk into her room. It's such a contrast to the sad clown face she makes when she cries. Her smile lightens the load for each of us. We hug, and she tells me the surgeon has an excellent bedside manner and she really likes him. He didn't have to puncture the lung to get the sample, which is a great relief to all of us. Pathology won't have the results for several days, so they will call Dr. Baranda with the test results and suggested next steps. That night we take Tommy out to thank him, and Steph eats better than she has all week. She is thrilled we are returning home tomorrow. Mark takes Caden's night shift as he has most of the week. It's a long night because the gas has returned and Caden can't sleep. The next morning, I tell Mark I'm sorry he had a tough night. He answers, "It's all right. That's what Dads have to do sometimes." I understand and smile.

Baby Stephanie is restless, sick, and crying again tonight. Colleen was up with our daughter often last night, so I tell her to get some sleep, and I will take care of the baby tonight. Steph is crying with arms and legs thrashing about as I lift her out of the crib. She ruts into my shoulder like she's looking for a breast, but won't take a bottle or pacifier. I walk her downstairs, so the crying doesn't bother Colleen. I change the diaper, wrap her in her fuzzy soft pink blanket, and then rock her. Slowly she settles down and falls asleep. I stop rocking, and soon she wakes up crying again.

I dance with her and sing, *"She'll be coming round the mountain when she comes."* I make up additional verses as I go because each time I stop, she starts to cry again. I wonder if she's testing my ability as a father or training me to bend to her wishes. It's two in the morning and based on last night's activity, I'm thinking she may be up all night. Accepting my fate, I focus on helping her feel better, and my goal changes from putting her to sleep to enjoying our time together. Changing my perspective makes all the difference in the world. We play, dance, sing, rock, and she responds by reaching up to touch my face, smiling, and holding on to my fingers. I'm in love. Around five, she drifts to sleep as we slowly rock. Colleen comes down at 7:00 a.m. and asks if I've been up all night. Yes, and I've never felt closer to my daughter. We have an understanding. I promised her I would always be here for her. Sometimes love grows slowly, but this night it bloomed.

Tommy picks us up early for our 7:00 a.m. flight. We say our goodbyes and board the G5, knowing we will miss him and all his help. I am so grateful our corporation has such a big heart in providing the jet. I shouldn't be surprised after observing their generosity during my career. They give away millions of dollars of product and funding each year to help those in need. I don't understand why pharmaceutical companies don't let it be known they are often in the first wave of help to provide medical and nutritional aid to disasters around the world. With that said, timing is everything. A few years later the executive jets would be liquidated as a corporate cost-cutting move.

Our trip proved to be both challenging and helpful. We are anxious about the liver results, but it's imperative we understand the full extent of Steph's disease. We are grateful for the help we received and know the Research Center is saving lives and providing hope to patients every day. Many believe it's a place where miracles happen.

At home, Colleen switches Caden to a new formula trying to get the gas under control, and tonight he sleeps for three hours, takes a bottle, and falls right back to sleep. Most of us sleep better with familiar beds and pillows. Steph is the exception as she worries about tomorrow's chemotherapy. Mark has used up his vacation, so the team decides I will take Steph to chemo, while Nana stays home with Caden and Mark goes to work. Each of us wants to be there with Steph, but we agree this is a better plan and I promise to update them throughout the day.

chapter 12

STEPH'S CHEMOTHERAPY BEGINS THIS MORNING, and she believes it's her best chance to kill any cancer still living in her body. She is uneasy on the way to KU's Cancer Center, but after we arrive, she settles down and becomes brave. The stress and anxiety that consistently stalk Stephanie account for the ten pounds she lost the past week and nausea now setting in. Nurse Practitioner Terri and Nurse Sue present Steph with a Chemo Binder that includes a personalized schedule, drug information, and other essentials. They review side effects and strategies used to help keep patients comfortable and safe during therapy. Chemotherapy targets fast-growing cancer cells, but also kills blood cells. With fewer red blood cells to carry oxygen, white blood cells to fight infection, and platelets to stop bleeding, Steph will become weak and fragile. We will need to be hypervigilant for signs of infection or blood clots during treatment.

The nurse uses Steph's port to deliver five pre-chemo medications used to reduce side effects, and then slowly runs the first chemo drug. Stephanie looks at me and says, "Okay, here we go" and gives me a thumbs up as I snap her picture. She is taking ownership of her disease and wants to know everything about what they are injecting, why, and the potential side effects. Steph asks about the equipment delivering the drugs and wants to understand all its bells and whistles. Steph tries to uncover any information she can about her disease and the tools available to overcome it. She is fighting for her life and determined to do everything in her power to shift the odds of survival in her favor. Nurse Sue is happy that Steph wants to be so informed and involved in the fight. It's unusual, and she tells us most patients simply become overwhelmed by the process. After the first bag empties, three additional chemo drugs are started. The staff is gentle and kind, and soon Steph is smiling.

✿

life lesson #8

Knowledge promotes understanding and confidence, allowing us the perspective to make adjustments and improve our situation. Become a student of life by learning about every aspect of it. Be curious and develop skills to improve your health, relationships, hobbies, and career. Learn from experts who are successful in areas of life that are important to you. Learning helps overcome obstacles, achieve goals, and adds depth to your life. My real education didn't start until after college, as I learned the importance of knowledge in a competitive world. It has helped me improve every aspect of my life, including my faith.

Stephanie calls Mark with an update, while I run out to the car and retrieve a cooler with our lunch. "So what do you have in there?" Sue asks. I proudly open the cooler and show her the fruit, drinks, and sandwiches I made earlier this morning. She shakes her head and says, "If it's cold she won't want anything to do with it. It's okay, this is your first time, and you're still learning, but chemo patients usually develop sensitivity to cold. Don't worry, we have something she will like." Sue guides me back to the staff kitchen and then shows me soups and snacks that are better choices.

Another chemo drug is started after lunch, and then Steph needs the restroom. I help her roll the IV stands to the bathroom, and when she's finished, I step in to hold the lines out of her way while she washes up. As her hands touch the water, she jerks them back in pain. Stephanie tells me it's colder than anything she has ever felt, and her hands still sting. The water is room temperature when I feel it. Steph mentions the reaction to Sue, who brings Stephanie a hat, scarf and gloves supplied by a pharmaceutical company. Since their medication sometimes causes the neuropathy and sensitivity to cold, the company provides these items to help patients deal with it. Steph wears them like a badge of honor.

The doctor and the staff here are personable and caring, making us feel like Steph is their only patient. They get things started, ask us if we need anything, and then give us our privacy as the drugs are infused. Stephanie and I enjoy our time together reliving memories like her driving lesson.

Steph is fifteen as we drive home from our country church and decide it's a good time for her first driving lesson. Winter has whitened the countryside with fresh snow and drifts are melting in the ditches, but the gravel road we travel on is dry. I stop the car thirty feet from an intersection and review everything Stephanie needs to remember while driving the vehicle. I notice Colleen in the r ear-view mirror shaking her head and realize I'm overdoing it. Steph tells me, "I'm not stupid Dad, and I know the brake from the gas. I drive the golf car and tractor all the time, so how hard can it be?"

"Okay." I reply, "Drive to the intersection and turn right."

Steph starts the car, puts it in gear, and quickly accelerates while asking me, "Which way do you want me to turn?"

"To the right."

"When do I start the turn?"

"When you enter the intersection."

"NOW?" she says as she jerks the wheel right. Everything moves in slow motion as the car lurches right, five feet short of the intersection. I'm shouting instructions. Steph's arms are locked on the wheel as I try to reverse the turn. Colleen and Scott are yelling in the back seat, and the car dives nose first into the ditch filled with snow and water.

Everything is quiet except the sizzle of the hot engine turning the ice water into steam. Then it happens. Steph begins to laugh hysterically and is joined by her mother and brother. I react differently, knowing if the car is high centered, I will be walking to the nearest farm to get pulled out. I don't believe I'm overreacting, but my wife tells me yelling at my daughter doesn't get the car out of the ditch. Steph and I switch places. I am happy the car starts, then I slowly ease it into reverse. A little gas and I am amazed the car slides out of the ditch as quickly as it went in. I look at my daughter and say, "Let's try this again."

"No way. I want Mom to teach me to drive." Scott chimes in that he does too. Fine with me.

I am surprised how light our mood is during chemo and how often we laugh. Stephanie is positive now and filled with hope.

I ask if she really feels that way or is putting on her brave face. A big smile tells me she really feels that way. I realize how much our moods reflect hers. If she has a good day or struggles, then so do we. I ask the nurses what patients read to stay motivated and help them win their fight? They tell us many patients read during chemo, but nothing really stands out. They will see what they can find out.

Steph naps and time passes quickly. She wakes, watches me journal, and asks me to write down the bedtime story about three field mice that I made up for her when she was little. She wants to tell it to Caden when he is old enough and asks me if I think she will be able to. I tell her without a doubt, yes. She smiles, closes her eyes, and drifts back to sleep.

Sue teaches me how to use the portable pump that Stephanie will go home with. It delivers the final chemo drug slowly over 48 hours to minimize the drug's side effects. I am taught how to hook it up, what to do if it stops running, how to disconnect it from the line, flush the port, and remove the needle. It's simple, but I have to maintain a sterile perimeter to eliminate the chances of infection by wearing a mask and chemo gloves. Sue shows me once, and then I try it. Steph is entertained by the questions I ask, being meticulous as I often am. When the lesson is over, Steph says, "My Dad rocks!" and we laugh with her.

Seven hours after our arrival, we walk back to the car. The slight breeze stings my daughter's sensitive fingers. She tells me how much she likes the doctor and staff and believes we have found critical members of the team we have been searching for. They are a great fit. Steph is excited to see Caden when we return home, and she tells him everything that happened at chemo. She snuggles him and promises, "I'm going to win this fight and live happily ever after with you, my baby boy!"

We learn that Steph and Mark's neighbor Page has called Colleen while we were at chemo. Page said the neighbors want to help and started a fund to offset some of Steph's medical bills. They are planning a dinner, raffle, and garage sale to raise the money and wanted us to know. Everyone wants to help, and the outpouring of love, cards, food and gifts is overwhelming. So many people care.

⚙

life lesson #9

Liz, a friend who knows from experience, recently gave me excellent counsel on our current situation. She said, "Take everything that anyone wants to give to you. Take in the love and concern they have for your family. It's a gift from their hearts. Over time they will call less and move back to their own lives and issues. It's a normal process, and we all have busy lives, so soak up their love now, for a time in the future when you need it." Liz also explains people show their love and concern in different ways. Some jump into the fray and stand by our sides while others are frightened to get too close or infringe on our privacy. People might bring food or send money, and others will pray for us. They may need to cry on our shoulder or need us to cry on theirs. There are no rules, so be careful not to judge. Everyone wants to help, but some don't know how to do it. They may simply be afraid, but that doesn't mean they love us any less.

chapter 13

THIS MORNING STEPH WAKES UP MOTIVATED. She sets appointments, organizes a document binder, requests records, and test results from the Research Center. Next, she sends a thank you note to the insurance company's Medical Director for approving her consultation. Steph's mood is light and hopeful. Knowing that the chemo is killing her cancer feeds her belief that she has a future again, and everything will work out. It's also the reason she wears gloves when drinking room temperature liquids and dresses in layers trying to keep the cold from settling in her bones. The neuropathy has spread to her feet, so she wears thick socks, and her legs are shaky when she walks. By afternoon fatigue sets in and her voice is raspy. The chemicals burn as they pass, yet she still wears a smile most of the day.

Nana and I are easing back into our work schedule, and the kids talk about spending more time at their own home. It's been challenging, but we hope the worst is behind us. Colleen never stops cooking, washing, cleaning, and caring for us all. A sign in our kitchen window quotes W. C. Fields, "I love to cook with wine. Sometimes I even add it to the food." Tonight my wife is asleep on the couch before her first sip. As I tuck her into bed, I realize it's the first day in a month that I haven't shed tears.

The Research Center is unable to reach us the next day, so they leave a message with the biopsy results. The cancer is in Stephanie's liver. Her diagnosis is now classified as Stage 4. End Stage. The oncologist stresses it's critical Steph gets immediate aggressive treatment. We are crushed and slide into disbelief and shock.

"Dad, am I going to die?"

"No, sweetheart. You have a great oncologist, a team fighting beside you, and you are going to survive. I believe it with all my heart." My tears return.

Colleen is lost in despair. She is tapped out and doesn't have any reserve energy to deal with this. We thought things were getting better, but now this destructive cancer is in her liver. How much of the liver is involved … can it be removed … how complex is the surgery … what about recovery … how much more can she take? How much more can any of us take? We don't have answers, and the questions keep coming.

After fear and anxiety and anger and uncertainty relentlessly attack the mind, despair moves in to finish the assault. Despair is the tubocurarine of emotions; it paralyzes its victim by stripping away all hope and joy. A black cloud descends, blunting the ability to think clearly. Uncertainty feeds indecision. The mind is lost in endless loops. Interest in sleep and food and life itself fade. Everything is gray. Nothing matters. Giving up and taking the path of least resistance promises welcome relief, but it's an empty promise.

Steph cries in my arms, and we promise each other we won't give up. She wears her sad clown face and is afraid she will die.

Will things ever be normal again? She tries to get her mind off the news and be positive. I watch her give Caden his bottle and wonder if he notices her warm tears dropping onto his cheek. Each of us needs to pull Steph through this and Caden is doing his part. There is no fear in his face, just smiles and unconditional love.

Can you look into the eyes of a baby and see God? Caden remains so calm throughout this ordeal. What does he know that we don't? He seems to see things that we can't. As I change him, he is focused on something above me, but when I look, I only see the white ceiling. Yet he stays focused, and his expressions support the notion he sees more. Colleen tells me he is so new to this earth that he still sees the angels. They reassure him everything will work out, and his mother will survive. It has become easy for us to believe in these things. You search for anything to hang onto when you risk losing everything. Faith needs nurturing to grow.

It's interesting how the mind works under stress. If it doesn't have the information to process a situation, it begins to speculate. My observation is that people often expect the worst if they don't know. Why the worst and not the best? Why be so cynical? I find comfort in believing Caden knows that his mother is going to be all right. I believe it to keep from falling apart.

I put on my mask and gloves, disconnect the chemo pump, flush the system with saline and heparin, then remove the line and needle from Steph's port. Round one complete. The kids take Caden to Steph's bedroom. They cuddle him and pray for an easy solution to the liver tumors. Terror has rushed back into their minds, but they keep it to themselves, trying not to burden Colleen and me. Caden is the only one of us who sleeps well that night.

Colleen and I leave the house early the next morning to focus on her needs for a change. I give everything to Steph, sometimes forgetting that Colleen also needs my support and love.. We run errands holding hands, talk, and pick up Chinese food for dinner. Steph's fortune reads *'You will receive pleasant news.'* Mark's opens his fortune cookie and finds the same message. We don't open any more cookies, deciding not to push our luck. We pick up our phones and update everyone about finding cancer in her liver. Steph's last call is to Teresa, and they talk late into the night.

Four days out and the chemo has Stephanie fatigued and lacking the interest to do anything. She and Mark are in bed by 9:00, but she can't slow her mind. At 10:00 Steph wanders into our room not wanting to deprive Mark of much-needed sleep. She is scared and nauseous. I search for the right things to say, but I don't know if any of it helps. I hold her tight like I did when she was a frightened little girl, and it seems to help as much as anything. It makes her feel safe, and I get comfort knowing that right now, she is alive and in my arms. I hum to her as we stand rocking together, locked in an embrace, just like we used to do when she was little.

I dance around the family room, holding my four-year-old tight in my arms. The stereo is playing *Every Breath You Take* by the Police. It's our song. As an adult, she teases me that the lyrics, "I'll be watching you" makes me sound like a stalker. Even so, it's her choice for the father-daughter dance at her wedding. I remind her of this now as we dance and her breath catches., "Dad we have so many wonderful memories. Will we have more? Will I get to make memories with Caden?"

"Yes, Sweetheart, I'm sure of it." I can't think of her future in any other way.

Stephanie wakes up the next day so fatigued that we have to force her out of bed. Colleen helps her shower, dress, and get into the backseat of the car next to Caden. Seeing them in the rearview mirror reminds me of Steph in her own car seat. I remember her dressed in a pink snowsuit looking out the window as we drive. I'm singing "I'm Popeye the Sailor Man" to her. She always adds "Toot-Toot" after that line, even if she is mad or crying. I sing the line now, but she has no response. Not this time. She's lost in thought about her appointment with Dr. Baranda to discuss the liver assessment.

The KU staff takes turns holding Caden, getting their baby fix, before handing him back to his mother. They take time to listen and answer each of our questions. Dr. Baranda has talked to the Research Center and tells us, "There is a significant increase in tumor growth and activity since the original CT scan was taken. Both lobes of the liver are now involved." This new information hits us hard. The doctor hasn't received the scans or test results yet and wants to review them before giving us a full assessment. She will present Steph's case and discuss options with a group of liver specialists. Her plan is for Stephanie to complete six to eight chemo sessions before surgery to shrink the tumors and save as much of the liver as possible. Dr. Baranda tells us this will be a significant operation, so she wants to use a liver surgeon who does this all day, every day. She also shares some good news. Stephanie's other organs are clear of cancer, and now that her diagnosis is Stage 4, Dr. Baranda can add the newest chemo drug, which may increase Steph's odds of survival.

The Doctor asks about side effects, and then prescriptions are written to help with Steph's nausea. She explains the chemo will throw Steph back into puberty. When the chemo is stopped for the surgery, she will experience menopausal symptoms with hot flashes and increased belly fat. Her hormones will be on a roller coaster ride. Steph taps her sense of humor and says, "Most women get to experience these changes only once, but I get to do it over and over again." Colleen smiles and welcomes her daughter to the old lady's club.

The doctor reminds us that Steph is now more susceptible to germs and infections. Caden will have to wait for some of his baby immunizations, because of the risk of spreading live viruses to Steph. Dr. Baranda discusses the specifics with nurse Nana.

We debrief on the ride home and try to spin things as positively as we can. It isn't good news, but we find comfort knowing that Steph is in good hands with Dr. Baranda, who has an aggressive plan to save Steph's life. Nana is quiet while we drive. She can't bear the thought of them opening up her baby girl again.

The team struggles at home as our emotions spill out. Stephanie is empty and walks around in a daze. In the hallway, we hug, and she begs, "Dad, please don't let me die. I don't want to die. I want to be a mom and raise Caden. That isn't asking too much, is it?" It tears at my heart when she asks me to save her, and I don't know what I can do to guarantee it. I promise and put on my bravest face, but she sees the fear in my eyes. We can't take much more. We need good news, not bad, and it's difficult not knowing what's coming next. As I release her, she won't let go, hugging me tighter, and then tells me, "Dad, you give me hope." I smile back at her and pray that it's enough. The girls go to bed while Mark and I talk, trying to build each other's confidence. Mark tells me we should focus on the chemo as a turning point. It's already killing cancer cells, and they will deliver wave after wave of the drugs until Steph is cancer free. Just saying it makes us feel better.

Mark is a wonderful husband, and we love and respect him. How many men could live with their in-laws, share hotel rooms, and allow us to take the lead on Steph and Caden's healthcare? Mark is always involved and jumps in anytime he can help. We make all decisions together after everyone discusses it, and that has made us a strong team. Pediatric Nurse Nana takes point on Caden's health, while I help with some of Steph's emotional care. She is my little girl, and we understand each other so well. As her husband, Mark is always there for Steph and as Caden's father, balancing the dirty diapers and late feedings with the baths and love that go along with it. He fills both roles with love, devotion, and attention, wearing many hats and doing it all so well. Our daughter made a wise choice in her life partner.

A husband willing to share the lead in his wife's health crisis with his in-laws reveals his inner strength. Mark is strong enough to recognize our medical expertise, and when added to our total commitment to Steph's survival, they combine to increase her chance of living. He is strong enough to realize his love and dedication are most synergistic when added to ours. He is strong enough to support or question our actions based solely on what will help Steph the most. There is no ego or selfishness on Mark's part. He consistently practices his beliefs and follows a positive moral compass. His strength and confidence in his marriage allow him to determine what's best for Steph without letting emotion rule over logic. Mark does the right thing. When a child falls in love and begins a new life with their partner, the previous parental relationship usually changes. Love is still alive and well, but priorities shift. The degree and timing of the shift are dictated by the depth and length of the relationship. Steph discovered early on that she has enough love for all of us. We didn't lose our daughter; we gained an awesome son-in-law.

Steph cares for Caden the next morning in a brief escape from her worry, then Colleen drives them to see Steph's OB/GYN. The office staff is following Steph's web page and anxious to see her. They come into the waiting room for hugs and fuss over Caden. The visit lasts for two hours as they catch up on details. There is so much support for Stephanie everywhere she goes.

In the afternoon, Colleen and I disagree about dusting and cleaning and priorities. We are run down, frustrated, and work is building up, which makes it easy to lash out at each other. I know better and have to try harder. I need to control my emotions, and Steph doesn't need to see us bicker. The fact is, doing chores keeps us busy and less focused on worrying.

That evening we sit down as a family and revisit the discussion Mark and I had the night before. The team is at a decision point and needs to agree on which way to go. We decide that from now on we can't waver from the belief that Steph is going to live. We need to stay positive and support each other because if we take care of the team, the team will take care of us. We talk about setting short term goals, like staying positive for the entire day, and how we can reward ourselves when we achieve them. We agree to focus back on things in our control, instead of those we can't impact.

Colleen and I tell Steph and Mark that we are going to send them on a reward trip after she is well. We will use my airline and hotel points to send them anywhere they want to go. They tell us it isn't necessary, but we say it's a done deal and won't take no for an answer. They get excited and talk about where they might go. It's easy to see this is a good idea and great use of the points I have accumulated over the last 20 years.

Steph asks me how my journaling is going, and I tell her it's very comforting. Then she asks what I'm going to do with it. I tell her it's for Caden because I want him to know how brave his mother is, and how hard she is fighting to win her battle with cancer. She smiles and tells me I should make it into a book and go on *Oprah* or *Ellen*. We laugh, and I remind her of my writing skills from college.

Entering college, my ability to write is sketchy at best. English 101 is a test out class. The rumor is that it's also used to weed out students who aren't college material and only attending school for the Viet Nam draft deferment. My draft number is 150. The newspaper suggests if a number is below 150, you should worry if above 150 you shouldn't. My draft number places me in limbo.

The English class covers six types of essays. Students are required to write a three-page essay in fifty minutes with five or fewer errors. Students passing on Monday have to also pass on Wednesday and on Friday to test out. The type of essay is revealed as the test starts. If you fail any of the three essays, you wait two weeks to try again.

It seems I only can write two successful essays in a week and sometimes only one. Many students struggle and some are kicked out for sneaking in completed essays in books, boots, and one cute coed in her underwear. She never returns. It's my first semester of school, and I am more embarrassed than worried after flunking the class. When I retake the course in my second semester, and that also proves unsuccessful, I receive an invitation from the dean to discuss my academic future.

I am admitted to the dean's office to find a balding middle-aged man wearing a tweed jacket and smoking a large carved ivory pipe. He ignores me for a time and then asks me if I would like to join the Army. I smile and answer, I would prefer to fly for the Air Force. He searches the paper in front of him for my name and proceeds to tell me I should take this seriously and shouldn't be wasting my parent's money flunking classes. I tell him I pay myself working thirty hours a week and was trying to pass the course. Four times I failed the Friday essay with one too many errors. Unimpressed, he tells me I have one more chance to pass the class before being expelled. I test out early the next semester and never see the dean again. If anyone is reading this now, I guess my writing improved.

chapter 14

THE NEXT DAY STARTS OUT BETTER for all of us, and there is a definite change in Steph's outlook. She is smiling more and so appreciative of the things everyone is doing for her. Caden smiles all the time, which provides a great diversion for us. We take turns dancing, singing, and playing with him. He loves to eat, and the word pudgy seems to capture his current look as he outgrows his clothes. I love to snuggle him after his bath. The fresh baby smell recharges my soul like nothing else.

In my office, I read through work email and product manuals. I complete several online tests. I am a field consultant for the marketing team, launching a new drug. Product launches are a big deal in our industry, and it's good for me to concentrate on other things.

While I work, Steph, and Caden smile and look pretty for a photographer. The session is a gift from Caden's pediatrician, Dr. Sheri Martin. The black and whites of Steph's hands cradling Caden's tiny feet are precious. Caden begins to fuss and won't settle down, so Steph asks me for help. I swaddle him, hold him tight, and sing as I slow-dance with him. He melts in my arms and falls asleep in a couple of minutes, just like my two babies before him. Colleen calls me *the sandman* and I enjoy the title. I feel a close bond with my grandson and couldn't be happier about it. We understand each other. The photographer, also a pediatrician, is impressed by how quickly I settled Caden down. Steph tells her not to make a big deal of it because my head will get even bigger and explode.

There are blessings usually mixed in with challenges if you look for them. Our family has always been close, and now Mark and Caden are a vital part of that. Colleen and I are thankful to have spent time with our grandson every day of his life. Mark leaves the house at 6:00 a.m. and works late into the night. When he returns home, he takes care of Steph and Caden's night shift. Colleen and I take on a few more night feedings so that Mark and Steph can get some sleep. We love our time with Caden. He's so joyful, and it's fun to have a baby in the house again. God gives us what we need.

We finally receive a book to help us with our positive thinking from Steph's cousin, Kristen. She spent a summer with us when she was young, and the girls developed a close relationship. Kristen is the big sister Steph never had. She sends us the book, *Chicken Soup for the Surviving Soul*, by Jack Canfield, etc. It shares positive stories about people dealing with cancer and references other books we can read. It's just what the doctor ordered, except that none of our doctors have seemed to know about it. The next day I pick up a copy for the cancer center to share with their patients.

The team is spoiling our patient. I buy her fancy jellybeans, Mark finds her favorite old movies, and Nana cooks the food she likes best. We search for ways to make her happy. Anything to bring her joy and get her to smile warms our hearts.

Nurse Nana drives Steph and Caden to his checkup at the pediatric office where she works. Dr. Martin says Caden is doing great and now weighs 13 pounds. Stephanie worked a few summers at the office, so everyone there knows her and enjoys catching up. That night Steph sends out a web update that reflects her positive attitude, while we make calls to those closest to us. Most answer fearing additional bad news, but we just want to talk and catch up on their lives for a change.

Colleen's brother and his wife are coming to visit this weekend. Bill and Kim are a few years younger than Colleen and I, and we began hanging around together after college. We've become close friends and often vacation together. Kim and I joke about being the responsible parents, always paying attention to details, while Colleen and Bill are spontaneous and just want to have fun. We've shared many adventures together. Kim will stay for a week to help out while I attend a company meeting. Colleen's excitement to spend time with her closest friend shows in her smiles and renewed energy. Kim will help replenish her spirit. I have mixed feelings about leaving. I want to be at the product launch for business reasons, but also worry about being separated from the team. I place one of Caden's little socks in my pant pocket, just to have something of his with me.

I talk to Steph and Mark about going home for the weekend to enjoy some private time with Caden. They agree it's a great idea and start packing. They are fighting this disease together, and the time alone allows them to revel in the strength of their marriage and the blessing of their young son. Arriving home, they find a surprise. The neighbors have cleaned their house from top to bottom, did laundry, filled the fridge with food, and left flowers on the kitchen table. The kids are stunned at the support and love they receive from these generous friends.

Bill and Kim are uncomfortable when they arrive. Their hugs are tentative, and they act nervous. Kim tells us they worried during the drive in about not knowing what they were walking into and what to do or say to help us. Colleen and I appreciate their honesty and explain we just need to be with friends. As we share everything we have been through and allow ourselves to relax, they do too. Soon we find ourselves laughing and acting normal again. Normal feels so good as we cook a meal together, have some refreshments, and catch up on their family.

We drop by the kids home the next morning so that Bill and Kim can meet Caden and hand out presents. Kim loves to shop and give away gifts. She has toys and outfits for Caden, warm fleece pajamas for Stephanie, and a little something for each of us. Steph has always been close to her aunt and uncle and enjoys their company. We talk about everything under the sun, but the discussion always returns to Steph's illness. They can't believe how well we work together and roll with the punches.

Bill leaves early Sunday for Minnesota while I pack for my trip. Aunt Kim volunteers to take Caden's night feedings for the week, so Colleen equips the guest room accordingly. The kids move back to our home just in time to join us for Nana's Sunday dinner.

I fly to the launch meeting with several members of my sales team. I am anxious about being separated from Stephanie and facing so many people at the meeting. I haven't had problems talking one-on-one, but I'm not sure how I'll do in a larger group. The conference will immerse me back into my job and allow me to thank friends for their support and prayers.

As I see people, I make it a point to hug them, tapping into their energy source, and recharging a little with each hug. Everyone is kind and concerned, so I keep my composure most of the time, but periodically, I have to slip away and catch my breath. I almost lose it when a friend tells me his five-year-old daughter remembers 'Miss Stephanie' in her nightly prayers. There are close to a thousand people at the meeting and it seems all of them know Steph's story. To escape attention, I skip dinner and hide in my hotel room. Back home everyone is doing fine when I call. I feel lonely and wish I were with them, but all in all, I'm doing fine too. I hold Caden's white and blue sock for a while thinking of his smiles, then set it next to the alarm and go to bed.

Colleen drives Stephanie to her second chemo session, while Aunt Kim stays home with Caden. I stand in the ballroom atrium waiting for the meeting to start when my cell phone rings. It's Stephanie. She misses me, is scared, and begins to sob uncontrollably. I'm not prepared for this and move to the backside of a large pillar in the open space before I lose control of my emotions. I don't care if anyone sees me cry, but don't want to create a scene. As I listen to my daughter struggle to catch her breath, my heart feels like it's being ripped apart, and I'm filled with guilt for leaving her. We talk, and she tells me she will be brave, but only after I promise to come home as soon as I can. We say I love you and it isn't until I hang up, that I realize that my body has slid down the pillar until I am sitting on the floor. There are people around me, but they are gracious not to stare and give me privacy to collect myself.

The chemotherapy goes smoothly as they administer the new combination of cancer-killing drugs. Dr. Baranda checks on Steph often, making sure she is comfortable and giving updates on the reports she has received concerning the liver tumors. They discuss timing and possible surgical options, which helps put things into perspective for our team.

Stephanie is chilled, so Colleen asks Sue for a warm blanket. The nurses keep extra blankets in a warmer since many patients are sensitive to the cold. Sue leads Colleen to the room where the blankets are stored, then turns to face her. Sue asks how a mother can hold up with this happening to her daughter. Colleen clenches her jaw and shakes her head, unable to answer. Sue hugs her as they tremble with emotion. Colleen confides, "I don't know how any of us are doing it. We just have to stay strong for Steph."

We are often asked how we do it. We don't feel strong or brave, but simply understand that we have to do everything in our power to save Stephanie. If we miss something or don't support her fight with everything we have and lose her, I can't imagine what would happen. We promised her the best doctors, hospitals, and drugs available. So far, we have delivered. Now we fight to stay positive, do our best, and keep moving forward. The chemo is harder on Steph's body this time with more side effects and stronger fatigue. Each treatment will grow in difficulty as her blood counts drop. It will also take longer for her to bounce back.

It's Stephanie who consistently shows the greatest amount of strength and bravery. She is the one who endures the tests, surgery, chemo, and side effects. She is the one whose young life with a new baby is a question mark. But even with those burdens, most of the time we draw on Stephanie as our role model for strength and bravery. She helps us put on our brave masks and get through each day. Her daily example of smiles and love allow us the luxury of hope and belief that she will survive. I can't imagine the additional challenge we would face if she was difficult, unwilling, or simply gave up.

The caretaker of a crisis victim quickly learns they must focus on the victim first instead of themselves. This is their opportunity to provide patience, understanding, and acceptance to someone in need. That focus, sprinkled with love, laughter, and support is what the patient often needs most. You have to feel sorry for yourself and deal with your emotions on your own time. That may sound harsh, but the ultimate goal is to overcome the crisis so everyone gets relief. Our team approach has worked well to share the load and give each other a break from time to time. It's vital to escape the stress of the crisis and recharge if you can. We quickly realize the team concept works to support each member of the team, not just Stephanie.

Colleen and Steph call that evening to fill me in on everything Dr. Baranda has discussed and they praise her gentle, caring bedside manner. Aunt Kim is doing fantastic with Caden at night, and it's such a relief to have her help. Colleen is doing better than she has in weeks. She has her best friend around to talk with, and Kim helps her escape the worry.

My week is filled with the technical information, medical experts, training, and marketing you would expect from a new drug launch meeting. I crash a private lunch to thank several top executives for their help in approving the jet for our trip. They downplay it, ask how Steph is doing, and wish our family all the best in the future. I enjoy time with friends and am told Steph will never fully understand how many people are following her progress updates and how amazed they are at her strength and faith. She has positively touched many lives, boosting their faith.

Back in my room, I think about the past week and realize everything outside of the meetings was centered on Steph's illness. There are times I find it difficult to talk to people who ask about my daughter, but I retell her story so frequently that I find efficient ways to encapsulate it, and that helps. Other times with closer friends, I tell more of her story, and that helps me deal with my feelings. I usually feel better after sharing. Sometimes I can't stop the tears. This is new territory for me, and I'm not sure what to do. I'm just trying to get through it and understand my friends will cut me a little slack if I make a fool of myself.

Finally, the long week is over, and I head home. I purchase a small Mickey Mouse at the airport to hang from the mobile over Caden's bassinet. When my kids were young I always brought home gifts after traveling and I want to keep up the tradition for my grandson. As I walk in the back door, Steph runs to me, and we hug and laugh. A minute later the rest of the team joins in. It's great to be home. Then the kids drive home to host Mark's parents for the weekend, and Bill returns to pick up Kim, leaving Colleen and me alone. We are not sure what to do. The house is too quiet, and we find the silence unsettling.

chapter 15

STEPHANIE NOW UNDERSTANDS what to expect from her two-week chemo routine. The day before chemotherapy is her best because she has more blood cells boosting her energy. Steph makes lunch of a peanut butter sandwich and canned soup for herself and the lucky one who will accompany her. After chemo, the cells begin to die off, and fatigue gets progressively worse for about eight days. Then Steph slowly rebuilds her cells along with her strength. She is nauseated most of the time. She is in pain much of the time, but you wouldn't know it. Stephanie works hard to stay positive and take things as they come. Steph reminds us often that she has a perfectly healthy little boy and is lucky to be alive. I am amazed watching my daughter grow into a warrior.

Scott is home for his colonoscopy. While we don't believe they will find disease, it's still a relief when the results come back normal. Oncology suggests Stephanie get gene mapping to understand the potential for cancer in her family line. Steph supports the idea, wanting to know if her son is at increased risk. They also suggest Caden has his first colonoscopy in his early teens.

Steph and Mark drive Caden home for the weekend to find their neighbors working their annual spring garage sale. The kids walk from garage to garage, and their day is filled with laughter and hugs. That evening these wonderful friends present Steph with the money they have made from the sale to help offset her medical bills. How do you thank people for something like that? At dusk, they release helium-filled balloons. Blue ones for colon cancer and white ones for hope. It's emotional and challenging, but Steph feels immersed in love.

When the kids return, Colleen is at work, so Steph enjoys a rare day alone with her son. Babies don't have much to do if you think about it. They look cute, eat, sleep, pee, and poop. It's that last thing that Caden is struggling with today. Stephanie patiently tries to help him feel better until finally, the dam breaks and caca flies. Literally. His reward is relief from the pain and a cleansing bubble bath with his mom. Colleen and I return home in time to dry Caden, slather on baby lotion, and delight in his clean baby smell.

Steph showers off and notices a mop of hair covering the drain. She wraps herself in a towel and walks into the hall. I see her sad clown face and water dripping off her as she stares at a fist full of long curly brown hair in disbelief. "This is from one shower." Looking at me, she asks, "Am I going to lose it all?"

"The doctor told us some patients only lose a little, and others more. Everyone is different. I don't know how much you will lose, but I promise it will all be back a year from now." She quits crying and tries to smile. I suggest, "Don't pluck your eyebrows anymore in case you need to do a comb-over." Her look tells me it's too soon for hair humor. I save a curly lock of Steph's hair that day. I'm not sure why. Maybe because we didn't save any of her hair as a baby. Perhaps I'm just grasping at straws again trying to hang on to her. I don't know, but I tie a ribbon around the curly lock of hair and stash it away like a treasure.

Stephanie's journey is grueling, but she is handling it well, and we're proud of her. God always gives her some good to offset the bad. She recovered from colon surgery faster than expected, traveled to the Research Center like a rock star, and now gets chemo from loving people at a cutting-edge clinic. She is losing her hair, but we love her just the way she is. Mark drives Steph to chemo, and mid-morning a dozen roses are delivered. Steph tears open the card, which simply reads, *Love you, Me.* The nurses tell her it's the first time a patient has received flowers during chemo. Steph hugs Mark's neck and plants a kiss on his cheek. She whispers, "I think I'll keep you around for a while."

Later in the week, Stephanie drives Caden to visit his pediatrician. While the nurse weighs Caden, Steph notices a flyer tacked to the office bulletin board. She is surprised to see that it's about her. The neighbors are hosting a fundraiser in her name. Her body warms as gratitude and love sweep through it. Many people don't know those living around them, but this neighborhood is different. They know each other well, feel a deep need to help their friend, and are working hard to achieve their shared goal.

Scott returns home for Easter and helps Mark, and I catch up on outside work. I enjoy their company and sense of humor, as we blend fun and teasing into our efforts. The physical labor feels good as we spread mulch and gravel and then trim trees. It's rewarding to see the finished results. We also feel good about the decision we make concerning Steph's tree. We planted half a dozen trees after the construction of our home and named each after a family member. Steph's oak tree stands in the front yard, but last year's ice storm broke off the top third leaving only lateral branches. Before Steph's cancer, I had planned to replace the imperfect tree, but that no longer feels right. The tree is alive and deserves a chance just like its namesake. We trim it up, hoping a lateral will become the new leader, and the tree will survive and prosper.

The team celebrates Easter day with good food, and welcomes the opportunity to rest and reflect on the meaning of the day. We skip church because Steph's blood counts are too low and we can't risk her catching a bug. She's exhausted from the chemo but keeps trying to help with the meal and play with Caden. When told to rest, she reminds us she doesn't know how many Easters they will have together. I am struck by the matter-of-fact way she says this, but I understand it's not because she's giving up. She just acknowledges the possibility and is determined to make the best of the time she is given. She writes an update for her webpage, thanking everyone for the cards, love, and prayers they send. Steph feels guilty about not thanking each one personally but she doesn't have the energy to do it.

Caden seems to change and grow each day. He coos and smiles whenever he sees us. He reaches out for a toy and tries to grab it until something else catches his eye. I watch him discover the world around him and find it fascinating. He's sleeping four to six hours between bottles at night, which is appreciated because we can too.

Late in the day, I talk to Steph's psychiatrist. Teresa informs me she had an abnormal mammogram. I tell her it's probably nothing and try to reassure her. She appreciates the positive thoughts but sounds frightened. She asks me not to tell Steph because she doesn't want her to worry, so I keep it to myself.

The next morning Steph's energy is depleted, so Nana stays home from the office to care for Caden while I travel for work. When I return, our team takes friends out to dinner to thank them for their ongoing help. Sensing our guest's uncertainty at what to say when we are seated, Steph fills the silence with a quick update and tells them how much she appreciates their help. She tells them she loves them, and with that, everyone relaxes and enjoys each other's company. As we leave, Teresa takes Steph aside and tells her she's having a biopsy tomorrow and explains why. They tell each other everything will be fine and not to worry, but both find that easier said than done. For a quiet moment, they communicate everything they feel by simply looking into each other's eyes and then embrace in a hug.

Later in the week as Stephanie's energy returns, the kids try four days at home without help. Nana and I work outside most of the weekend and are surprised when they return with a picnic lunch. After they leave, we finish our work, enjoy a fire on the pond's peninsula, and then sleep until 10:00 the next morning. The kids have us over for burgers, and it becomes apparent that we are so used to being together, it doesn't feel right to be apart. We haven't heard anything from Teresa yet, so I call to find out the test results. The biopsy confirms she has breast cancer, and with the diagnosis comes fear and uncertainty. Teresa tells Steph, "I get so much strength from you. If you can fight your cancer and be brave, so can I." The physician and patient are now friends fighting a common enemy. They talk through tears and promise each other to be brave and win their battles together. Teresa is at the beginning, without an understanding of the extent of her cancer or what the next steps may be. Stephanie tells her about the excellent treatment team she has at KU and promises to identify their best oncologist for breast cancer. She also encourages Teresa to move as fast as possible to start the most aggressive and quickest way to treat it.

At her fourth chemo session, Steph's neutrophil counts are

low but still within the acceptable range to receive therapy. Her bone marrow isn't able to replace the red and white blood cells as fast as the chemo is killing them off. After each session, the cells take longer to rebuild than the previous treatment, and her energy levels are directly tied to the recovery of the cells. The doctor reminds us that Steph's risk for infection continues to rise, and we must minimize her exposure to people and places that could pass on germs, a cold, or worse. Stephanie mentions the lower back pain she's had lately, so Dr. Baranda schedules a nuclear bone scan to make sure her patient's cancer hasn't spread. Then we collect the names of their top breast cancer oncologists to pass onto Teresa.

As we gather our things to leave, the nurse practitioner tells us she has some good news. The tumor marker blood test from Steph's first chemo session registered at 4.7. The normal range is less than 3.0. Dr. Baranda is excited and can't believe today's numbers have dropped to 1.1. The cancer isn't gone or in remission, but this is the first indicator that the chemotherapy is working and creating a positive effect. We are so excited that we hug everyone and feel like we are walking on air.

In the car, Steph and I are giddy as we discuss the great news. Then it hits me. The nurses have said they were so happy the chemo was working and having a positive effect, and in fact, they acted surprised. It never crossed my mind that the chemo wouldn't work. I had naively believed that it always worked. The more I thought about this, the more foolish I felt. I've sold prescription drugs most of my life and fully understand that no medication works every time. Somehow my mind completely blanked that out. Maybe my subconscious wasn't sure I could handle it.

Stephanie is thrilled and gains strength from this fantastic news. She wants to share it and starts calling everyone. "Guess what? I just got new tumor marker numbers and the chemo's working! Woo Hoo!" On the way home, we pick up a copy of the *Chicken Soup* book for Dr. Varanka.

Teresa and her husband Voyteck join us for dinner, bringing gifts for Caden and Steph and a homemade pie for dessert. They are also generous with their time. Teresa holds Caden while we visit after the meal, telling us that she is so ready for grandchildren. Steph shares the oncologist names we collected and promises we will help any way we can. Teresa answers she is already drawing strength from Steph's courage and example. As they leave, I am reminded we now have two patients to keep in our prayers. Both are members of the Cancer Club. If you survive the initiation, you graduate to the Survivor Club. Those members share first-hand knowledge of what it's like to stare death in the face.

Over the next week, Stephanie talks about the tumor marker often, always giving us high fives and exclaiming, "Hey I'm fighting this cancer and winning. I'm kicking cancer's ass! Woo Hoo!" It's so motivating for our team to see her excited and filled with hope. We are reenergized, and the relief is liberating.

I drive Stephanie to her Nuclear Bone Scan the next morning and am allowed to stay in the room during the procedure. Twenty years ago, I sold nuclear medicine and have retained a basic under-standing of the process. The tech injects radiated phosphorous into a vein and then tracks the rate of its absorption into the bone. The radiologist looks for areas where the uptake is abnormal. I see the monitor that shows Steph's skeleton and the phosphorous being picked up.

Sometimes a little knowledge is dangerous. As I watch my daughter's joints and skeleton register hot spots, my first thought is, the cancer is showing up everywhere. My heart begins to pound, I break a sweat, and my anxiety quickly rises as emotion blocks out logic. Then the analytical side of my mind notices the symmetry and mirrored image on each side of her skeleton, making it more likely to be a normal uptake and not cancer. My lesson for the day is not to react quickly to things I don't fully understand. Especially when it comes to Steph's health. Two days later, the scan comes back normal.

Nana and I have fallen victim to the grandparent delusion that Caden is the best looking, smartest, and most talented child ever. But in this case, he really is. We enjoy his playful personality, which matures each day. He lies on his back, kicking and cooing as I walk by. He looks up, then smiles and makes faces. The best part of Steph's day is in the morning when she wakes up to find him happy, laughing, and wanting to play. She can't wait to pick him up and let her worries fall away. She looks into his big brown eyes and knows what she is fighting for. "You are loved little one, and always will be." She whispers while kissing the bottom of his toes.

We receive the first chemo bill today and are surprised at how high it is. Her insurance is paying for most of it, but the planned chemo sessions will consume much of the lifetime limit of her coverage. If we add the cost of hospitals, surgeries, doctors, lab work, scans, prescriptions, etc. she may exceed that limit. We decide there isn't much we can do except stay positive and hope it never happens. It's not much of a plan, but we don't see many options.

chapter 16

STEPHANIE VISITS THE CANCER CENTER for a blood draw and finds her counts just high enough to attend the fundraiser. The center's staff is supportive and believes she needs to be there, but asks her to minimize direct contact with people and the risk that exposure brings. They know Steph is a hugger and ask her to be selective. Good luck with that.

The neighbors work hard on last-minute details for the spaghetti dinner, silent auction, and casino night. Everything is well organized with people cooking, setting up tables, and displaying the items for auction. They wear white t-shirts that read, *Bet on STEPH*, with pictures of cards and dice on the front and the *Preventable, Curable, Beatable* cancer message on the back. What we can't see are the endless hours they have invested getting businesses to donate items for the auction, securing a site for the event, and generating the large attendance.

Steph and Mark arrive with Caden and immediately draw a crowd. Mark's parents are here, along with many of our friends, and others who join in to support Steph's journey. Everything flows smoothly as people eat, talk, and place their bids. Steph enjoys a salad and a little spaghetti and then walks around with Caden thanking as many people as she can.

Page asks me to say something to the gathering before the casino games start. I enjoy speaking to groups and do it all the time, but this is different, this is about my little girl's survival, and I'm not sure I can do it without breaking down. Steph stands beside me and says, "No problem, Dad, I want to do it." Page leads Steph up onto the stage, introduces her, and Steph begins to talk.

"I want to thank everyone who helped put this event together. We have the most amazing neighbors, and they worked very hard to make this happen. If you were involved in any way, thank you so much for everything that you did. The turnout is absolutely incredible, and it means the world to me that you took time out of your busy lives to come and support me. I love you all. I am fighting Stage 4 Colon Cancer. I found out I had it two weeks after the birth of my son Caden. He is the reason I am fighting so hard to survive."

Emotion sweeps through the room. Tears flow down her cheeks as Stephanie struggles for the words and soon can't continue. I help her off the stage as another speaker tells the audience how the neighborhood developed a plan to help their friend. It's evident to anyone listening that the camaraderie and friendship this group has is uncommon. Someone in the audience says, "If there is a house for sale in the neighborhood, I want to move in." The comment is met with nods and smiles.

Stephanie composes herself and then continues to thank people until she is forced to sit down from growing pain in her gut. Its intensity grows until she has to say goodbye and leave for home. I ask her how bad it is and she answers, 'It's getting worse, but I'm okay.' At first, we don't pick up on how frightened she is or how bad she feels. After a few phone calls with her mom, its clear things are getting worse, so Colleen and I leave to join her.

When we arrive at their home, Steph is weak, shaking, and begins to vomit. Over the next two hours, we talk to Dr. Baranda three times. The doctor doesn't think we need to go to the emergency room since there isn't a fever and none of the recent scans showed anything new. That's fine with Steph because she doesn't want to visit the ER unless she has to. At 1:00 a.m. her pain finally settles down and she dozes off with the help of a sleeping pill. Nana and I camp out on the floor in Caden's nursery to take night duty and let his parents rest. Steph feels fine in the morning and wonders if she just reacted to the excitement and stress of the night before. Colleen and I head home so I can pack for a business trip.

On my flight to San Francisco, I catch up on my journaling about Steph's illness and experiences the other team members have shared with me. I enjoy writing to Caden but struggle to find the time as work becomes demanding again. My goal is to record everything about Steph's fight with cancer so he can view it through my writing, in case she can't tell him herself. I want to capture his mother's will to survive and the incredible love she has for him and life itself. Hopefully, this gives him a glimpse of her spirit and soul. When he reads it, he will be proud of her. This reminds me of how thankful I am to be part of the strong team that is helping Steph. This disease makes it clear that life should never be taken for granted. It's easy to get caught up in everyday stuff and lose perspective on things most important to us, the blessings of love, life, and the souls around us. Journaling also gives a grandfather the chance to pass on some life lessons and advice to his grandson.

Something happens that I never expected. The time I spend

writing to Caden helps me deal with my daughter's illness and has become therapeutic for me. There are so many things to keep track of that it quickly became overwhelming. But when I write them down, it's like plucking them from my mind and filing them away for safekeeping. It makes me feel lighter somehow. I feel less stress without them spinning around in my thoughts, yet I know exactly where they are if I need them. Trying to help Caden know his mother has also helped me appreciate her more myself. Thank you for that, baby boy.

At the hotel, I notice toys in the gift shop window and that reminds me of Caden. A couple checking in makes me think of Colleen, and a family walking through the lobby together looks like our team. I'm meeting with a hundred people on this work trip, but I still feel alone and miss everyone at home. I miss Stephanie the most because I can't see for myself that she is okay. All I need is a hug, a kiss, or to see her smile and give me a thumbs up. I have just arrived and can't wait to get back home. I reach into my pocket for my room key, find Caden's sock and smile. And ever since that product launch, I always carry his little white and blue sock with me.

Mark takes Steph to her fifth chemo treatment, where they use five drugs to combat her nausea. Dr. Baranda sets up CT and PET scans for the day after Steph's sixth chemo session. Those results will be reviewed at KU's Liver Rounds (a regular scheduled educational meeting where experts discuss cutting edge liver research and treatment), and then Dr. Baranda will discuss the next steps with us. Waiting for time to pass is challenging. We try to make the best of each day and live in the moment, but often our thoughts drift to the future. Stephanie and Teresa are in our prayers every day. Teresa will undergo surgery first and then start chemotherapy after she recovers.

Steph's fatigue is increasing and lasts longer. The list of side effects grows to include weak shaking hands, a faltering voice, and more hair down the shower drain. The cold sensations are stronger, and the skin on her knuckles has grown dark. She seldom complains about these things, just casually mentioning them to us, so we know what's going on. We wish we could take the burden ourselves and lift it off her shoulders, but she tells us it's hers to carry. The toughest part for her right now is the inability to pick up Caden and take care of him. Steph is learning the importance of staying positive while having cancer. She still gets down and feels sorry for herself sometimes, but who wouldn't wish to wake up to a healthy life again? She reminds herself to stay positive and believe that the chemo is working. Most of the time, she fights her cancer with all that she has. Her boys help keep her going every day and are a constant reminder of what she is living for.

I am happy to return home after my trip and am welcomed at the door with hugs and kisses. I haven't slept well in the hotel but still look forward to taking Caden's night shift so I can spend time with him. During dinner, everyone tells me about the week's activities and the plans for Mother's Day. Colleen has been hinting she would enjoy a fountain beside the gazebo. She loves the sound of babbling water and the sense of peace she gets from listening to it. She seems to get the opposite feeling when I babble.

At midnight Nana goes to bed, and Mark takes Caden upstairs for a bottle. Stephanie and I walk up last, turning off the lights as we go. Halfway up the stairs, she complains that her left leg feels heavy. The chemo has her so weak that she crawls up the last six steps, and I help her into the bed. I walk to my room and kiss Colleen goodnight. After lying in bed for a minute, for no particular reason, I decide to tell Stephanie a good night a second time. When I walk into her room, she again tells me how heavy her leg is. I turn on the light for a better look and notice the leg is swollen and mottled with red and white blotches. The color concerns me, so I get Nurse Nana to have a look. We call Dr. Baranda, and she tells us to get Steph to the nearest emergency room as quickly as we can. Steph, Mark, and I hurry to the car while Nana stays at home with Caden.

At the ER, we summarize Stephanie's history and the oncologist's orders to be seen quickly. They tell us they understand and will be with us as soon as possible. We remind them of the oncologist's concerns twice over the next hour until she is finally taken back. The ER doctor takes one look at the leg and immediately suspects a blood clot. She tells us if it breaks off and goes to a lung, Steph could die, and there wouldn't be anything they could do to save her. I fear for my daughter's life and hold back my anger at waiting an hour to be seen. It's easy to see Mark feels the same way. The doctor puts in motion a flurry of activity with nurses hooking Steph up to monitors, starting IVs, and blood thinners to prevent additional clots from forming.

The physician steps out while a nurse accesses Stephanie's port. She isn't wearing a mask, puts gloves on halfway through the procedure as an afterthought, and doesn't swab the tail line before placing a syringe in it. Mark and I watch, our minds distracted with fear, and things happen so fast the nurse is finished by the time we realize she didn't use sterile technique. We know this from the port access training we received at chemo, where sterile technique had been stressed to be so crucial in protecting Steph from infection. It's too late to change the nurse's actions, and we hope it won't matter.

We wait for the on-call tech to arrive at the hospital, complete a sonogram, and then place the information online for a radiologist to review. We keep Nana updated, and she is just as anxious as we are. It's harder when you're alone, so she puts Caden in bed with her and holds him tight.

The waiting is nerve-racking and frustrates each of us. Getting upset won't help, and we quickly learn pacing doesn't help either. We can't get our minds around the issue because we don't know what we are dealing with, so emotions build and I just want to scream. Mark walks outside to the car, gets in, and finds out that screaming doesn't help either. We pray, and that helps some, but time is moving so slowly, and all we can think about is the danger Steph is in. The only consolation we have is hoping the blood thinner is providing the protection she needs. I find myself wishing I had learned how to meditate. I desperately want to escape into the silence.

The procedure begins when the tech arrives. He allows Mark and me to stay and then glides the Doppler ultrasound equipment over Steph's legs and torso numerous times, checking blood flow. The radiology report states there is extensive Deep Vein Thrombosis in the Femoral & Iliac Veins extending into the Inferior Vena Cava. Stephanie has a massive blood clot that starts above the knee in one leg, continues up to a point just below her heart and then flows back down to the knee on her other leg. The doctor tells us if we had waited a few more hours, Stephanie would have died. Instead of being thankful, I want to scream at someone for the unconcerned way the ER treated us when we arrived. Three flu patients were seen while we waited. I keep wondering if their mismanaged triage will impact my daughter's life.

Steph receives additional blood thinners and is admitted to the hospital's cancer floor at about 5:00 a.m.. The goal is to thin the blood enough to keep it from clotting, but not so thin that it will cause bleeding complications. We take Steph home late that afternoon and all of us crash. Caden is the only team member to have slept in the last 38 hours.

We are aware of our luck in catching the blood clot when we did. We don't talk about it, but each of us knows how close we have come to losing Stephanie. My mind is spinning. What if I had gone to sleep instead of telling her good night a second time? What if she hadn't told me her leg was heavy walking up the stairs? Instead of playing what if, I realize I should be on my knees, thanking God that my little girl is alive. She was being looked after even if we didn't see it at the time.

chapter 17

FOR STEPHANIE'S FIRST MOTHER'S DAY, Mark cooks breakfast and dinner and still finds time to make a card for his wife. I put in less effort taking Colleen shopping, but we do see a small rock fountain that is just what she wants. When we get home, Colleen picks up Caden and he giggles at the silly noises she makes for him. She tells me this is what Mother's Day is all about. After kisses and hugs, she returns him to his blanket on the floor where he grabs onto a rattle and delights in its noise.

Stephanie still hates needles but doesn't fight the blood thinners injected into her gut every 12 hours. Nurse Nana sets the alarm, quietly enters her daughter's room and gives the injection quickly. Steph knows it bothers Colleen to stick her and tells her mom she can hardly feel it. It's a lie, but the pain and burning don't last long, and Stephanie is growing tougher. The pain in her swollen legs is another matter. We raise the foot of her bed and use pillows to elevate her legs, but the swelling isn't going down. We worry about long-term damage to her legs from the obstructed circulation and wish the swelling would just go away.

I tell Colleen the next time we have a child, let's pay extra for the extended warranty.

Steph and Colleen meet with Dr. Baranda, who tells them any combination of cancer, chemotherapy, or birth control pills may have caused the blood clot. She schedules a hematology appointment to see if anything can be done with the existing clot and to keep others from forming. Dr. Baranda stops the birth control pills used to manage Steph's migraines and tells her to exercise and increase her overall activity. She needs to walk often to increase her heart rate and blood flow and can't sit in a car or on the couch for very long. The doctor also reminds Steph not to shave her legs with a razor because a nick could get infected.

The cancer center is having a hard time achieving the blood-thinning target as they move Steph from the injectable to an oral drug, but there is also some good news. Steph is excited and relieved when told her white counts are high enough for a cookout this weekend. The kid's neighbors are coming over, so we can thank them for everything they did at the fundraiser.

After the appointment, Colleen and Steph talk over pizza and agree that the team needs additional help. They call Steph's cousin Kristen, who flies into Kansas City that night. She wants to assist and is happy we called. Kristen offers to take Caden's night duty, allowing our team to recharge. We quickly realize that another one of Steph's angels has arrived to help.

Saturday morning Mark and I prepare the cookout while Kristen helps Steph bathe and get Caden dressed. Nana finishes the side dishes and makes sure all the food is ready. The neighbors arrive for the celebration late afternoon, and soon everyone has a plate of barbeque and a beverage. Caden is the star of the show with smiles and giggles and everyone taking turns holding him. It's a beautiful evening without wind, so I start a fire out on our peninsula and light the yard torches. Steph sits in the Gazebo with her legs propped up to keep the swelling down. She has two blankets wrapped around her to warm up and stays outside for the entire celebration.

At the end of the night, the neighbors present Steph and Mark with a giant five-foot check like the lottery winners get. It's made out for $22,000. The kids are stunned at the amount. Steph's emotions show while Mark jokes about walking into the bank and cashing the giant-sized check. The closeness of the group is seen in their embraces and laughter. I gain their attention and thank them for their generosity and all the work they have done. "You wanted to help and created a whirlwind of activity in your busy lives to help a friend in need. You are genuine friends, and this time I am happy I'm able to tell you so." With moist eyes Mark thanks them and Steph adds how much she loves them. As the neighbors begin to leave, a girlfriend hugging Steph tells her she feels warm. Probably just from the excitement and being bundled up all night.

In the morning, I shovel river rock around Nana's new fountain to complete the landscaping. As I clean up, Steph tells me she can't quit shivering. Nana covers her with blankets and takes her temperature. It's 101.7, so she gives Steph some Tylenol®. Thirty minutes later, the temperature has climbed to 103.7. We call Dr. Baranda and again are told to get Stephanie to an emergency room as quickly as we can. We hurry to a different hospital this time.

Mark and I check Steph into the ER and wait forty-five minutes to see a doctor. As we wait, Steph's fever reminds me of a night when she was a toddler.

Little Stephanie wakes up crying and has a temperature of 103. Nurse Nana tells me we can't let it get higher and runs a cold bath hoping to bring it down. Stephanie feels the water and cycles between crying and laughing, not wanting to get into the tub. We tell her why she needs to and promise it won't take long, and she will feel better after. Steph's afraid and shakes her head no. Will you join me if I get in? She smiles and nods, yes. I enter the cool water with my daughter watching my every move. She wants to be brave like me and slowly gets in. After thirty seconds, she says, "'Kay let's get out now." I laugh, sit her in front of me, and bring in toys to divert her. Her fever drops, and an hour later she's sound asleep. Colleen tells me I'm a great dad. I nuzzle up to my wife and say, "It's easy when you're in love. By the way, I think my temperature is too low. You have any ideas on how we can warm me up?" "Well, you could take a hot bath or we could …" "Yeah, let's do that one."

The ER nurse takes vitals and brings out a large syringe. Steph takes one look at it and blurts out, "Holy Shit." The nurse tells her not to be scared, and Steph answers, "I'm not scared, I just don't think I have that much blood to spare." Blood samples are taken from her port and forearm to be screened for infection.

Normal white blood counts range from 4,500 to 11,000, but Steph's are below 450. The doctor believes she has sepsis, which develops rapidly in people with weakened immune systems. He tells us sepsis is extremely dangerous because the blood becomes poisoned from a bacteria source and can quickly lead to multiple organ failure and death. Without white blood cells to counter the bacteria, she can die in a matter of hours. We look at each other and can't believe it. This is the second time in ten days a doctor tells Stephanie, she is within hours of death. The three of us are shocked and confused. The reality of death has never been more apparent to Stephanie than at this moment. She is terrified, begins to panic, and sobs uncontrollably. I try to calm her, but she doesn't respond. Mark holds her and talks to her, and slowly, she settles down. I call Colleen with an update and then try to settle her down.

The ER doctor consults with an Infectious Disease Specialist and then starts IV fluids and a powerful broad-spectrum antibiotic. Our company developed it, and I was on the training team at its launch. I know how serious sepsis is, and this time, I remember that antibiotics don't always work. Stephanie is admitted to the hospital's cancer ward.

Steph is still frightened when we arrive at her room; Mark and I are also struggling. She tells us she's afraid she won't leave the hospital alive. Death is stalking her and she doesn't know how to protect herself. The ID specialist reviews the lab results and quickly adds a second antibiotic to increase the bacteria coverage.

It's late, and there isn't any more I can do, so I drive home. Mark stays with his wife. He needs to hold onto her, both literally and figuratively. At home, my mind is filled with worry as I try to get some rest. Nana comforts me and tells me she has faith that the antibiotics will work. I pray she is right.

Early the next morning, the hospital Oncologist places Stephanie into isolation to protect her from additional germs. A sign on the door dictates, 'No visitors, no children, no flowers, no fruit or vegetables.' When Steph hears about it, she becomes aggressive and challenges the nurse saying, "I am not going to be separated from Caden. You can't stop me from bringing my baby boy in here."

The nurse answers, "I guess we can't lock the door to stop you, but you need to realize we are just trying to protect you." Steph apologizes for her bluntness, explaining that Caden and her team have lived together for months, and because of her uncertain future, she wants to spend every precious moment with her baby. The nurse relays Steph's message to the physician, and he stops by to talk. The doctor listens and decides that based on the circumstances, the team and Caden can stay. He is very gracious and sorry for the misunderstanding.

Colleen, Kristen, and I arrive to reunite Caden with his mother. Stephanie's face brightens and she reaches for him as we enter her room. She holds him close and becomes lost in the moment, with kisses and whispers of love to his smiling face. Anyone else watching this intimate moment between mother and child would believe their world is perfect, but I can't forget that their world is under attack again. Our team has been shaken hard, and we are all afraid.

Steph is wearing down and tells me she can't take it anymore. I hold her, kiss her on the cheek, and stroke her hand, but she's numb to it. I feel like I am failing her and don't know what to do. We say we were lucky to catch it early, and it will get better, and let's stay positive, but our words seem empty. In contrast, Caden gives his mother relief without any words at all. He captures her attention so thoroughly that she escapes her fear and joins him in the moment. What a blessing.

Stephanie's temperature slowly begins to drop as the antibiotics slay the bacteria. The oncologist tells us we are lucky to have caught the fever and move so quickly because her counts were so low there was no defense to stop the infection or the ensuing sepsis. He remarks that in another six hours she would have died. After giving us a minute to absorb this cold hard fact, he stresses the importance of decreasing her exposure to germs. Stephanie can't be around anyone who is ill or has been close to someone not feeling well. She can't eat any food prepared outside of our home, and everything must be cooked thoroughly. She also can't be around children since they don't know when they are sick. The oncologist starts a new medication to boost her white blood count.

When asked if he knows where the infection started, the doctor answers that they haven't located anything specific. I tell him about the nurse who accessed Steph's port the week before and her lack of sterile technique. "That certainly could have done it," he says, and then he does something that surprises me. He apologizes for that nurse. After I explain it happened at a different hospital, he tells me it doesn't matter, they are all part of the medical community and accountable to their patients. In a time when many people don't take responsibility for their actions, this physician is very refreshing. What caused the infection isn't more important than the fact we caught it in time. Approximately one-third of all sepsis cases in the United States are fatal.

The Infectious Disease specialist stops to see Stephanie on his rounds. His entourage of a dozen residents reviews Steph's history and diagnosis and then discusses the lab results and antibiotics used. He tells the residents he is seeing a lot of our antibiotic used in the hospital, so there must be pharmaceutical rep with a short skirt running around selling it. They laugh, but I can't help myself and add, "Actually the rep is a 55-year-old immigrant who escaped communist Poland with his wife, and now works for me." The residents seemed to enjoy the truth even more. The immigrant is our friend Voyteck, and the story of how he and Teresa escaped from the KGB to their freedom is incredible.

That evening after Mark and I take Caden home and things settle down, Steph walks into the bathroom to take a shower. She doesn't notice the drain isn't working, so water quickly flows into her adjacent room. Colleen sees the water and calls a nurse, who puts down towels and pages maintenance. Two men arrive, but their drain auger doesn't work, so they page a second team.

Colleen helps Steph dress and dry her hair, while a parade of people came in and out of her room. When the drain is finally opened, housekeeping cleans up the dirty mess of hair, gunk, and who knows what else would be found in a hospital drain. The ordeal lasts a couple of hours and really isn't a big deal, other than completely compromising Stephanie's isolation. After being instructed to stay in a germ-free environment, this adds to Steph's fears. Nurse Nana tells her not to worry, the antibiotics should provide all the protection she needs.

Steph calls Mark at home, while Colleen takes a short walk down the hall. She makes it to the restroom before breaking down. Her mind replays Stephanie walking out of the shower. Her body is swollen from the steroids, and black and blue tracks running everywhere document the needles and surgical scars. She limps from the blood clots in her legs, and as Colleen dries Steph's hair, it falls out in clumps. How can this be happening to my young daughter? Colleen allows herself to cry for a while then washes her face in cold water and walks back to the room. Nurse Nana spends the night, but neither of my girls sleep well.

Stephanie's sixth-grade class is graduating from elementary school today. She has planned on attending and is disappointed not to be with them, but sends congratulatory e-mails instead and explains why she's not there. The children reply with gratitude and wishes for her quick recovery. Steph's interest in teaching was sparked even before she became a teenager.

A neighbor noticed how well Stephanie interacted with her young children playing in the back yard and called Colleen to ask if our daughter ever babysat. Steph had watched Scott and a few others, but she was only ten and didn't have much experience. The neighbor wondered if Steph would like to watch her kids. Colleen wasn't sure and said she would talk to Steph about it. The neighbor had four children, two in diapers, and one autistic. Steph was excited to try it, but Colleen wondered if she was taking on too much. Steph thought she could handle it especially since our homes backed up to each other, and Mom would be close by if needed. Colleen reluctantly agreed. Steph watched the kids for five hours. She changed diapers, heated up dinner, and read stories to them in bed. Afterward, Steph ran home excited. "Mom, guess what? They gave me money." She hadn't even thought about being paid. Steph enjoyed babysitting so much that she began watching other kids in the neighborhood and some of the physician's children from Colleen's work. She would read stories, compete in board games, and play school with them.

Soon our ten-year-old was making over $100 a week. Colleen and I agreed our daughter needed a lesson on economics. The three of us sat down, and I suggested we get her a bank account and told her half of what she earned would go into her college fund. As she thought about that, I told her we would match dollar for dollar everything she put into the account. "Wait, I have $100 and put $50 into savings, and you put $50 into savings so there will be $100? And I still have $50 to spend?" I nod yes and can see the gears in her brain turning. "What if I put all $100 into savings?"

"Then we will match it."

"So, I put in $100, and you give me $100, so I really have $200?"

"Yes."

"That doesn't make sense, why would you do that?"

"It's an incentive for you to save your money for college when you need it."

Steph shook her head, saying. "It isn't fair for you, and you don't have to match it. You need your money to take care of us."

Laughingly I tell her, "It's okay, and there's more good news.

The bank will pay you interest while the money sits in the bank." It took another half hour to answer all the questions. In the end, our daughter couldn't believe it but was willing to accept money from both the bank and us. It's my belief the enjoyment she received from babysitting laid the foundation for her interest in becoming a teacher.

The Infectious Disease specialist stops the second antibiotic and replaces it with another. He is happy with Steph's progress, and if it continues, she may be able to go home tomorrow afternoon. Steph is determined to make that happen and is beginning to feel like things are moving forward again.

✣

life lesson #10

The obstacles people face in life do not define them,
but the way they deal with them might. Stephanie
has been challenged more in the last year than I
have in all of my life. The assaults come in waves
knocking her down, but she keeps getting back up.
She is not fearless, but she meets each test head on
telling herself: Keep moving forward. One day at
a time. Never quit trying. I am simply amazed at
how strong she's become.

Kristen and I bring Caden up to visit his mother, and it's hard to tell who is more excited. Kristen plans to spend the night with Steph, and after visiting hours, Mark will bring Caden home. Midday Nana and I leave the hospital, I drop her off at home, and leave town for work. Our patient's mental health is refreshed when she and Kristen have a comedy movie marathon in the hospital. It also helps the time pass quickly.

Driving has often been part of my job, and I enjoy it because it gives me time to think. I reflect on everything the team has been through and wonder how we can prepare for the future. How do you prepare for the unknown? The only thing I can think of is to live each day as well as we can and stay focused on that. We can't change the past; we can only learn from its lessons. We can't control the future; we can only plan for its probabilities. We can, however, choose what we do at this moment. It's really all we have. For my sanity, I will try to remember that and hope it makes things simpler. I think about the people who stepped up to help us during this crisis. What would we have done without them? Maybe each of us really can make a difference in this world simply by helping those around us. As the miles drift by, I find myself at peace and remember how blessed we really are.

Stephanie is released from the hospital after the oncologist reminds her to take additional precautions against exposure to germs. He tells her, "You can't eat any food prepared out of your home, it must be fully cooked, and you should wear a mask when you go out. If there is any concern about what to do, err on the side of safety. Questions?" Steph tells him she understands and appreciates his help. She continues to receive multiple IV antibiotics at home and leaves the hospital with enough for the next 24 hours. Mark and Kristen bring her home at the same time I return from my trip.

That night I tell Steph about my thoughts in the car, and she agrees we need to focus on what's happening now and do our best. It worked with the surgery, the blood clot, and the sepsis. We didn't know what to do but did our best with a lot of help from those around us. Something continues to guide us through the terrifying maze of her illness. Is it faith, love, or God? Neither of us knows, so we agree to embrace and cherish each of them. Someone this week told me to hang in there, no storm lasts forever. I tell Steph I like that advice and she agrees. Our faces fill with smiles instead of tears for a change, and we both feel better. Nana hangs a fresh bag of antibiotics, and we all head to bed.

chapter 18

CADEN LIES ON HIS SOFT BLUE BLANKET in the hearth room looking around, stretching and then rolls over by himself for the first time. His expression is, *hey, what just happened*, and then he starts giggling because Steph makes a fuss over it. She turns him back, and Caden does it again so everyone can see. He continues to change and learn, which we find entertaining and a great diversion. His little hands reach out to anything near him, and after getting ahold of it, shoves it in his mouth. He prefers the blanket with a small white bear on it from Aunt Kim.

Caden and I have a new game. He lies on his back and grabs one of my thumbs in each hand. I slowly lift him up until they slip from his grip. He enjoys the game and holds on longer as he gets stronger. The moment he drops down, he reaches for my thumbs to do it again. It's like mini sit-ups, but he only gets inches off the thick blanket. His face has a big smile as he grabs my thumbs, then turns serious when I start to lift. He works hard to hold on and then giggles when he drops back onto the blanket. Nana thinks I like the game more than Caden does and she may be right. It's delightful to have him in our lives. A moment with him makes all the fear and uncertainty disappear for a while, giving us a welcome escape. That's a gift no one else can provide us with. Thank you, my precious grandson!

Steph is still fighting the infection, so chemotherapy will be rescheduled until she is strong enough to receive it. I hope this allows her the time she needs to rest up and catch her breath. Nana is worn out, and I don't know how we would have made it through the last week without Kristen's help. She has developed a strong bond with Caden, and her photographs capture his budding personality. We will miss Kristen when she returns to her own family tomorrow.

Home Health Care delivers the new antibiotics Stephanie needs to complete her treatment. They teach us how to prep and attach the pressurized delivery units to the IV lines, and each of us feels comfortable starting or stopping them. One injectable is given four times a day, and the other three times a day, so Steph's sleep is disturbed each night to flush lines and start the drugs. Mark sets his alarm almost every hour to deliver the night schedule while Colleen and I take Caden's night shift.

When Steph and I leave early the next morning for her CT scan, she wears a mask to help protect her from any germs we might encounter. A nurse starts an IV line with the first stick, causing Steph to smile and tell me it's a good sign that things will go well today. She drains two 450ml bottles of barium prep for the scan. The expression on her face tells me she never wants to experience that taste again. The tech completes the scan and has Steph out in ten minutes.

On our way home, we joke about something silly, and it feels good to laugh. I tell her I am proud of her because she doesn't complain and usually has everything under control. Steph smiles and tells me, "Everyone says that, but the fact is, I'm scared and often close to crying. I try not to think about it, but everything in my life right now is focused around the cancer, so it's hard to ignore it." She covers it well most of the time, which makes it easier for the rest of us. Being brave doesn't mean you aren't scared; it means you don't let the fear paralyze you. You keep trying to move forward and work hard to overcome the obstacle. The situation would be so much harder if she fought us, the process, or just gave up. We've already seen others that have fallen into each of these categories.

When we arrive home, Nana sends us to the Gazebo for some fresh air and sunshine. Steph is a little stronger with a break in the chemo and grabs Caden while Nana makes lunch. We are surprised when Dr. Baranda calls with the preliminary CT results because they weren't supposed to be read until Monday. The oncologist knows we are anxious to hear the test results and calls us the moment she receives them. She tells Steph the tumors are showing significant shrinkage compared to the last scan. One tumor can't be seen at all, while the others are smaller. Dr. Baranda's excitement is contagious. Steph calls Mark, and then we share the great news with family and friends. Steph's prediction this morning had been right, things do go well today.

The next afternoon Steph feels warm, and her temperature quickly climbs to 102.6. She puts on her mask, and Mark and I drive her to the emergency room where the doctor tries to uncover the cause of the fever. He reviews the test results and believes the antibiotics change made in the hospital isn't working as well as the original, so he switches them back. After five hours in the ER, we head home and monitor Steph's temperature closely. This is the third weekend in a row we visited the ER. At least this one didn't end in hospitalization or someone telling us death was closing in on her.

Home health services is so busy that they drop off the new antibiotics at 12:30 a.m. Steph now takes medication or has lines flushed in sixteen of every twenty-four hours, so I create a schedule to help us give the right drugs at the right time. We're using so many needles at home that the cancer center gives us a Sharps Container to safely dispose of them. Strangely, we are now used to having needles, IVs, and so much medicine in the house. Mark's Mom, Jeanne, arrives from Nebraska to help for the week with Caden's night shift.

Steph and I meet with Dr. Baranda and discuss the scan. The doctor is excited about the tumors shrinking and wants to follow up with a positron emission tomography (PET) scan. She is scheduled to meet with a liver surgeon to discuss our next steps. Since the IV antibiotics are still being used, the sixth chemotherapy is delayed for another week. Steph's temperature is normal again.

Mark returns from work with a dozen roses for Steph in celebration of their third wedding anniversary. After dinner, we recall all the events surrounding their wedding in our back yard.

Planning an outdoor wedding quickly changes to planning two weddings – the one you want to happen and the alternative if it rains. The day starts out dreary with heavy cloud cover. A large tent is up in the back yard while the white chairs and rose-covered trellis are set up on the pond's peninsula. Guests arrive, and because the parking attendants haven't shown up , several relatives jump into action and guide traffic to a parking area at the back of our property. The wedding party is ready, and most guests have arrived when the clouds break apart, leaving nothing but sunshine.

The stringed trio plays music while I accompany my daughter in a horse-drawn carriage to the ceremony. We stroll down the grassy aisle, whispering secrets to each other until we join the wedding party waiting at the trellis. I completely forget to kiss my daughter and turn to join her mother as Steph tries to grab me. The assembled guests laugh at my cluelessness as she misses my arm, shakes her head, and joins Mark. As the ceremony ends, Mark kisses his new bride, and they take a ride in the carriage to steal a quiet moment together.

After the toasts and dinner and festivities, the music begins and so does the party. A cheer rises up from a group next to the bar where I see Stephanie doing a beer bong in her wedding dress. I take her aside and remind her this will be a night she will want to remember. She replies, "Hey Dad, I'm a big girl now, bet I can out drink you. Just kidding, this is my first beer and somebody bet I couldn't do Scott's beer bong, so I proved I could. By the way, at the wedding, you just handed me over to Mark without so much as a kiss. What's up with that?" Shaking my head, I say, "Too many things running through my mind, I just blanked out." When the music stops, the kids sneak off to their honeymoon suite, and the guests head home.

Now Mark tells us the "for better or for worse, in sickness and in health" part of their wedding vows should have been highlighted, underlined, and explained in greater detail. He kisses his laughing wife, telling her there isn't anything they can't overcome as long as they do it together.

❖

life lesson # 11

Choosing a life partner is one of the most important decisions a person ever makes. Find the right person, and everything else seems to fall in place.

Steph walks in from school and asks, "Dad, when did you know you were in love with Mom?"

"So, you like a boy?"

"No, just wondering."

"We started dating and never broke up. Before I knew it, we were spending all our time together. Mom became my best friend and more important to me than anyone else in my life."

"So how will I know if I am in love with someone?"

"Because you can't live without them. They become as essential to you as the air you breathe. You can't just make it happen. Take your time and choose wisely. Marry a Boy Scout."

"What does that mean?"

"You know the Boy Scout Laws. Trustworthy, friendly, kind, thrifty, clean, good looking, and ... I can't remember the rest."

"You just say that because you were a Boy Scout."

"Probably, but here's my point. When you begin falling in love, your emotions go off the chart, and it's easy to overlook things. Figure out what's important to you now and see if he measures up. Does he have a sense of humor? How does he treat you? Are you friends and have similar life goals? Do you want to spend the rest of your life with him over all others? Remember, till death do us part, is a very long time. Go through your checklist, be honest with yourself, and you will know."

"Thanks, Dad."

"You're welcome. I love you, Sweetheart."

"I love you more."

"Because I am sooo cool?"

She smiles, "Yeah, that."

chapter 19

STEPHANIE TAKES HER SON OUTSIDE for fresh air whenever she has the energy, and this morning I join them on the deck. Caden looks at the blue sky dotted with pillow clouds until a pair of geese landing on the pond draws his attention. He responds to the bird's honk and the wind chimes with a look of wonder on his face. Steph watches him, smiles, and pictures him walking, and talking, and growing up with her beside him. "Dad if we believe in something strong enough, will it really come true?"

"Remember how you dreamed of becoming a teacher and getting married and having a baby?" She nods, yes. "Then I don't know why your other dreams wouldn't come true as well if you work hard to achieve them." She smiles and reminds me that when she was ten, her dream was to live in the castle at Disney World. I laugh and tell her, "Just because it hasn't happened yet, doesn't mean it never will."

The next morning starts with an early PET scan and finishes with a hematologist appointment. The specialist says the extensive blood clot quickly calcified and nothing can be done to dissolve or repair the damage. Stephanie's left leg, having more obstruction, will continue to swell, but may improve over time if the blood circulation around the clot increases. She needs to continue taking blood thinners for a year to prevent new clots from forming. Steph now gets blood draws every three days as they struggle to keep the blood thinned at optimal levels with the oral drug.

Jeanne heads back to Nebraska after Steph returns from her PET scan. We appreciate her help and are happy that she's had some quality time with her newest grandchild. Stephanie's cousin Heather drives down from South Dakota to help us this week. The girls are excited to see each other and catch up while Nana makes dinner, and Caden enjoys a nap. Heather will take over Steph's night duty of administering antibiotics, utilizing her nursing degree. She will move into Steph's room and sleep there, just like when they were little, so the rest of us can catch up on our sleep. No one notices the black cloud brewing on the horizon.

As happy as we are to see Heather, an emotional storm overwhelms each of us at the same time. After dinner, Steph and Mark argue and then Colleen and I join in. All hell breaks loose as we shout at each other. It's a free-for-all unlike anything our family has experienced before. EVER. Our beloved team implodes as we unload emotional baggage that we've each been carrying around. The spectacle lasts an hour. Everyone takes part, and some of it is ugly. When the storm passes, we sit together in silence. Our hearts are beating fast, we are exhausted, and angry at the world. Poor Heather has sat quietly on the couch, watching it all unfold. I don't know why she hasn't run to her car to drive back home. Who needs Jerry Springer when you have this?

The reality of how fragile Steph's future is has hit us like a one-two punch when the blood clot and sepsis each try to steal her away from us. Tension has built up over the last few weeks until the dam had to burst, and it thundered out. No one wants to admit how terrified we are, because we're supposed to stay strong for Steph and have faith that everything is going to be all right. After a little time passes, we agree not to let hurt feelings or anything else derail what we are working so hard to accomplish. Each of us apologizes, and we agree that this isn't about us; it's about something much bigger, saving Steph's life. She doesn't need drama; she needs our unconditional love and support.

In the days following, each of us goes out of our way to be kind and help each other. The truth is that our blowout brings us closer together. We will have tough times ahead, but never again will we attack another member of the team. To make steel stronger, you temper it by adding extreme heat. I believe that was precisely what happened to our team tonight.

❀

life lesson #12

When you are caught up in the emotion of the moment, it's easy to say or do things that are wrong or hurtful. Worse yet, these things are often directed at those we care about the most. If we are honest with ourselves, we realize our mistake, which presents an opportunity. By sincerely apologizing, you can begin the healing, and make up for it. Fill your heart with love and your words with forgiveness. Be accountable for what you do. Life is too short to live it in anger, especially with those you love. Forgiveness is one of the greatest gifts you can give or receive. And remember, sometimes you also have to forgive yourself.

The team sits down with a liver surgeon who reviews Steph's scans. He tells us the liver tumors are small, and the PET scan didn't pick up any additional activity, so that's good news. He doesn't want to remove the section of liver growing tumors in case something appears on the other lobe in the future. Her liver won't be able to do its job if that happens. He plans to consult with a radiologist about using radiofrequency ablation (RFA) to burn out the tumors. If that is possible, it will be less traumatic for both the liver and the patient. He explains that a CT helps the doctor guide a needle into the tumor, where electrical impulses kill the cancer cells. If RFA is used first, he will still have the option to go in later for surgery if necessary.

The doctor tells us that it takes a large number of cancer cells to be seen on a CT, so there may be more activity in the liver than we think. He is concerned since so many lymph nodes removed during her colon surgery tested positive for cancer. The surgeon explains Stephanie's options and takes his time answering all of our questions. We thank him and head home.

Mark sits down on the couch and sings Caden a song that his grandpa sang to him as a little boy. It follows the melody from *Here we go round the mulberry bush*. He sits Caden on his knee like he's riding a horse and slowly bounces singing two rounds of "This is the way the little girls ride, the little girls ride, the little girls ride," then he bounces faster and higher while singing, "This is the way the little boys ride." Caden always giggles and definitely prefers riding faster, 'all the way to town.' At four months he's growing so fast that he needs a new car seat. Everything is a game to him, and he communicates so much with his eyes and facial expressions. He is cutting teeth, so the jolly mood we are used to is interrupted from time to time, as he provides his updates on their progress. From my observations, I think the teeth hurt his mother and grandmother more than him.

Kim and Bill visit from Minnesota, and over the weekend we have a campfire, relax, and search for our regular routine again. Kim is staying with us for the next two weeks. I kid her that she is the sister I never had, and she always answers, you're my brother from another mother. She has brought a bag of presents for Caden and two more sets of pajamas for his mom. Since the Valentine's Day surgery, Kim has sent Stephanie two cards every week reminding her to hang in there and keep on fighting. We are sorry to see Heather leave on Sunday, but she has work and a family of her own to take care of. Aunt Kim covers night duty, and Caden really takes to her. When he makes a fuss while waiting for his bottle, she calls him 'Starvin Marvin,' then picks him up and coaxes a smile out of him before he attacks his bottle.

For years my closest friend Stan and I have taken our sons walleye fishing in South Dakota. While in college, Stan and I worked at a music store together where the owner taught us to fish using homemade bucktail jigs and whippy rods while wading in the state's northeastern glacial lakes. I have planned to skip our annual trip this year, but Nana and Steph insist we go, especially now that Kim is here to help. After the nine-hour drive, Scott and I meet up with Stan and his son Michael at their cabin. The weather is cold and windy, kicking up large whitecaps, which makes our wader fishing more challenging. We work our jigs in eight lakes but release the few small fish we catch. The quality of these trips is measured in fun, not filets.

Fishing usually allows me to forget about my responsibilities and stress, but this trip is different as my mind continually drifts back home. Stan provides relief by listening patiently to my fears, telling me things will work out, and that we are doing amazingly well with the crisis we now live in. The two days of fishing, story-telling, and bonding with our sons pass quickly. In the past, when we leave there is bragging about the biggest fish and those that got away, but this goodbye is filled with emotion and promises of prayers for our little girl. My excitement to get home builds, as we drive through five states and get closer to home.

chapter 20

COLLEEN JOINS STEPH THIS MORNING for her sixth chemo treatment. Two drugs are added to the seven-hour regimen to help Steph's bone marrow produce more red and white blood cells. The drugs also add new side effects of muscle and bone pain. Stephanie is now receiving over thirty drugs to help her quest. Dr. Baranda starts the examination, and after noticing her patient's legs are a little too smooth, she asks, "Are you shaving your legs with a razor?" Guiltily Steph nods yes, adding there was so much stubble on her legs you could grate cheese on them. The good doctor fights back a smile and delivers a stern talk. She reminds Steph not to use a razor since a cut could cause infection and her thin blood doesn't easily clot. It's like being scolded by her mother, who has already bought her daughter an electric razor and delivered the same message the night before.

Dr. Baranda suggests that Steph get a second opinion for the liver surgery from either the Research Center or the Mayo Clinic in Rochester, Minnesota. We like the idea of going to Mayo since it's one of the top cancer centers in the country and a day's drive from us. Dr. Baranda tells us to provide a copy of Steph's scans to the Research Center, so the oncologist and surgeon there can review them and offer treatment recommendations. Colleen agrees to Federal Express them on her way home. The doctor plans to have Steph finish two more rounds of chemotherapy, get an updated CT scan, and then set a date for surgery.

Aunt Kim and I bring Caden to the cancer center around noon to surprise his mother with a visit. You would think she hadn't seen him for a week by the way she carries on and kisses him. The nurses love it when we bring our little guy along. One of them picks up Caden and walks to the nurse's station, where they fuss over him and shower him with love. A baby brings joy wherever they go, and Caden is such a willing ambassador.

The next day Caden has his four-month check-up. His pediatrician travels to him so that baby and mom won't have additional exposure to germs. Dr. Sheri Martin completes the check-up, and then Nurse Mary gives Caden his shots. Afterward, everyone enjoys the lunch and cookies this thoughtful medical team has brought along. Later Dr. Teresa stops by bringing flowers and chocolates with her. Who says doctors don't make house calls anymore? Both Mother and child are doing fine, and once again, we are reminded of the incredible support we have around us and how much they love Stephanie. Teresa and Steph talk for a long time, comparing notes and building up each other's spirits. Their relationship grows, sparked in part by the fact they find themselves on a similar path, fighting a common enemy.

Kim seems to have a bottomless source of energy. She watches Caden most nights and then helps with chores around the house. She's leaving soon, and we will all miss her, but none more than Colleen. Nana is losing her helper, but more importantly, her best friend and confidant. The rest of the team meets to discuss what we can do to lighten Colleen's workload. Steph commits to doing the mom stuff, as long as her energy holds out. Mark is working overtime on a work deadline, but will back up Steph with Caden, and help where he can. I will help keep the house in order, both inside and out, and hold Caden more often. Steph smiles and quickly corrects me, "No, Dad, that falls under my duties." We hope by each doing a little more, we can lighten Nana's load.

Bill returns and the kids take Caden home to have a quiet weekend as a family. That night, Mark inflates a blowup mattress so they can camp out in their living room. Steph cuts up meat, cheese, and vegies for a cold plate, and everyone lies down to watch a movie. Mark walks into the kitchen for Caden's bottle and steps in water that's leaking from the dishwasher. He turns off the water and cleans up the mess before telling Steph the camping trip has been rained out. The next day Mark celebrates his first Father's Day by installing a new dishwasher.

Bill and Kim depart for home in the morning, and we are sad to see them leave. Kim fits into our family so well that it seems routine to have her around, and Caden adores her. She's like the fun sister you want in the family. Kim is Nana's closest friend and playmate. They love to shop, grab a bite to eat, and then shop some more. Kim has grown closer to Steph, listening and understanding like friends do for each other. We all love her so much.

The kids return to our home base on Sunday, and we are happy the team is together again. When we're not overwhelmed by lack of sleep or some new challenge, the five of us do great together. Steph posts a web update on her progress and thanks her readers. 'The power of prayer is amazing, and I feel your prayers working in my life. I wish I could hug you all!' She is reminded every day with cards or phone calls how many people are following her journey and rooting for her. She tells us her fatigue is making the updates harder to compose, so she begins to write them monthly instead of weekly. Her readers interpret this as a turn for the worse, and many reach out to her.

chapter 21

STEPH IS IN THE BIG CHEMO ROOM for today's treatment, enjoying the comfortable oversized chair. Nana sings *This Little Piggy* to Caden on the adjoining bed as she plays with his toes. They appreciate the extra comfort and private bathroom the large room offers. . The nurses try to make it available any time Caden is along. It's a small thing, but we welcome anything positive.

The girls update Dr. Baranda on the hematology appointment, and she is pleased to hear that the blood clot is stabilizing, and that pain and swelling aren't getting worse. Steph's blood is too thin today, so she is directed to skip the blood thinner for two days. They still can't maintain a therapeutic window, possibly due to the other medications that come and go with chemotherapy. Colleen tells Dr. Baranda of our desire to go to the Mayo Clinic for the liver assessment and surgery and the doctor approves. Nana will set up the appointments. Steph tells Dr. Baranda she is struggling with the idea of more surgery, fearing the risk of the operation and painful recovery afterward. The doctor understands but gently reminds her patient that *all* cancer must be removed to save her life. Steph knows the surgery isn't optional, but can't block out the fear.

What defines a hero? Is it someone without fear, or believes they can't fail or has a superhuman trait of some kind? I recall a story about a man who was labeled a hero but didn't think he deserved the title. He simply found himself in an unexpected situation and did the best he could to make it better. Stephanie finds herself in an unexpected situation and tries to do the best she can to survive. Steph has become our hero.

Colleen calls the Research Center about their assessment but is told they have never received the scans or information. She provides the Federal Express confirmation of delivery, time, and who signed for it. They will look into it and get back to us. Colleen then follows up with the insurance company to gain approval for the assessment and surgery at the Mayo Clinic. She receives confirmation that the liver assessment has been approved. After reviewing the surgeon's evaluation, they will decide whether or not to cover the operation. The insurance employee on the phone assigns Steph a case manager, which should streamline future communications since that person will already be familiar with Steph's case. Colleen is excellent on the phone. She is patient, polite, asks clarifying questions, and always thanks each person she talks to. Her nursing experience with phone triage has taught her to take notes, including names, times, and dates of conversations. She volunteers for many of the tough assignments, never complaining, and always gets them done.

Steph walks down the stairs smiling, so I ask, what's up? She answers, "I started to wash my hair less often since I don't like to see it collect around the drain. The good news is it's getting easier to fix because there is less of it." It's the first time she talks about her hair loss with any hint of humor. Then our daughter tells us, she has come to grips with the liver surgery. Her exact comment is, "Why would we do a half-assed job and take the risk? I am already doing the chemo, so once the surgeon removes the tumors, I will be cancer free." She makes the statement with conviction and absolute belief; that is the plan, end of discussion. Attitude is so important, and Stephanie understands it is one thing in her life she can control.

⚜

life lesson #13

Our attitude is similar to a compass helping us stay on course. A positive attitude promotes thoughts of belief, faith, and action. A negative attitude promotes anxiety, frustration, and worry. We experience both, but the secret is to tip the scales quickly to the positive. Henry Ford said, "If you think you can do it, or you think you can't do it, you are right." Belief and attitude determine action. We are much more in control of our destiny than most of us realize.

chapter 22

TONIGHT, COLLEEN AND I WATCH OUR GRANDSON while Steph and Mark have a date night at their home. As we play, Nana suggests this is what typical grandparents do with their grandkids. I smile and tell her, "It's okay, I think we adapted rather well to the roller coaster we're on. Besides, most grandparents don't get to see their grandchild every day as we do."

In the middle of the night, our little guy wakes up with zero interest in going back to sleep. Nana takes him out onto the deck for some fresh air, where she sees one little star peeking through the clouds. She tells Caden she will help him make his first 'wish upon a star.' Nana whispers the request into his ear and then sings *Twinkle, Twinkle Little Star*. When she comes to bed, I see her wiping her eyes and ask what's wrong. She tells me, "Nothing. Caden just made his first wish on a star, and I hope God makes it comes true."

Mark and I are working more hours now, and Stephanie is trying hard to do what she can, but the medicine saps her strength. That leaves Nana to get things done. This morning she cleaned the kid's house, then packed their things and moved Caden and Steph back to our home. Nana often tells me, when she keeps busy she doesn't have time to worry. Her favorite activity is to cuddle up with Caden and take a nap on the couch. It gives her pleasure and Caden is always a willing partner.

I travel to Dallas for a week of meetings while Colleen watches over Steph and Caden. Her job is more challenging now that Caden is cutting teeth. Nana is exhausted when Mark returns from work and relieves her. Shortly after dinner, Steph starts to feel pain in her abdomen and chest. Nothing seems to help, so Mark takes her to the ER. As they drive, the doctor's warning replays in their minds. "If a piece of the blood clot breaks off and lodges in your lung, it could result in death."

Within minutes of the kids leaving the house, Steph and Colleen each call to tell me what is happening. I hear the fear in their voices. It's hard not being there to help and worse yet not knowing what's going on minute to minute. Time stands still as I wait in my hotel room for half hour updates, without any change in the pain. Filled with emotion, I ask God to please make this something simple and not life-threatening for a change. Something that can be solved quickly and easily, so that Steph can just go home, instead of enduring tests or time in the hospital. My little girl doesn't need any more on her plate, so please just make it go away. Afterward, I realize it sounded more like pleading than praying.

In the emergency room 500 miles away from me, Steph waits for two hours, running to the restroom periodically to get sick. After her gut is empty, she feels dramatically better. Steph tells the staff she is no longer in pain and wants to go home. The discharge nurse checks her over and agrees Steph can leave. As Mark leaves the hospital parking lot, Steph calls me with the good news. I am so relieved and tell her about the prayer, which was heard and boosts our faith. She tells me, 'I love you so much,' my answer, 'I love you more.' I wake up often that night but find myself at peace knowing Steph is asleep at home.

Later the puzzle pieces come together. Tonight's problem was the bacon, lettuce, and tomato sandwich she ate for dinner. Salad is difficult for her compromised gut to move and digest, which creates cramping and pain. This is the same gut pain she had at the fundraiser, which was caused by the dinner salad. In time Stephanie identifies additional challenging foods and learns to manage them through portion control.

Today is Steph's 28th birthday, and I forget until she calls and reminds me. She teases me saying, "Only a terrible father would forget his daughter's birthday!" but quickly adds, "Don't feel bad Dad, I forgot too, until Mom wished me Happy Birthday when I got up. Do you remember when we found out about my cancer, and I wondered if I would get the chance to celebrate another birthday?" "Yes." "Well, I guess now we know that I will!" Her comment makes me smile. We will celebrate when I get home, but for now I am so happy she is alive and remind myself to enjoy each day with her.

Colleen tells me how difficult it is for Steph when I'm gone and how my presence provides her strength. I understand because I know that I feel weaker when away from the team. I start calling home twice a day in the hope it helps both of us. Colleen also tells me Caden's first tooth has broken through today and a second is close behind. He is growing up so quickly.

This morning Steph and her mom drive to the Cancer Center for a blood draw. Steph's blood is too thick, so the dosage of the blood thinner is adjusted again. In preparation for the liver surgery, Dr. Baranda will substitute the oral blood thinner for short-acting injections to protect Steph from further blood clots. The injections will be discontinued before surgery, so her blood can help heal the surgical wounds. Her blood pressure is high, so an antihypertensive is prescribed. She will continue the drug until chemo is completed because the high blood pressure may be a side effect of the cancer drugs. Steph tells me she feels like an old lady, taking pills for blood pressure and blood thinning. Then she adds, I just hope I'll be an old lady.

The Research Center confirms that they signed for our Fed Ex package, but still can't locate the test results and scans we sent to them. They ask us to resend them. This doesn't sit well with me because they also lost the original tissue slides, test results, and scans when we flew there. Colleen calls the Mayo Clinic and learns they have already reviewed the information we sent. With time running out this solidifies our decision to use Mayo for the liver assessment and surgery. They suggest we come prepared to spend two or three weeks at the clinic. Our research into their oncology department and liver surgeons increases our confidence that we are making the right decision. To keep Steph safe from blood clots, she will walk for fifteen minutes every two hours on our eight-hour drive to Rochester.

On Friday I return home exhausted, but take the night shift because I have missed Caden. As I rock him to sleep, the stress from my workweek melts away. I find myself at peace and alive in the moment while Caden dozes and holds my finger. I am content merely watching him breathe. His breathing is soft, calm, and somehow comforting. He radiates the peace we are desperate for. After an hour holding him, I lay him in the bassinet where he sleeps soundly for ten hours. I am the Sandman.

Steph gives Caden his bottle the next morning, and her eyes fill with joyful tears as she plays with a wisp of his hair. She feels so lucky to have him in her life. "Dad, I loved him when he was born, but can't believe how that love has grown and strengthened." His bright eyes stare at his mother as he smiles and enjoys the bottle. The eyes shut, the bottle empty, a burp and the smile returns. "I love you, baby boy, with all my heart and soul." He is now 5 months old, weighs 20 pounds, and is already wearing 12-month clothes. Two teeth are in, and he rolls over from front to back. When Steph feels up to it, he loves joining her in the swimming pool. He's a little fish in the water, kicking in his whale float and squealing in delight at the splashing water.

Stephanie struggles emotionally and grows quiet as she loses ground to anxiety. She worries about having a new medical team and her liver surgery. I tell her these concerns are reasonable for anyone in her situation. She opens up, and we talk through it. We deal with it now, so she's ready to fight when we get to the Mayo. After our talk, she tells me she's ready. The team packs up the car, then we try to get some sleep.

Sleep is a welcome friend, but lately, it taunts us by staying just outside our reach. Some of us get help from medications for sleep, depression, or anxiety. A cardinal greets the dawn at 5:30 a.m. each day and prefers to do this perched on the eves outside Colleen and my bedroom window. The joy I usually feel from his sweet song is replaced with frustration as it robs me of my rest, so I start using a sound machine. This electronic helper becomes a staple for each member of the team, as it buffers the outside distractions and wraps us in its comforting embrace.

chapter 23

WE SHARE A BALANCE OF EXCITEMENT and apprehension as we drive to Rochester, Minnesota, to consult with the Mayo Clinic about Steph's liver surgery. Two hours into the trip, Steph walks carrying Caden, telling him about all the fun they will have with Daddy when she feels better. Caden brings out the best in his mother, and it warms our hearts to see her smile and focus on a positive future.

We have packed for a week filled with tests, appointments, and possibly surgery. The operation concerns us, but the tumors are shrinking, which we hope will require less surgery on the liver. We also hope the new treatment team will be a good fit. The Mayo Clinic's reputation for cutting edge research and treatment is widely respected and draws presidents, royalty, and run-of-the-mill people like us.

Our hotel is attached to an underground tunnel leading to the clinic and downtown Rochester, making it easy to get around without regard to the weather or parking. We drop our bags in the room, put Caden in his stroller, and explore the tunnel system. The hour walk helps us get our bearings and burn off the nervous energy built up on our drive. We turn in early and sound like *The Waltons* telling each other good night. The purr of the sound machine helps nullify the noises frequently heard in a hotel.

The morning starts on a positive note. Stephanie takes the lead to the Registration Desk, where they pronounce her last name correctly. She smiles and tells us it's a good sign. The receptionist confirms that Steph is fasting and then prints the appointment schedule. She reviews the printout, asks us to wait a minute, and then calls to reschedule the last test. She hangs up the phone smiling and tells Steph now she will be able to eat two hours earlier. Every person we talk to smiles and acts like they've been waiting for us. There aren't any issues using the port, and if the tech isn't qualified, they quickly find someone who is. When we have a question, they stop what they are doing and find an answer. As we finish each appointment, they direct us to the next one, often walking us to a place where the directions are clearer to follow. The Mayo is very patient-friendly.

In the first waiting room, we sit next to a young family. Steph starts a conversation, and they share the stories that brought them to the clinic. Everyone has a story. The young father from a distant country listens while Stephanie tells him that she is frightened. He smiles and says, "Sometimes we don't understand what is going on, because it's all above our heads. But we must remember, if it's above our head, it's still below God's feet." This man is so kind to take the time to boost her confidence. A few minutes later, I receive a text from a work friend. "In the presence of light, darkness recedes. Keep the faith!"

In a second waiting room, I watch my daughter sing and read to Caden like it's a typical day. I'm proud of her for living in the moment. Caden flirts with everyone around him, especially the women. My grandson already has my love, but now he's earning my respect as well. Caden is very welcome here. Many patients are older, and they light up when he looks at them. They make faces, and then he giggles. A woman watching him turns away, smiling to herself, lost in thought. I'm sure she's thinking of a child in her past. For the moment I escape the worries that shadow me, and feel content and happy.

Babies are the great equalizer. They fill a room with love. Their pure soul shines bright, and every little thing they do is captivating. They make eye contact, smile, or wrap their tiny hand around your finger, filling you with joy and excitement. Care is not given to color, sex, or religion. Instead, the focus is on love and happiness. Holding a baby fuels hope and dreams and appreciation. There is much to learn from these little souls. They live in the moment, they don't judge, and they get over things quickly. They cry to seek help, but stay resilient and keep getting up when they fall. They show genuine excitement over little things and don't hold grudges. They make the best of their situation. In a world where role models often disappoint, babies consistently practice unconditional love.

Everyone at 'The Mayo' is professional and friendly – and I mean every single person we encounter. It's a big campus like other facilities we've been, but this is different for some reason. It's odd, but each of us feels comfortable here. We are smiling and joking more. I mention it feels like we are in a healing environment, and the team quickly agrees. Everything seems right, and this is where we need to be. I can't explain why, but it's more than things just going smoothly. The tests and scans are finished, and we stop to eat. The long day leaves us exhausted, but our mood remains positive and light.

In our room Colleen bounces Caden on the bed singing, "Five little monkeys jumping on the bed, one fell off and bumped his head. Nana called the Doctor, the Doctor said, no more monkeys jumping on the bed!" Caden won't let her stop, and Nana doesn't want to. Steph warns her mother that if Caden gets wound up, Nana can stay up with him. Not a problem, everyone sleeps.

We arrive at oncology early and talk to a member of the staff. The woman tells us the department reviews new patients as a group and places them with the physician best suited to help them. In time we find out the Mayo health system uses a team approach on just about everything they do. Steph's Oncologist is Dr. Axel Grothey.

A Nurse Practitioner calls our team back, checks Steph's vitals, and takes us into the examination room. The room is slightly larger than average with an exam table, work desk, counter with sink, and one corner curtained off to change into a gown. The team sits tightly together on a small cushioned bench, and Caden chews on his favorite toy – a brightly colored cloth giraffe. We give the Nurse Practitioner two documents. One lists the thirty plus drugs Steph is currently taking. The second provides a timeline and summarizes the events of her illness from mid-pregnancy to the present. We've learned what a new medical staff wants to know and how to provide it in their language. She reviews the documents and asks which one of us is in medicine. We smile and point at Nurse Nana.

Dr. Grothey joins us and spends a moment asking about Caden. We introduce ourselves, and Steph gives him a quick rundown of her history and care at the Research Center and KU. He already knows both oncologists from research symposiums they've all attended. After a physical, he summarizes her history from the documents and scans we provided, as well as the procedures completed yesterday. He is entirely up to speed with every aspect of her medical history. Unlike our previous experiences, Dr. Grothey tells us he has treated five females under age 30 whose diagnoses are similar to Steph's, and two of them had babies. That was why he took her case at the department review. What a great strategy. Don't just assign the new patient to whoever has an opening, look at their individual situation, and determine if they would benefit from a particular physician's experience. We are excited to find someone with experience treating patients just like Steph. Our hope is growing, but we are afraid to inquire about other patients' outcomes.

This physician is kind and gentle with Stephanie. He is also honest and straightforward. He tells her, "We will do everything we can to help you, but this is something you will struggle with the rest of your life, and you need to be committed to the fight. It appears the chemotherapy is working and the shrinking tumors are a great sign. We will try to get her cancer under control and put it into remission." I will never forget what the doctor did next. Looking Stephanie in the eye and taking her hand, he said, "I will never be able to tell you that you are cured." The room is silent. My heart races, and I feel like the oxygen is being sucked out of the room. Our eyes reveal our fear, but we hold back the tears. We know Steph's condition is serious, and we also expect a difficult fight, but no one has ever told us what we've just heard.

The Doctor says everything Steph has done is right on target. He would have liked to do liver surgery after six chemo sessions like Dr. Baranda had suggested, but when the blood clot formed, that was no longer an option. Dr. Grothey had talked with researchers in the Netherlands about the newest oncology drug added when Steph was diagnosed as Stage 4. They suggested we wait for six weeks after the last dose was given before doing the surgery. This ensures the drug will be out of Steph's system and not hinder wound healing or liver regeneration. Dr. Grothey tells us that liver surgery is definitely the next step. He discusses four available liver surgeons and has one in particular in mind. He tells us he likes Dr. Que for this surgery because she is very aggressive and will connect well with Stephanie. She also prefers to work on livers being treated with the specific chemo cocktail Steph is receiving.

Dr. Grothey says that for Caden's sake, Steph should have genetic testing to identify the cause of her cancer and help determine his level of future risk. The Doctor has young children of his own and it shows in his attention to Caden. He tells Stephanie she's lucky to have a family committed to helping her.

The Doctor answers our questions and treats Steph like she is the only patient in his practice. We speak with him for more than an hour. As we leave, I tell him our Mayo Clinic experience has been very positive. Everyone we've encountered has been incredible. He smiles and says, "We have to be that way." I expect him to say something about being a leader in medicine, but to my surprise, he adds, "We have to be the very best to get anyone to travel to Minnesota in the winter." This oncologist is friendly, kind, smart, connected, and has a sense of humor. What else could we ask for? There is one other thing: As we walk to the elevator, Steph and Colleen both agree that he looks a little like Russell Crowe.

As we leave the appointment, there is much to think about and digest. We feel great about choosing Mayo and find the staff friendly, professional, and understanding of what is truly at stake. We are impressed with Dr. Grothey's bedside manner and skill set, but are haunted by his telling Stephanie she will never be cured.

On the way back to the hotel, we discuss everything we had been told. It still amazes us how four people at the same meeting can hear different things. One of us can be thinking about something said earlier and miss the next statement, or two of us can listen to the same thing and interpret it differently. We find these debriefing sessions valuable, and as always they keep our team on the same page.

We have dinner at an Italian restaurant that is a local favorite. As we continue to discuss the appointment, we make a team decision about expectations. We decide that Stephanie is going to be a miracle and beat this thing. She is going to be cured and not settle for remission. Steph likes that idea. She also likes Dr. Grothey's approach to her disease and that he is direct, honest, and cares about her. She tells us, "I think we found another great fit!" We toast our decision with wine and enjoy a wonderful meal. Just like the Mayo, the restaurant doesn't disappoint us. We walk back to the hotel understanding the difficulties that lie ahead but believing that Mayo will help all of us survive it.

Caden seems at ease with everything in his life and is fascinated by his toes when he can grab them. We take him everywhere, and he sleeps easily in hotels, hospitals, or in anyone's arms. He's happy in restaurants, the stroller, and even in his car seat. We are lucky to have this perfect little boy. Last night Caden surprised his mother by rolling over and sleeping on his tummy for the first time. She gets excited at anything new, and it's heartwarming to see her happy. Caden is now eating some real food like bananas and peaches. Steph tries vegetables at dinner, and he loves them. Her son hasn't met a food he doesn't like, and it's beginning to show. Plump comes to mind, but Nana corrects me saying he looks like he should for his age. Thank you for your presence in our lives little man. You strengthen us all.

We meet with the liver surgeon, Dr. Florencia Que. She is friendly and Steph connects with her quickly. The Doctor reviews the scans with us in detail and tells us the locations of the tumors are not ideal. Even if she removes half of the liver, she won't get them all, and removing any more won't leave enough to meet Steph's needs. She educates us on the liver, telling us it's the only organ that can regenerate itself after surgery and actually replace some of the missing tissue. Her surgical plan begins with a scope looking for additional cancer, and in her experience, she usually finds some. This isn't what we want to hear. Next, she will open Steph up to get full access to the organs in the abdominal cavity and examine each of them. The surgical team will do a sonogram directly on the liver, while the surgeon tries to locate the tumors by touch. Dr. Que will share the results with Dr. Grothey and a radiologist to determine whether to use radiofrequency ablation, cut out multiple liver sections, or remove half of the liver. Stephanie will be hospitalized for seven days and then taken home for six weeks of recovery. Chemotherapy will start again four weeks later.

Dr. Que answers all of our questions, but she stays focused on Stephanie throughout the entire appointment. The Doctor said she operates on livers all day long and is confident the surgery will go smoothly.. We comment that our Mayo experience has been excellent. Dr. Que smiles and tells us, "It's probably due to all the corn fields. They tend to give you a sense of peace and order in this crazy world." As we leave her office, the team agrees that Dr. Que is another great fit for Steph.

Both the oncologist and surgeon have mentioned the likelihood of more cancer and surgery in Steph's future. They will monitor Stephanie diligently to allow them to move quickly if things develop. It's unnerving, but in their expert opinions, it's a fact that Steph must be watched closely for the rest of her life. It's enough for us to focus on one day at a time and live it without becoming overwhelmed. We need to keep our eyes on the prize and enjoy every moment of life we have together. Even the ease of writing these words does not reflect the fear they place in our minds.

We have found the Mayo Clinic to be an amazing place. In three days we have had all tests completed, results analyzed and met our oncologist and surgeon, who presented us with a concise plan. We've heard unsettling facts, but discovered a medical team we believe can help us overcome the obstacles. Mayo is the last piece of the puzzle we need for Stephanie's Medical Dream Team – a team we can trust to take our hands and lead us down the road to recovery. This health care system is a beautiful fit and replenishes our hope. Never underestimate the importance of hope and belief.

Steph wants to see Grandpa Bill and our other relatives in the twin cities, so we call Bill and Kim and invite ourselves to White Bear Lake for the weekend. They are excited to see us, and happy Steph has a positive outlook. We recharge and put our worries behind us. Steph gets excited when she sees less hair on the drain than she's seen in months. Her hair has thinned by a third. She has gained seventy pounds since starting the steroids.

Bill and Kim throw together a backyard party. Colleen's brother and sister and their families are here, along with Grandpa Bill. My buddy Stan and his wife Linda are in the area visiting their son and also stop by. Their son Michael is named after me , an honor I did not repay when our son was named Scott. I've taken a bit of static about that over the years, but Mark has an idea and writes 'Stanley Jr.' on Caden's tee shirt with a sharpie. Stan loves it and carries Caden around showing everyone. We spend the day in the sunshine, talking with friends, and enjoying great food. It grows late, and everyone hugs us hard and long before they leave.

It's great to see them, and our spirits are boosted. Our trip home the next morning is uneventful and quiet with everyone lost in thought.

Back home the team joins Steph for her appointment with Dr. Baranda. Mayo has copied her on everything, and she is both surprised and pleased that Dr. Grothey has joined Steph's team. She tells us that he's tough to get in to see, and asks how we did it. Steph explains that he chose us and summarizes everything from the visit as well as the date selected for surgery. The Doctor is pleased with the plan and agrees we made the right choice selecting Mayo.

Stephanie's story continues to spread. There are Mass's said in her honor both here in the States and in Europe. Her name is added to dozens of prayer lists, and children's nightly prayers. So much support and love from so many people.

chapter 24

TWO WEEKS LATER WITH A BREAK IN HER CHEMO, Steph's energy has returned, and she is ready for surgery. We drive to Rochester following the two-hour schedule set on our first trip. Cappuccinos at the first stop, tacos at the second, and the girls decide to walk through a mall at the third. At first, I haven't realized this for what it really is – an excuse to shop and get money flowing along with the blood. We grab an early dinner since Stephanie needs to fast for morning tests, and then check into a hotel.

With Steph's blood work complete, we meet again with Dr. Que. She reviews her plan, reassures us everything is set for the next morning's surgery, and reminds Steph to remove all her jewelry. Stephanie says her wedding ring won't come off because of swelling from the steroids. Dr. Que tells her the nurses will have some tricks they can try when Steph is under anesthesia. If that doesn't work, they will cut the ring off for Steph's safety. The Doctor sees my daughter's reaction and explains it's better to cut the ring than lose a finger. Steph assures the Doctor that we will get it off somehow.

Afterward we explore Mayo's Plummer Building across the street, which opened in 1928. Dr. W. W. Mayo settled in Rochester after the civil war and joined the Sisters of St. Francis in the late 1800s to create Saint Mary's Hospital. His two sons became doctors, and the clinic grew to what it is today. One exhibit shows the first surgical table and instruments used by Dr. Mayo. Looking at it, Steph says she's happy she wasn't born 100 years earlier. Fear and anxiety grow as the surgery gets closer, but we reassure each other that Steph is in good hands, and everything will be fine. One of us is brave and positive for a while, and then someone else takes over sharing the load, just like a flock of geese in flight

Steph doesn't want her wedding ring cut because Mark had it inscribed before giving it to her. We try ice, Crisco, Windex, and soap, but nothing works. The harder we try, the more her finger swells, so we hope the nurses have better luck.

At 5:30 the next morning, Stephanie, Mark, and I walk across the street to Saint Mary's Hospital. Colleen stays at the hotel to let Caden sleep, but it isn't easy for her to stay behind. She wants to be with us, but sacrifices her needs for the child, because that's what mom's do. Stephanie hands her sleeping baby to Nana, repeating the request from her colon surgery, "Mom if something happens, please take care of Caden for me." With watery eyes, Steph kisses Caden on the cheek, and we leave.

We check in for surgery, and the staff confirms the direction of her living will. If they lose her in surgery, they will try to revive her once, then a second time, and then let her go. We know the directive, but my stomach turns as I hear it. It's essential for the staff to confirm this information, but our thoughts move to dark places.

Steph changes into a surgical gown. She's frightened when the nurse comes for her. Mark and I get long hugs, then watch her walk down the hall, wishing we could join her. As the surgical doors close behind her, Steph turns back to us and we see tears and fear on her face. We want to run to her and save her, but the doors close, and the hall is empty. Mark and I hold each other. A husband scared for his wife, a father fearing what she will have to endure, and both uncertain about what the surgeon will find. I walk Mark to the waiting room, then leave him to go help Nana with Caden.

The staff gives Mark a patient number to track Steph's progress. He stares at the monitor while the strain of waiting wears on his soul. Someone calls his name and then asks him to come to the Nurse's station. His heart is in his throat. It's too early for the surgery to be finished, and he's alone to deal with what? What could have happened to Steph? The last time he saw her, she was crying. Does she need me? Is something horribly wrong? The nurse doesn't have any information but leads him back down the long corridor to the surgical doors. His anxiety grows with each step. He walks through the entrance and is told to wait by another set of doors where the hall is dimly lit and cold. Mark is alone and lightheaded. His mind races through the trauma of the last eight months. So much pain and despair and fear. How has Steph handled it so bravely?

The door opens, and a woman dressed in scrubs walks up and asks if he is Stephanie's husband. Yes. She hands him a small box. He doesn't understand and then sees the wedding ring inside. They didn't cut through the three simple words that symbolize so much to Steph and Mark. *Love you, Me.* That's the phrase they ended every card, phone call, and e-mail with while dating and living in different states. Mark walks back to the waiting room, feeling some relief. Holding the ring makes him feel like part of Steph is with him again.

Nana, Caden and I join Mark in the waiting room, where the monitor shows us the surgery has started. I try reading, but soon find myself walking the hallway. I need space and time alone. I find myself in the Chapel and sit down with my thoughts. I whisper a thank you prayer for all the blessings we've received on this journey. Slowly my mind settles, and I realize I don't need to be alone; I need to be with my daughter. To hold her hand, comfort her, and know that she is all right. Returning to the waiting room, I sit down and put my arm around Colleen. She lays her hand on my lap, and automatically I tickle her palm and fingers. Colleen also appreciates the power of touch.

When Colleen and I first married, an average weeknight consists of her studying and me watching TV with a beer and pretzels. After hitting the books, she lies down on the couch and then settles her head on my lap while I work on her back. Colleen loves it when I rub her shoulders and neck, or gently massage anywhere she has skin. She delights in my touch, and it comes so naturally that many nights I do it for an hour, even continuing after she's fallen into a deep sleep.

One evening I hear a small voice speaking jibber jabber come from my lap. I try to understand what my wife is saying in her sleep, but her high pitch and quick delivery make me laugh so loud it wakes her up. Half asleep, she asks me, "What's your problem?" I explain and mimic her, but she thinks I'm making it all up. Over the next month, the sleep talking continues, and her conversations get longer and more animated with exaggerated facial expressions. I have to leave the room since she has become less tolerant of waking up to her husband laughing hysterically at her. Still, she doesn't believe she talks in her sleep, so I hide a cassette recorder under the couch and push record when the entertainment begins. I tape her for five minutes and then play it back as she lies there. She wakes up with a start wondering who's talking and then begins laughing at the silliness she's hearing. I wish I still had the recording because after hearing the tape, she never does it again. The power of touch continues to infuse our life-long bond as I tickle her back almost every night since we married.

The waiting room monitor informs us the surgery is finished and Steph is in recovery. We are gathered up, escorted into a tiny room, and told to wait for Dr. Que. The room is silent as we wait behind the closed door. Our minds fill with questions and race from highs to lows in seconds. The air feels thick, and the room claustrophobic. We give each other empty smiles and wait. A knock at the door and Dr. Que walks in still wearing her surgical scrubs. She tells us the surgery went as planned and Steph is doing well.

The surgeons and radiologist have worked on Stephanie for three and a half hours. Dr. Que scoped Steph and biopsied multiple areas she thought were suspect. Pathology found no signs of cancer. They cut through Steph's abdominal wall and completed a sonogram directly on her liver, finding two tumors, which were also biopsied. The third tumor was too small to harvest a sample. The physician team performed radiofrequency ablation on all three tumors. Each was burned out with minimal damage to the liver. Dr. Que checked the abdominal cavity and organs within it, finding nothing but scar tissue. The Doctor tells us she can't believe there wasn't any new cancer! Even the cancer cells biopsied from the liver were already dead from the chemo. It's an 'Oh my God' moment as we gasp and laugh and look at each other in disbelief. The news is so good that we ask her to repeat it to make sure it's real.

Dr. Que compliments the colorectal surgeon's work as being

very thorough and well done. That confirms what we already know – he is a great fit. The Doctor smiles and says that Caden looks like a Cherub. We agree and feel blessed he's our Cherub. Caden is happy as he has been all day and now, we share his feeling that things are right in our world. We thank Dr. Que for everything and give her hugs as she leaves for her next procedure.

Eight and a half hours earlier, a nurse took Steph for surgery. Now our excitement fills Steph's room as we wait for her. She reaches out for Caden, and her face fills with joy as she's rolled into her room. She moves in and out of consciousness as the anesthesia wears off and falls asleep mid-sentence, which makes us laugh. She wakes up smiling and asks, "What's so funny?" We explain, and then Steph tells us she wants to say a prayer. "Dear Lord, thank you for this beautiful day and thank you for letting my surgery go so well. Thank you for killing all the cancer in my body and letting me live to raise my son and be with my husband and family. I want to thank you for my family and all of their love and support; I couldn't have done this without them. Amen." I fill with pride. My daughter can hardly stay awake, hitting the Morphine button to offset the pain, and yet takes the time to thank God for this beautiful day.

I was raised in the Lutheran faith and converted to Catholicism when I married Colleen, who had two uncles who are priests. For me it was more about my relationship with God than the building I worshipped in. That belief and awareness of other faiths led me to embrace the ideals they share and the spiritual life I live today.

❀

life lesson #14

The subject of religion can quickly stir up emotion
and controversy, yet most cultures throughout
history believe in a power greater than ourselves.
It has many names and is supported by different
teachings, but even as they differ, most have some
shared ideology. It's inclusive to gain a basic understanding of many teachings and focus on what they
have in common. Most believe this greater power is
loving, peaceful, and virtuous. Surround yourself
with loving people doing good for others and be at
peace. Ask for guidance and help by moving into
the silence through meditation and begin a spiritual
journey filled with discovery and blessings.

After a 12-hour day, Dr. Que is needed in the ER and sends
her fourth-year surgical resident to check on Stephanie. Steph's
memory of her time in recovery is foggy, so the resident reviews
the day's surgical results. Stephanie can't stop smiling when she
hears the chemo is working. She is excited, filled with energy,
and tells each of us how much she loves us. She calls Teresa and
Grandpa Bill with the great news and reaffirms her love for them.
They cry and laugh and ride the adrenalin high.

Steph tells us that on her way to the operating room, she
became overwhelmed and asked God, "Please take the wheel, I
just can't handle it anymore." The stress and worry again lifted
from her body, giving way to immediate peace in knowing everything is all right.

Colleen and I walk Caden back to the hotel, while Mark stays with his wife. Steph wakes up almost every hour, each time nudging Mark and telling him, "Hey, wake up, I'm Cancer Free!" She is so happy to be alive and believes everything is getting better again.

chapter 25

STEPH IS DETERMINED to heal up quickly and get back home. She starts this process by impressing the nurses with her ability to walk further than asked. They want her to walk to the hallway, so she adds another 100 feet down the hall and back. Each walk is further than the last. Steph's pain is present, but her smile and positive attitude camouflage it. Excellent nursing care also helps. This staff is skilled, gentle, and attentive, making sure Steph and her entourage stay comfortable. They are consistently happy and seem to enjoy their jobs. That is so refreshing.

Stephanie's pain has increased this evening, and her breathing is labored. We hear her lungs rattle as fluids build up. She struggles to cough up the liquid because of her incision pain and can't get a breath to cough with. The morphine on demand makes her drowsy, and she drifts in and out of consciousness. Two pharmacists come in and discuss pain-reducing options with us.

Steph's oxygen levels begin to drop while her heart rate climbs, so the resident increases her oxygen flow and begins to monitor her heart rate. He updates Dr. Que, and they decide to check the lungs for pneumonia but are more concerned about a pulmonary embolism because of Steph's history with blood clots. An x-ray rules out pneumonia, and they adjust the pain meds. The CT comes back negative for pulmonary embolism, and everyone is relieved. A heparin drip is started to protect Steph from blood clots.

The change in pain meds seems to help, and everything begins to settle down. We are impressed by how quickly the evening staff have assembled from five different departments over the last two hours and how well they work together as a team. Neither Colleen nor I have ever seen a system run so smoothly and efficiently. Steph quiets down and falls asleep. After 18 hours in the hospital, Colleen and I take Caden back to the hotel for some rest.

Caden falls asleep after his bottle. So do we. He wakes up crying four times in the next two hours and then hourly after that. Maybe it's the stress or that he misses his mother. It's a long exhausting night as we try one thing after another to settle him down. Hotels are a challenging place to quiet a crying baby, and we hope he isn't keeping others awake. We get about three hours of sleep, but Caden still gets up happy, as he always does. Steph sleeps peacefully through the night. She wakes up alert and breathing better, leading us to believe it was the morphine that put her in distress the night before.

Bill and Kim visit, bringing presents for Caden and pajamas for Stephanie. Steph takes us all for a walk around the hospital. She's quiet. I ask why, and she tells me it's nothing. I know better, but don't push it. Later she admits the pain increased, but she doesn't want to make a big deal of it. "Dad, short-term pain is nothing when you consider I'm cancer free." She understands that fighting this disease is a marathon, not a sprint.

Bill and Kim take Colleen, Caden, and me out to eat while

Mark dines with Steph. The waitress brings a plate of sliced lemons with our iced tea. Caden grabs one, and like everything else, he shoves the lemon and half his fist into his mouth. He tastes it, pulls it away with a sour look, and then shoves it in again. While Caden is in his own world sorting out taste sensations, his body language puts on a show for everyone around us. When I take the lemon away, he immediately lets me know I've overstepped my authority with a face that shows disappointment and questions my love for him. I swap out the pulverized lemon slice with a fresh one, and he forgives me.

That evening after Bill and Kim depart for home, Colleen helps Steph take a shower, and Caden and I take a walk outside. We stop by the chapel. Saint Mary's Chapel is old and beautiful inside with its rich wood and granite pillars. I enjoy the quiet, while Caden looks around and plays with his giraffe. I long for quiet in my life but remind myself that Stephanie is alive and doing well and everything else is secondary.

Recovery proceeds normally the next few days with tubes and medications being removed, and Steph's strength and stamina returning. Changing from the IV blood thinner to an oral proves to be as challenging here as it was back home. Caden isn't himself, waking up fussy multiple times each night. After trial and error, Nana lays him between us in bed while he clutches Lambie. Bingo, that's what he wanted. I guess we all like someone close to us as we sleep. Mark understands this. He sleeps uncomfortably in the hospital each night, just to be close to his wife.

Steph continues walking further to increase her strength. She walks to the elevator, rides it down to the first floor, and finds the gift shop. She's a sight to see pushing her IV pole in her newest flannel pajamas covered with polar bears from Aunt Kim.

She rewards herself with a roll of Butter Rum Lifesavers. That's my girl.

As the week passes, our appreciation of the Mayo team and Saint Mary's Hospital Staff continues to grow. The residents and physicians become closer to us and seek out Caden when they visit. The IV, Lab, and Catheter teams are specialized and excellent at their jobs. With three to four patients, the floor nurses have time to provide personal care. And to top it off they all seem genuinely happy with their jobs. This is a healing place, more than any other we have experienced. A quote from William J. Mayo captures their goal. "The best interest of the patient is the only interest to be considered." It's odd, but each of our team agrees that Mayo somehow feels like home. Maybe it's because we just feel safe here. Whatever the reason, it's welcome, refreshing and feels so very good to have them care for Steph.

chapter 26

A WEEK AFTER STEPHANIE'S SURGERY, she is given a choice to stay and get the oral blood thinner stabilized or leave using an injectable. She wants to go home, so we pack and are driving two hours later. It's Mark's birthday and taking his wife home is the best present he can imagine. Caden gives him a bonus gift, by settling back into his routine of sleeping soundly again.

August in Kansas City brings heat and humidity. The house is set up in zones to increase heating and cooling efficiency. One of the air conditioners quits, and since we've used up most of our money cushion, we try to get by with only one. After a few days in a warm house, I borrow some money until my bonus arrives and replace both units, making the team comfortable again.

The team is wearing down again, and we'll need help to care for Steph and Caden. We call Kristen, and she says it's no problem; she flies in to help us for the week. She mothers us, takes Caden at night and does anything to help, always with a smile on her face. She has a take-charge attitude, fits into the team well, and we enjoy her company. Deciding that we could use some diversion,

Kristen throws a birthday party for all of us with two cakes and presents for everyone. At the party, Caden enjoys the cake and drinks from a straw for the first time. Steph thinks it's so funny to watch him figure it out and doesn't seem to mind the cake crumb backwash floating in her glass. When Kristen flies home, we miss her smiles and her positive attitude.

Stephanie is recovering quickly. She doesn't have problems walking stairs or other issues that challenged her after other surgeries. Her incision is healing well, and the latest cut changed the picture on her tummy. It starts at the top of the anchor handle and curves down to the edge of the smile line. It now looks more like a sailboat; hopefully, that forecasts smooth sailing on the horizon. Steph's attitude is positive. You can tell the chemo is out of her system by her high energy level and less hair around the drain, but some side effects remain. The neuropathy and tingling in her hands, arms, and legs continue to increase. It's difficult for her to pick things up, and she is always cold. While sitting in our Gazebo, she wraps up in a blanket wearing gloves even though it is 95 degrees outside.

The month passes quickly, and we head back to Mayo for Steph's checkup. It seems strange, but our team is excited to get there and see the doctors. Steph tells us she has 'scanxiety,' which she defines as anxiety about the scans showing new cancer. At the same time, she understands the doctors can only fight what they can find. All of us believe the tests will be clear, but we've had bad news after good enough times to be a little nervous. We check into the hotel, and Caden jumps on the bed with Nana. We walk to the Italian restaurant for dinner and have the same waiter from our first visit. He remembers everything we ordered a month ago, including the wine. The food and service are wonderful, and Caden can't get enough of their dinner rolls.

Early the next morning Steph and Mark take the tunnel to her blood draw and CT, while Colleen and I keep Caden at the hotel. The same tech Steph had last time struggles to get the IV started because scar tissue continues to form from the chemo and past sticks. Finally, she finds a vein that works. She tells Steph she's thought of her often in the last month, wondering how she and her baby were getting along. She is genuinely happy things are progressing well.

We arrive early for our appointment with Dr. Que. It's unsettling what happens to you emotionally when you get called back and are placed into an examination room. The door closes, and you wait. Everyone experiences this at the doctor's office, but it's different when you're fighting a life-threatening disease. It gives your mind time to worry and play, *what if.* Each of us feels it, and our team even has a name for it. We call it 'Behind the Door Syndrome.' BDS is the feeling you have waiting behind the exam room door for test results. The syndrome includes anxiety, fear, lack of control, anger, instant religion, and a willingness to bargain with God. The antidote to BDS is good news delivered quickly.

Dr. Que walks in and tells us the CT is clear even before she sits down. She clearly understands BDS syndrome. The team is excited, and so is she. Steph asks, "Do you want to check my incision?" This prompts Dr. Que to ask, "Why is there something wrong with it?" Steph smiles, "No, in fact, things are great." We talk with Dr. Que for half an hour and find out she has performed over 5,000 surgeries. She tells Stephanie she is releasing her since there's no more surgery to complete.

"You can start doing anything you feel comfortable doing. You can pick up Caden, go swimming, or anything else you want to." We are so pleased she's been Steph's surgeon, and we tell her so. Dr. Grothey was right, this surgeon is a great fit for our daughter.

Our appointment with Dr. Grothey is in three hours. Colleen suggests we see if they have anything earlier, so we can get on the road. They don't have any cancelations, but the doctor works us in between patients two hours early. This medical system continues to differentiate itself. In less than eight hours, Steph gets lab work, scans, test results, and analysis from two doctors. Amazing!

Dr. Grothey is delighted with the surgical results and today's tests. He reviews everything with us, and Mark tells him he has made our day. The doctor smiles, and looking at Steph says, "No, actually she made my day." He tells us he expected Dr. Que to find more cancer during surgery and was surprised when nothing was found. He is delighted they were able to do RFA and save Steph's liver. The doctor spends 30 minutes with us and is genuinely happy and excited for us. He has squeezed us in, and yet we feel like he doesn't have another patient on his schedule, only Steph. He suggests Dr. Baranda restart the chemo cocktail, stay with the aggressively high doses, and complete four more chemo sessions, for a total of 12. He will see us again in January for another round of tests and follow up.

The plan moving forward will be to complete CT scans and blood work every three months for the next two years, then every six months for an additional five years. I thought cancer patients were usually monitored for five years after treatment and ask him about it. He said in Steph's case, he might want to follow her for seven. The oncologist tells us 85% of all re occurrences happen within the first two years and Steph has a 50/50 chance of reoccurrence. He tells Stephanie that exercise may improve the odds, but not to overdo it.

Our team enjoys the Mayo experience and has a difficult time saying good-bye because we honestly believe it's a healing place for us. We feel confident and safe here. We thank Dr. Grothey, head home, and debrief during the drive. The trip is a happy one, and the miles fly by as the team updates family and friends and then drifts to sleep. Except for me– I drive. Cross-country driving is therapy for me and gives me a chance to think things through. Lately, there's been a great deal to think about.

chapter 27

STEPHANIE, CADEN, AND I MEET WITH DR. BARANDA to review the Mayo visit. The doctor hasn't received any information yet and gets excited at the positive results we share. She takes her time listening to Steph's experience, reviewing the next steps, and cooing over Caden. It's taken months to find the medical teams we now have at KU and Mayo. Now that we have two amazing oncologists providing leadership and expertise, we no longer feel alone and illiterate when making decisions that may impact survival. These professionals guide us and fill us with hope. We depend on their knowledge and skill and love them for who they are and what they do for us.

Everything proceeds smoothly with Steph's ninth chemo session, and we leave with the chemo pump slowly delivering the last drug. I drive Steph home where she fixes meatloaf for the team while I play with Caden. The kids have been living at their home but will return to ours tomorrow since chemo has resumed, and Steph will be challenged again with the side effects.

Caden now has five teeth with more on the way. If his teeth

don't bother him, he sleeps soundly, which is appreciated by everyone. Caden loves eating the table food that Steph grinds up. He tips the scale at 22 pounds and has just turned 7 months. Caden is so good that everyone asks if he is always this happy. He is and helps us get through many tough days.

The chemo pump is disconnected. Steph's blood is too thick, so the blood thinner is adjusted. The chemo drains her strength, while the drugs boosting her blood cell production create bone and muscle pain. Fatigue sets in and Steph swells up from the steroids. Nurse Nana monitors her daughter's blood pressure since all medications are once again on board. A mixture of depression and fatigue quiets Steph. Two days later, the blood is too thin, so meds are adjusted. Steph tries to stay positive and upbeat, but doesn't have much energy to work with.

Tomorrow is Colleen's birthday. Nana and I have Caden's night shift, and he spends most of it cutting teeth. At 5:30 a.m. we bring him into bed with us, and he drifts off. Later his eyes open and he rolls over to Nana, waking her with one kiss after another. Laughing, she tells him he couldn't give her a better birthday present. Colleen doesn't want cake for her birthday, so I take a Skinny Cow and stick a candle in it that plays happy birthday. She smiles telling us, it's just what she wanted. It's a quiet day, and everyone enjoys the downtime.

Another blood draw confirms Steph's blood is still outside the therapeutic window. It's decided Steph will use inject-able blood thinners until her chemotherapy is completed. This will provide consistent protection against the blood clots, but it requires injections in her gut twice a day and is much more expensive. The medication burns and creates a four-inch black and blue circle around the injection site. The surgical scars and needle marks make her tummy look like a battle zone, reflecting the fight going on in her body.

I travel for work and Mark works nights against a deadline, which leaves Colleen alone to do everything again. She takes Steph and Caden to chemo, deals with meals, and stays up with Caden every night as he cuts teeth. She is completely wiped out when I return on Friday. I'm happy to take Caden, and we practice his sit-ups as I change him. His strength grows, and now when he pulls himself up and giggles, I can see all his new teeth. Something has changed while I was gone; my needle-avoiding daughter is injecting herself twice each day. I can't believe it. She tells me, "It's no big deal. You guys have enough to deal with, so I just started doing it myself." Will wonders never cease?

The neuropathy in Steph's hands and feet is getting worse, moving up her limbs, making them cold and numb all the time. When she bathes Caden, we check the water first to make sure the temperature is okay since she can't tell. When she makes bottles she tastes them, making sure they are not too hot. The doctor prescribes an antibiotic for an infection in Steph's toe. She can't always feel her feet and doesn't know when she stubs or injures a toe, so we start checking them more often. The drugs mess with her hormones, so her body can't decide if she is in puberty or menopause. So many changes are going on, but Stephanie continues to be a trooper. Two more rounds of chemo remain.

Caden grows faster than bamboo, changes each day, and now wants to crawl. He gets up on his hands and knees, rocks back and forth, but isn't sure what the next move is. Caden snorts when he laughs, which makes us laugh with him. At chemo he pulls himself up on the hospital bed rail, so we realize it won't be long before he begins to walk.

Stephanie is exhausted and feels guilty that she can't care for Caden. She asks me if I think he notices. That's a loaded question since I want to assure her that all his needs are being met, but only one person is his mother. I tell her Caden loves his Mommy so much, that no one can ever replace her, but he also loves the team and understands when Mommy needs to rest. That seems to be the right answer, but she tells me to write it in my journal, so Caden knows for sure. I am certain Caden knows how much she loves him, and I'm just as confident that he is the best medicine for her recovery. Caden keeps her going and reminds me of how important love is in our lives.

The chemotherapy is much harder on Stephanie this round. Steph remembers what Dr. Baranda told her at the first appointment, 'We will take you as close to death as possible to kill your cancer with chemo, and then bring you back again.' Now Steph is experiencing what the doctor described. None of the side effects take her entirely down, but they stack on top of each other and add up. Steph is in more pain than she admits to, usually nauseated, and doesn't sleep well. She remains dedicated to Caden, telling us, "Don't worry, everything is okay, as long as I have my baby boy. I am so lucky to have him in my life." Seeing her great attitude makes me feel guilty complaining about not getting enough sleep. Steph is a living reminder to wake up and be happy for what I have. Things could be so much worse.

The kids drive to their home on Friday night but return early Sunday. The side effects are worse, and Steph needs everyone's help. Stephanie sits with Caden in her lap, thinking she has a runny nose, but its blood. The nose bleeds occur daily now, likely a side effect from one of the chemo drugs.

Our team is worn out after a stressful week of Caden not sleeping, me traveling, and Mark working each night. Colleen works three days and somehow keeps up with the laundry, meals, and cleaning. Exhaustion and frustration build up, but we rest when we can and work through it.

It's easy for emotions to run high when the body is exhausted. Two of Stephanie's cousins are expecting new babies. She is happy for them but feels sad, reflecting on her own experience. Much of her time with Caden has been a blur. She and I talk, but I don't know what to say. She fills the silence, remembering how lucky she is. What if they had discovered her cancer early in the pregnancy and started chemo? How would Caden have been affected? Her eyes glass over for a moment, and she's gone, then she's back with me. "Dad, things could have been so much worse. Caden is here and healthy, and I'm alive." She's wearing her brave face now and tells me how fortunate she is to have this baby boy in her arms. She knows what to say and helps us both through the moment.

Like many people, our lives are busy. Mark, Colleen, and I work long hours to meet work obligations and keep up with the house. Steph and Caden also need more attention, so everyone is spent by the end of each day. It's very demanding again, and none of us sleep more than six hours a night. We tell each other to hang on, that chemo will be done in a month and all will get better. I hope so. I have never liked roller coaster rides, and this one seems unending.

I can't believe it's October as I drive my grandson and his mother to her eleventh Chemo session. Dr. Baranda adds a flu shot to other vaccinations ordered by Dr. Grothey. Everything goes smoothly with the treatment, and our patient even sleeps for an hour. Caden decides not to sleep and takes the opportunity to bond with his Papa. He owns me as his mother did at this age. I talk to him in baby talk with a goofy smile on my face. For a while, there is nothing else in our world but each other and silliness.

The kids host Mark's parents for the weekend, then return to our house on Sunday.

Dr. Baranda examines Steph's skin and checks her cell counts, thinking she may delay the last chemo session until Steph heals more. A second toe is infected, so a stronger antibiotic is ordered. Adding to Steph's burden are weight gain, a puffed-up steroid face, and new blood pressure medication. The doctor asks Steph how she's dealing with all the side effects. She bravely answers, "I'm okay because I'm cancer-free." It's difficult for me to understand how she does it, simply because I don't think I could. She owns her disease and understands she can't feel sorry for herself because it makes her weaker. She's become a warrior. Her positive attitude is her armor, and her actions become her weapons. Sometimes her efforts are minimal, but Stephanie understands that when the direction of a journey changes by just one degree, time reveals an entirely new destination.

Mark is on a deadline and works through the night at his office. Colleen sees Steph's disappointment and suggests they camp out in her bedroom. The girls play games with Caden until he gets tired. The next morning Mark finds all three asleep on the floor.

As the last chemo treatment nears, Steph's anxiety increases. She's concerned that her body won't be able to kill new cancer cells if they develop. We remind her that a great medical team watches over her, and we believe she is going to win her fight. She listens and understands, but still worries. Who wouldn't? Restless Leg Syndrome keeps her awake at night, allowing her mind to dwell on the fear for hours. We try sleeping pills, but they don't help her escape the endless loop of anxiety.

Caden is on the verge of crawling. He rises up on hands and knees, rocks back and forth sliding forward a bit, then drops down on his tummy. He moves a hand or foot and tries again, determined to make something happen. I try to show him what to do by crawling on the floor, but he laughs at me along with the rest of my family. He gets better with each try until he finally moves forward, rocks unsteadily side to side and moves again. He giggles and drops like a rock. Stone-faced, he pushes himself up and travels twice as far on the next try.

Soon he is crawling everywhere, going further and faster each hour. His face is tense as he struggles, then softens as everything comes together. He looks around making sure we are watching, loses focus, falls on his side, and lies there giggling. Steph couldn't wait for Caden to crawl, but now that he's mobile, she doesn't know why she was in such a hurry. Caden enjoys the exercise and needs it since his baby fat has moved his body description from a cherub to full-fledged Sumo Wrestler. He quickly masters patty-cake, waving bye-bye, and making noise. He now says Mama, Dada, Nana, and Papa, which we make him repeat over and over, imagining it determines who he likes the best.

Mark drives Steph to her last planned chemo session. With Dr. Baranda, Steph shares her excitement of completing the drugs along with the fear of losing their protection. The oncologist explains there is clinical data to support the continuation of the Stage 4 drug for an additional six months, which she plans to do. Steph supports the idea, willing to do anything to improve her chance of long-term survival. She mentally checks off the side effects she hopes to be rid of. Her fingers are so numb and weak that now she needs help getting dressed and half her hair is gone. She might also eliminate some of the drugs used to offset other side effects.

Our patient puts a smile on her face that stays there most of the day. With most of the chemo drugs discontinued, they decide to try the oral blood thinner again. On the way home, the kids stop at the pharmacy for refills and find her prescription benefit has now maxed out. They will pay full price for all prescriptions until the end of the year.

Mark's architect firm takes the kids to dinner to celebrate the end of her first round of chemo. Everyone asks how Stephanie is doing, which reminds her to post an overdue web update on her progress and thank her many supporters.

chapter 28

STEPH, MARK, AND CADEN MOVE BACK to their house perma-
nently. It's too quiet around our home, so most days we find an
excuse to visit them. It also helps that Steph calls several times
each day. They join us over the weekend to plant three Sunset
Maple trees, one for each member of their family. We will enjoy
their red foliage in the fall.

Caden sits on my lap as I drive the tractor and trailer to the
planting site across the pond. He enjoys the ride, and his head is
on a swivel looking at each tree and the geese on the water as we
drive by. Caden crawls around in the dirt and plays with hedge
apples as I auger out the holes. Steph watches her son telling
Nana, "He is all boy." Mark rolls a hedge ball near his son. Caden
is thrilled, quickly crawls to it, and then wants to do it again. I
enjoy watching him experience everyday life. It takes me back to
the simplicity of my own childhood. Caden giggles as I scoop him
up and plant him on my shoulders. He wraps little arms around
my neck as we walk. We hide, and Nana finds us, making him
laugh. His eyes beg, please do it again, Nana, and she does. A

smile is usually on his face, and the giggles come so effortlessly. I will miss him on my trip.

I drive to South Dakota to visit my parents and hunt with Stan. My parents were raised on farms and started their own when they married. A year later, my brother was born. Mom wanted a different future for her kids, so eventually, she talked Dad into selling the farm. They bought a small store where two highways crossed and sold groceries and gas, and did a decent business. They doubled their money when selling it a year later, and moved to a small town of about 18,000 people. After I was born, they purchased a corner grocery and lived above it. Business went well for a few years, but Dad was too trusting when handing out credit, and eventually, they had to sell the business. Dad managed a department in a large grocery store while Mom worked at JCPenney's. Her determination and hard work eventually earned her a spot managing a department, which at the time was unusual for a woman.

My parents overcame their limited education by working long, hard hours, and built a respectable life for their family. They are honest, salt of the earth people. Their answer to any need that surfaced was to work more hours, so most days they were gone before I went to school and often they worked nights. I was a latch key kid before there was a name for it. I didn't know any better and enjoyed the freedom I had. I walked the mile to grade school and always felt safe, spending most after-school time at a friend's home half a block down the street. Looking back, I remember a great childhood. I always felt loved, taken care of, and thoroughly enjoyed the freedom I earned as a good kid who seldom caused trouble.

Dad now lives in assisted living, doing well for being in his early 90s, and happy to have company. Mom is in her early 80's.

Her dementia has progressed, so she lives in a nursing home and no longer recognizes us. At least her delusions and hallucinations have stopped, and she isn't burdened by Steph's illness. I feel helpless when I am with my mother, but she seems to get some comfort when I hold her hand and stroke her arm. I know it comforts me, again confirming the power of touch. It's difficult with them six hundred miles away, but they want to stay where they are, whenever we try to move them closer.

Stan and I enjoy our time together walking the harvested fields. My mind quiets as my legs carry me through miles of cornfields and sloughs. I lose myself in the moment and enjoy the company of my oldest friend. We've been friends since 1970 and never had an argument. I attribute that more to him than to myself. We don't always agree on politics, and he is six inches taller, but we are similar in our approach to family and the enjoyment we get from hunting and fishing. When we're together, it's like we are eighteen again having fun without responsibilities or stress.

Today the geese aren't moving off the water so Stan naps in his blind. I quietly crawl up on my prey and pounce. After a minute wrestling, he uses his size to pin me and makes me promise to be good or he'll take my lunch away and eat it. I enjoy the part of us that has never grown up. It's effortless for us to work or play together, and we both understand how unusual it is to have this close friendship throughout our lives. The long drive home gives me time to appreciate my blessings, think through Steph's ongoing fight, and the various challenges at work. I treasure the quiet time to think.

The next three weeks fly by. Steph's insurance rejects the Mayo surgery bill, saying they didn't pre-approve the RFA, so we appeal the decision, hoping it's just miscommunication. A new CT scan is cancer free providing her welcome relief. Stephanie receives her single-agent chemotherapy, which only takes an hour. They adjust blood thinner doses, but still can't maintain the therapeutic window. Afterward, the kids travel to Nebraska to visit Mark's family. Steph's legs swell up in the car even though they stop and walk every two hours. When Dr. Baranda hears this, she is not happy that her patient placed herself at risk and makes it clear Stephanie can only travel for medical treatment. Steph promises it won't happen again.

The next morning Steph trips on a toy block, stumbles and hurts her knee. An hour later, she falls again hurting the same knee and her shoulder. We try not to overreact but have become hyper-vigilant after the blood clot and sepsis incidents. Nana checks for injury and internal bleeding, but nothing develops. Steph is placed back on the injectable blood thinner since the orals can't provide consistent safety. She doesn't complain and injects herself.

Thanksgiving generates a full house of family. Scott is home from college and Bill and Kim drive down from Minnesota. Colleen and Bill cook a wonderful turkey dinner, while Scott tries his hand at making California Rolls and sushi. Steph can't eat the raw fish, and Kim never, ever eats anything she can't fully identify, but the rest of us enjoy it. We make the best of the warm weather by setting up Santa's sleigh and reindeer, along with Christmas lights on the gate and garland on the driveway light poles. The holiday weekend is a welcome break to the stress Bill and Kim are currently experiencing; a colonoscopy has revealed a large tumor in Kim's colon that needs to be removed. Monday morning is filled with hugs and prayers as Bill and Kim depart for home, and I fly to New Jersey to prepare for another product launch.

Some of our friends and family learn that Steph's prescription insurance has run out and send money to keep the drugs flowing. I am taken aback by their generosity. They don't want a fuss made about it, they just want to help, and Steph and Mark appreciate it so much.

December brings Stephanie additional leg pain, and the swelling and her limp get worse. We are concerned about the blood clot decreasing circulation to her leg. Worse yet, if a piece breaks off, it could still trigger a heart attack, stroke, or sudden death. It's difficult not to think about it and harder yet waiting to see if something happens with so much at risk. We try to return to our regular routine, but it's easy to imagine things going wrong. Will this be a good Christmas or Steph's last? Thoughts appear in our minds from nowhere, and we feel guilty not being able to block them out, or that somehow thinking about them will attract problems into our lives.

Steph talks to her oncologist about the increased leg pain and swelling. A sonogram shows veins in her right leg have narrowed, likely causing the problems. The blood thinner should help, and over time, we hope the veins will construct new pathways around the problem areas. After chemo Steph and Mark meet with Dr. Lynch. They ask him about having more children. The physician has strong concerns for the health of both mother and child due to the potential damage to her eggs from chemo and her extensive blood clots. The words are difficult to hear but not surprising. Steph feels guilty, and it all seems so final. They leave the appointment with heavy hearts, after confirming the reality they have both feared. As their emotions settle, they remind each other how lucky they are to have Caden and each other.

Nana introduces Caden to *The Polar Express*. She sings along with the movie and Caden is mesmerized by the experience. They cuddle while watching it together, and it becomes Caden's favorite thing to do. Christmas is always more fun with little ones around. Caden is cute crawling around with a bow stuck on top of his head. He is standing now, loves to rip open presents, and follows his soccer ball around the room, not so much kicking it as taking it for a walk. We take time to count our many blessings and try to catch our breath. The last year has taken a toll on each of us, but Steph is alive, and that is our long-term goal.

The day after Christmas, Steph and Mark leave early for chemo. Scott and I work outside clearing trails, and it's a pleasure to spend time with my son. We take breaks and talk, neither of which we usually do when we work the chain saws. We even shoot 22's at the new target I received for Christmas. My son has grown up, but I still watch over him. I want to keep everyone I love close to me where I can protect them. That is my flawed plan to keep them safe.

❖

life lesson #15

I have heard that if you genuinely love someone, you would do anything for their happiness, even if it means letting them go. Try to do what is best for them, even if it's difficult for you. A mother bird coaxing her chick out of the nest, so they learn to fly. A father releasing the bike his child is learning to ride, hoping they won't fall. Parents seeing their sixteen-year-old daughter picked up on her first date by a twenty-year-old boy in a van. Nope, that's never going to happen. End Of Lesson!

chapter 29

STEPHANIE AND MARK HOST A SURVIVAL PARTY to celebrate her living through the last twelve months. All the neighbors attend, and the night is filled with laughter, friendship, and thanks. Nana and I are excited to watch Caden. We read nursery rhymes and play games into the night. At bedtime, Nana gives him a bath and then lays him between us in bed to play until he falls asleep. She tells me we can spoil him because that's what grandparents are expected to do. Her plan includes forgetting to take Caden home tomorrow and keeping him a second night.

The next morning Colleen and I write a second letter to Steph's insurance company about their rejection of the RFA surgery. We believe it's a misunderstanding since they preapproved surgery and then rejected RFA. We are on top of it, but stay patient with them, since they have covered most things so far.

On Monday Steph's pap test comes back abnormal and the doctor wants to repeat it. They tell her it's probably nothing and not to worry about it, but that's easier said than done. Some of our team has started to diet and count points staying true to their

New Year's resolutions. Last year's grueling schedule wasn't built around exercise or a balanced diet, and now it's caught up with us.

Mid-afternoon, we hear that Aunt Kim's colon resection has gone well. Doctors removed a large polyp and fortunately didn't find any cancer. Kim also starts a Nicotine Patch to try to quit smoking again. She tells us, "I want to be around to watch Caden grow up." Kim also decides the best medicine for her recovery is to look forward to something fun. She and Bill invite Colleen and me to vacation with them in Mexico. We need a break and agree to join them.

Stephanie has recently heard that some patients with cancer develop something called chemo brain. She asks Dr. Baranda about it during her next appointment. The doctor tells her that cancer patients can experience a foggy thought process, sometimes labeled chemo brain. Symptoms may include problems with memory or processing thoughts. There isn't very much data published, and it's uncertain if it's a side effect of drug therapy or part of the disease. It was believed to last up to a year after treatment, but newer data suggests it may last much longer in some patients. Steph says some days she just feels like an airhead. We notice her sense of urgency has diminished, she is less organized and forgets more than in the past, but that could simply be fatigue. However you define chemo brain, Stephanie thinks she may have it based on the timing and symptoms. Hopefully it will disappear after she completes chemotherapy. Steph's second pap comes back normal.

Scott returns home to watch the house and pets while we visit the Mayo Clinic again. It's hard for him to be away from family, and I worry about him dealing with Steph's illness alone. He doesn't want to talk about it when I ask, telling me everything is fine. The self-reliance and sense of freedom that college has given Scott may mislead him to believe he has to deal with personal feelings on his own. Or maybe it just isn't any of my business. Scott has already experienced extreme loss after losing several close friends. He tends to internalize it, which I worry about. We're just part of the ongoing struggle of kids trying to find their way with parents attempting to help and protect them.

In Rochester, we check into a hotel. Nana sings about monkeys while Caden jumps on the bed, then everyone calls it a night. None of us sleep well. We think everything will be fine, but anxiety still shadows us. We complete the morning CT and blood tests and then pass time shopping before meeting with the oncologist. We all take turns changing Caden, but it seems Mark and I get the duty, no pun intended, more often than not. We locate a men's room and quickly make Caden comfortable. I don't see men changing babies frequently in public restrooms, but we do it so often, it's like a tag team. One of us starts the removal process while the other is pulling out wipes and a fresh diaper. A well-oiled machine as they say and people notice. As we walk out, I tell Mark that everyone thinks we are partners, and I'm his Sugar Daddy. He laughs and tells me I really am his Sugar Daddy since they live with us so often.

We ride the elevator at the center of the Gonda building to the ninth floor and take a seat in the large south waiting area. Small areas of computers and educational materials divide up the room, but most of the space is set up in pods of comfortable seating to wait your turn. Caden's favorite place to sit is by the floor to ceiling windows near the elevators. He likes watching the clouds and birds drift by.

Dr. Grothey tells us the tests don't show any cancer activity. The liver lesions haven't changed, and he is delighted with the results. As Steph continues the newest chemo drug for an additional six months, there will be a risk of not knowing what long-term side effects may occur. Because this drug alters the body's natural systems, it could produce issues with blood flow or increased cardiovascular risk. Since early research suggests better results when the drug is given longer, the choice is relatively straightforward. Our priority is to keep Steph alive now and then deal with complications if or when they arise. The team agrees with the physician's logic and priorities.

The oncologist appreciates our willingness to use Mayo for checkups. He believes it benefits Steph to keep consistency in the scans, and if anything is detected, he will move aggressively to remove it with surgery. He comments on the importance of a positive attitude, a strong support team, and that Steph is lucky to have both. The doctor recalls how positive and upbeat Stephanie has been from the beginning, and it's obvious how much support her family provides to her. He tells us there is nothing concrete by way of studies to document the value of a positive attitude and a support system, but he believes both are critical to her long-term health. We find this physician to be a caring and personable man.

Our appointment is interrupted as the doctor leaves to take a call from a referring physician. When he returns, he explains a young pregnant woman just diagnosed with colon cancer was trying to determine her next course of action. What an incredibly difficult decision for the mother to be faced with. Wait to start treatment until after the birth or start it now? How do you balance the health of the mother and child? Hopefully, with the guidance of a great medical team, both will do well. We keep the family in our prayers and are reminded that everyone has a story.

We thank the doctor, and on the way out, Mark receives a call from work that they were just awarded a large government project. Mark is excited because he designed it and will be very involved throughout the build. Steph is proud of him. She knows how much time he invested in the planning.

Steph dials Dr. Varanka's number, and they share emotions of relief and happiness. Teresa is also making progress in her cancer battle. She thanks Stephanie for convincing her to take the most aggressive, effective course of action to fight the cancer. Steph is her inspiration and source of strength as she helps her friend set clear goals and work through her struggles. Teresa tells Steph she will keep fighting with her and for her. The team jumps into the car and debriefs on the way to visit Aunt Kim.

Kim and I have grown closer this last year with all the time she's spent helping us. It feels great to hug her and see that she's recovering quickly from her surgery. She gets around fine, grows stronger every day, and has a great attitude. Kim attributes her strength to Steph's example, saying, "If Steph can go through all the crap she has and stay positive, so can I." Kim has lost interest in smoking and tells us food tastes funny now that she has quit. She thinks it's probably because the tobacco had tainted her taste buds. We visit for a few hours and then head back to Rochester. On the drive Caden throws up, which creates a lot of activity in the moving car. The girls clean him up, and then we stop to pick up food, detergent, and a toy for the little guy, before going to the hotel. After washing clothes and cleaning the car, we go to bed and sleep soundly through the night.

On the drive home, Steph plans Caden's first birthday and writes in his journal:

My precious sweet boy, I can't believe you turn one tomorrow! You sleep beside me, and my heart is full of joy. The year slipped by so fast, and we have been through so much. I don't know if I could have done it without you. I am so blessed to get a second chance at life to be here with you. You grew up so fast, and there have been so many challenges, but I spent every day of your life with you and feel so grateful for that. God blessed me throughout this hardship. Everyone you meet tells me how good you are. I tell them you are an angel and my miracle. Thank you for everything. Peanut, I couldn't live without you and love you so much.

— Mom

Today is Caden's first birthday, so we take him out to lunch to celebrate. He enjoys sampling food off our plates and is thrilled with the cake and ice cream. He digs in with both hands and seems to delight in wearing it as much as eating it. Steph talks about the day he was born and the two conventional weeks she had before her diagnosis. He has added so much to our lives in the last year, and we are thankful for the timing of his arrival. He wobbles as he walks, but drops to the ground and crawls when he wants to move fast.

When Caden was born I brought him a big blue 'It's a Boy' foil balloon that plays the song *Baby Face*. I loved it, but Steph said it was annoying and it quickly became a joke between us. When we were leaving the hospital, she even tried to leave it behind the door, but I grabbed it. Today after lunch, I find the balloon in Caden's closet and play the song. We laugh, but Steph quickly reminds me, "It's still annoying." I ask her why she didn't just pop it and throw it away, and immediately know my mistake as she stares daggers at me.

It's young Stephanie's birthday party and she sits in the highchair, watching me clean up after everyone leaves. I bounce balloons at her as I work and she giggles until I pop one to throw it into the garbage. The unexpected noise terrifies her, and she won't stop crying. I feel horrible about it, and it takes forever to settle her down. Unfortunately, her fear of loud bangs doesn't go away. We leave baseball games early if they have fireworks, she hates thunder, and she joins the dogs in the house shielded by music on the fourth of July. This fear continues into her twenties.

Caden's real birthday party takes place over the weekend so family and friends can attend. He giggles ripping the paper off his gifts as his dad helps open the boxes. Children take turns hitting the piñata until candy pours out, and everyone scrambles for the goodies. Caden cries when his little friends have to leave. He points and sobs 'NO' to express his displeasure. Minutes later, he falls asleep exhausted in Mark's arms.

At chemo, Steph tells Dr. Baranda about recent migraines, which occur almost daily. An MRI is ordered to rule out a bleed in her brain. The results are normal. Genetic testing is also arranged. Steph struggles as the genetic doctor lists the cancers she's at increased risk to get because of the colon cancer. She breaks down as they leave the appointment and Mark tries to console her. He diverts her attention by shopping for a Muppets movie that Steph loved to watch as a child. She wants it for Caden and hopes he will enjoy it too. She doesn't tell Mark, she's afraid she won't be alive to watch it with her son.

One year ago, today, our world was shattered as we learned our little girl had cancer. Steph is more emotional and weepier, and we're not sure if it's from reliving last year's memories or adjustments to her antidepressant. She tells us not to worry about it because she's still alive. Steph is consistently exercising and the weight loss, which is important for her overall health, reminds her that some things are still in her control. She has another migraine tonight, and we don't have a clue why they happen so frequently.

Stephanie has her first colonoscopy since the colon resection.

The doctor finds and removes one polyp from the short colon stump. Her new GI doctor from KU tells us her colon must really like to grow polyps. He find the surgical location connecting the small intestine to the colon stump fully open and healed. She will have this procedure every year for the rest of her life.

Last year at this time we learned of another woman whose disease was similar to Stephanie's. She was young and had just given birth to her second baby when they found advanced colon cancer. It soon spread to her pancreas and our team is shaken today when we hear of her death. She only survived ten months. It feels like someone punched us in the stomach. Stephanie struggles the most and can't stop thinking about the children left behind. We say a tearful prayer for the woman and her family and wonder why one person lives, and another dies? It's unfair, and so many questions flood our minds. Were the doctors aggressive with treatment? What chemo did she have? Did she own the disease and believe she could overcome it? Did she have a support team helping her? Was there faith and belief in her heart? We don't know the answers but understand she may have had all of these things and still lost her battle. We do know how lucky we are to have Stephanie alive and with us. We say a second prayer for all of the beautiful souls helping our team overcome the challenges we face. Thank you, God, for bringing all these angels into our lives, we are so blessed.

chapter 30

THE KIDS ASK NANA AND ME to watch Caden while they have a date night. The three of us have fun stacking blocks until Caden trips on one and falls into the couch. He cries as Nana cleans up a little blood on his lip, then gets over it and starts playing again. Later, Nana gives him a bath in the laundry room's oversized sink. It's just his size, and he watches the trickle of water she keeps running. Caden puts his hand into the stream of water and then into his mouth and acts surprised like he's never tasted the water before. He retreats into this wet world, oblivious of everything else around him. Caden splashes and soon his fingers and toes look like prunes. After the bath, we join Lambie in bed where Nana reads to us. When Steph and Mark pick him up the next morning, it doesn't cross our minds to tell them about his fall.

At home, Mark notices a tiny chip on Caden's front tooth. He shows Steph, and she immediately calls us with questions, like "What the hell went on last night? How could you let something like this happen to our baby? Weren't you watching him?" I thought she would ask if we threw him off the roof. "No sweetheart, we didn't notice the chip. He tripped on a block... Of course, we were watching him... I don't think... Okay, I give up, when you think of a suitable punishment just let us know." The lesson here is simple; there is no winning when you get between a mama bear and her cub. After several attempts to explain, I realize this incident will be dredged up and talked about for a long time, just like Steph's baby tooth.

Stephanie wiggles the front baby tooth for days before Colleen decides it's time to get it out. Steph says, "I want Daddy to do it." She follows me upstairs and sits next to me on the bed as I pull off my tennis shoes. Cycling between nervous laughter and fear, she asks me how I am going to do it. I tell her my mom used old rusty pliers and Steph fearfully replies, "I changed my mind." At the same moment she stands to leave, the shoe I am struggling to pull off gives way and flies up hitting Steph in the face. I jump up saying, "I am so sorry," as she reaches down and picks up the tooth from the floor. Now, as tears mix with the laughter, she asks, "Why did you take it out with your shoe? that's a lot worse than rusty pliers!" Steph loves to tell the story about her mean father using a shoe to knock out her tooth. I am sure she will also enjoy telling everyone how Caden's wicked grandparents chipped his tooth.

Steph calls this morning to say she has to run some errands. Since I'm working in my office at home, she offers to stop by with sub sandwiches for lunch. Steph walks into the house and puts Caden down. He sees me sitting at my desk and does the best thing a child can do. He yells Papa and then runs to me with his arms open. As I pick him up, he hugs my neck and giggles. He has never run to me like that before, and it's one of the strongest memories I have of raising my own children. Coming home to see Steph or Scott stop what they were doing and run to me with open arms is like being showered by pure love that permeates the skin and settles into my bones. For that moment nothing in the world is more important. Worries disappear. I feel loved, the sun is brighter, and everything is right with the world. If captured and bottled this feeling could be sold at any price, but here it is, unselfishly given away by a one-year-old.

Our team makes a conscious decision to stay away from researching Steph's disease on the Internet because we're afraid it's more likely to be negative than positive. Our goal is to remain positive, and while we know the odds are against her, we don't know by how much.

March is Colon Cancer Awareness month, and frequent news reports highlight the disease's symptoms and the importance of having colonoscopies. Colleen is first to see the newspaper article and brings it to me. Using American Cancer Society statistics, only 8% of patients with Stage 4 Colon Cancer survive five years. My heart is pounding as my brain realizes 92% of patients with Steph's diagnosis die. That's 92 lives and families out of 100 that are destroyed. It takes my breath away. My skin is cold and clammy, and I feel like I am having a panic attack. Colleen gently reminds me Steph has a medical dream team, she is a fighter, and truly believes she will live to beat the odds. She settles me down, and we agree to keep the article from the rest of the team. God, please help her overcome the odds.

The insurance company finally approves payment for the Mayo RFA surgery. They also cover genetic testing, which provides some welcome news. Stephanie's cancer isn't hereditary, so it shouldn't be passed onto Caden. The physician believes her cancer likely started from a mutant gene. She explains most people have mutant genes that never really impact them, but in Steph's case, it did. The testing also confirms something we already suspected; Steph has an increased risk for other cancers.

Steph finishes 18 months of chemo today, and the team celebrates at lunch. She continues to lose weight and looks healthier all the time. Life may never be the same as before her cancer, but it's getting better. Her health will always be on our minds, but we try not to worry about it and choose to fuel our faith and live for today. A mammogram and sonogram are completed as baselines for future comparisons.

At Stephanie's three-month Mayo evaluation, she completes testing in the morning and is scheduled to see Dr. Grothey that afternoon. We arrive at the appointment and are told he is sick at home. Steph looks at us and says, "I didn't think physicians were allowed to get sick." We are disappointed not to see him, but his nurse practitioner fills in for him. While we wait, the syndrome sets in. We hoped the Behind the Door Syndrome would skip this simple checkup, but it usually shows up to one degree or another. Steph worries that her cancer will return now that her chemotherapy is finished. Some level of anxiety and fear are never far away, even as we try to distance ourselves from them. Good news delivered quickly is what we hunger for. The nurse practitioner walks in and tells us none of the tests show any evidence of disease. Colleen and Steph shed some tears as they release tension, and there are hugs all around. Nana smiles, telling Steph, "What a great Mother's Day present."

Throughout Stephanie's illness, we have increased our communication with family. Colleen and Steph realize that her cousins haven't spent much time together since they've grown and started busy lives. Steph's solution is to have a cousin's weekend at our house. The invitations are accepted, and twenty-four members of Colleen's family descend on our home for four days. We fish, swim, and celebrate birthdays. Three generations catch up on each other's lives, and everyone agrees this is a tradition to continue.

Stephanie is now one-year cancer free. Eighty-five percent of recurrences happen within two years, and we hope the next twelve months pass smoothly. We celebrate the milestone and reflect on everything that's happened since Steph became pregnant. We're proud of the way we have met each challenge head on and done our best. At the same time, it's surreal and feels like a bad dream. Everything has happened fast and kept coming at us in waves for so long. It's hard for us to understand how we were able to plow through it. We talk about it, and it becomes clear there is much we we've lived through but haven't yet dealt with emotionally. Each of us carries around unresolved emotional baggage. Some of us take antidepressants to help us along the way, but these buried feelings will have to be dealt with eventually. Steph thinks getting away from everything may help, so the team plans a trip to Stan and Linda's lake cabin.

We arrive at Pickerel Lake, unpack, and are in the water in less than an hour. Caden has his own life jacket and loves this new wet experience. There is plenty to eat and drink, and as the sun drops, Stan helps Caden catch sunfish off the dock. He is thrilled, and Caden loves it too. We boat, float, and relax. Steph and Mark try their hand at water skiing, each taking turns drinking lake water as the boat pulls them up. My mind drifts back thirty years earlier when Stan, Linda, Colleen and I learned to slalom the same waters and I'm reminded that life moves so quickly.

Linda plays with Caden in the yard the dogs run around. Anyone observing us wouldn't think we had a worry in the world. The Kolb's are wonderful hosts and great friends. I don't think they realize the importance of the gift they have given us this week. They've provided us an escape that allows our minds to find peace. Lake time always passes quickly, and too soon it's time to go. There are hugs and tears and promises to get together soon. The drive home is happy and filled with reminiscences.

Just days before Steph's next checkup, the team visits family in Minnesota. We have a fun weekend, but the upcoming tests are on our minds and feed our anxiety. We learn it's better to deal with the results and then have fun instead of the other way around. The tests are completed, and Dr. Grothey gives us the thumbs up. Our faith is recharged again. A vascular expert provides his perspective on the blood clots in Steph's legs and agrees with the steps we are taking. We pack and Caden thinks the best part of the trip is riding the luggage cart from our room to the car.

Fall turns into winter, and fortunately life goes on. Mark's Florida project is progressing well. He takes Lambie along and sends pictures of her back to Caden. She looks out the airplane window, waves from the taxi, and sits on the hotel desk while Daddy works. A clever way of keeping in contact with his family and Caden loves it.

In December, Steph's visit to the Mayo Clinic includes additional workups. Dr. Grothey tells us he is pleased with the way everything is progressing and wants to move from three-month checks to four. That's good news, but Steph would choose to be checked more often than less often. Dr. Grothey takes time to address her concerns and balance them by limiting her radiation exposure. She understands and tells him she doesn't mean to make a big deal of it. He smiles and tells her he always wants to know what is on her mind, so he can help. It's snowing when we leave, and the roads are snow packed and icy, adding an hour to our drive home.

It's January, and the kids host Steph's second Survivor party. Caden is tall for his age and continues to captivate our team. We take him out to celebrate his birthday, and he's fascinated when we bump our glasses together and say 'Cheers.' Now anytime he takes a drink, he says 'Cheers' and wants to clink glasses. Steph has her yearly colonoscopy, where they remove several polyps from the remaining few inches of her colon. The counter tracking visits to Steph's website for updates is now at 6,641 with good wishes from all.

chapter 31

WE ARE FORTUNATE CADEN TRAVELS SO WELL. He sits in his car seat without a fuss and easily rolls with the agenda. His happy soul inspires each of us. It's four months since Stephanie's last Mayo visit, and she is relieved to be back for her checkup. Steph doesn't like waiting for the extra month, because she needs ongoing confirmation that her cancer hasn't returned. After dinner, Caden runs down the tunnel, playing hide and seek with his father. He snickers when he finds Mark, then runs to a doorway, peaks out, and waits to be discovered. We enjoy watching him run off the energy he's stored up on the drive.

The kids leave early the next morning for her tests, while Colleen, Caden and I sleep in and eat breakfast. The radiology tech has a difficult time getting the IV started for the CT, but after several sticks, she finds a vein. The procedure begins, and immediately, Steph's arm begins to swell. A pump automatically injects the 120 ccs of contrast media into the interstitial tissue of her arm, instead of her vein. Another IV is started, and a second infusion of the contrast is successful.

When we see Steph, her arm above and below the elbow is so swollen it resembles Popeye's. She isn't in much pain, but the skin is stretched so tight it's uncomfortable. She has full use of her hand and fingers, but the Radiologist is concerned and consults with plastic surgery for their opinion. To reduce the swelling, they place Steph's arm in hot packs to increase circulation and disperse the contrast media across more tissue. Over the next hour, Steph is seen by two plastic and two orthopedic surgeons, and each is surprised she isn't in more pain. Their main concern is that swelling could restrict blood flow or cause nerve damage to her arm and hand. The last plastic surgeon, a hand specialist, says that he will be on call at St. Mary's and gives us his cell phone number with instructions to contact him anytime day or night. The doctor tells Steph to keep a heating pad on it and spend the night in Rochester in case anything develops. As things settle down, I realize while most of our team is reacting, Steph stays utterly calm and lets everything play out.

We meet with Dr. Grothey a few hours later and tell him about the incident. For the first time in our experience, he seems upset. He checks Steph's arm and then makes a phone call, but doesn't get an answer. Dr. Grothey then turns to Steph and says, "There is something else. The CT shows a mass that was not seen on the last scan." He isn't sure what it is and quickly reviews the scan with us on the computer. The apple shaped mass is about 1.5mm in size, and located midpoint between her pubic line and belly button. He tells us when it's less than 1 mm it's common just to monitor it, but when it's larger, it becomes a high concern. He has talked to Dr. Que, and they agreed to do more tests over the next two days and then possibly surgery.

As this information hangs in the air, the doctor takes Steph's hand and asks, "No tears?" The floor has been pulled out from under us, and we are free falling. We don't understand. This isn't really happening. Slowly the information registers and the tears begin to flow. Steph first wonders if the additional month made a difference, then if she's going to die, She sees her life slipping away and holds Caden tighter. How much time do we have left together? I can't leave you. Her face is blank and distant.

Dr. Grothey reminds us that we come back for checkups to find problems early so they can quickly be dealt with. He is supportive, and his face and actions show a fatherly concern for Stephanie. We understand what these trips are for, but balance our expectations by staying positive and believing everything will be fine. Balance is a difficult thing to achieve on a roller coaster. The emotions are overwhelming. I remember 92% of stage 4, colon cancer patients die within five years, and Steph is one year and eight months out from her liver surgery. I feel foolish and guilty to have squandered my time at work, instead of spending it with my daughter. I need to be emotionally strong and focus on the present, but instead, find myself feeling lost and disoriented.

Our past experience has helped us condense these trips down to two days of driving, testing, and meetings. This time we've efficiently packed for two days and now find we don't have the clothes, hotel reservations, or time off work needed for this trip. These things seem so trivial now, but still need to be handled, so we take time to make the necessary arrangements.

Steph's arm is back to normal in the morning. We fill the day with activities to keep our minds off the uncertainty until more tests are completed. We walk around the mall and play with Caden, who is oblivious to our concerns. He runs off so much energy that Mark has to carry him. Colleen is struggling and afraid. Steph finally tells her, "Please stop it. I can't always be the strong one for all of us." It's true, so often we draw our strength from her. She is making the best of it, and we need to do the same. If we don't, it just adds to her burden.

After a PET Scan, we meet with Dr. Que to discuss the results, which come back inconclusive. She explains this sometimes happens after chemo, and there are two ways to proceed. Do a biopsy and see if it's cancer or do surgery and remove it. Without hesitation or further discussion, Steph decides, "I want to have the surgery to get whatever it is out of me as soon as possible." Cancer is the enemy, and she wants all of it destroyed. The surgeon agrees and schedules surgery in one week.

Walking to the elevator, Stephanie tells us, "I felt sorry for myself yesterday, but that's over. I am ready to fight and want to get this thing out of me." It helps when there is a plan in place to attack the problem. Our warrior is back and leading her team. Hope slowly begins to return.

chapter 32

THE LONG TRIP HOME IS FILLED WITH EMOTION, and the cold rain we drive in fits our mood. The team vows to overcome whatever stands in our way, and we act positively for each other. Still, our anxiety builds, and much of the trip is quiet as we digest the news. Steph beat it... how did it come back... didn't the chemo work... is it deadlier now? Each time we stop, Steph takes Caden out of his car seat and walks alone with him. His smile and happiness lift her spirit, and together they escape to a special place all their own.

My mind keeps telling me it's not fair. Steph is our hero and leads the way for all of us. Time and time again, it's harder than it should be. She's experienced too much worry and pain, and now more is on her doorstep. My mind drifts back to when Steph was seven. I accepted a promotion, and we are in the process of moving. Colleen and the kids stay in South Dakota for three months as I shuttle back and forth to Kansas City while our home is being built.

Mobile phones aren't yet in general use, but a realtor tracks me down, telling me that something has happened at home, and I need to call the hospital. I try not to panic and make the call. Colleen is scared and tells me to get home as soon as possible, something is wrong with Stephanie. She slurred her words and lost all feeling on one side of her body. The doctors don't know why and are running tests to find out. Colleen spent years in this hospital's ICU, and I ask her what she thinks it is. She tells me Steph's symptoms mimic those seen with a stroke or aneurysm. She starts sobbing. I tell her I love her and will get home as soon as I can. I ask to talk to Steph, but they have taken her away for more tests. Colleen tells me she will pass on my love and kisses. She also tells me to hurry, because Steph may not live long if it's an aneurysm. There is one flight that can make the connection, but I still won't get home until midnight. Driving would take even longer.

On my way to the airport, traffic comes to a complete stop due to an accident. Everything is in slow motion. I sit helpless, with tears running down my cheeks, and wonder if I will see my baby girl alive again. All I can do is wait and pray. At the airport, I buy a stuffed monkey for Steph and hold it tight until I walk into the hospital at midnight. I have no idea what's going on and run to my daughter's room. I'm rewarded by finding Steph sitting up in bed. She puts her arms out to me, and we hold each other tightly. It feels so uplifting after the hours of uncertainty and worry. Colleen joins us, and we grow stronger together.

As the symptoms subside, the doctors still haven't uncovered the cause. We fly Steph to a children's hospital in Kansas City. There are so many tests and needles that Steph tenses up when anyone enters her room. As a parent, it's hard to watch her fear but understand the tests that need to be done. We try to be reassuring and explain it to her, but she's seven and afraid and the needles hurt. I tell her it comes down to a simple decision on her part. The needles can be done the easy way or the hard way, the choice is up to her. After I explain the difference and add a reward of ice cream, she agrees to try sitting still and not fight the needle. She never fights it again. Stephanie is still afraid, always crushes our hands, and cycles from crying to nervous laughter, but she also becomes stronger.

A children's neurologist wants to monitor and test Steph during an episode, hoping it will help determine the cause. Based on previous symptoms, he begins treating her for seizures. The medications change Steph's demeanor, and she experiences dramatic mood changes and acts out. A few weeks later, there is another episode. She loses her speech and sight, as well as the ability to use her left arm or leg. She is locked inside herself, doesn't understand what is happening, and can't tell us her fears. Colleen and I are terrified, as Steph slips away from us. Colleen holds her daughter, stroking her hair as I rush us to the hospital. The symptoms are gone by the time we get there.

Tests and episodes continue for six months until Stephanie is diagnosed with a hemiplegic migraine disorder. One side of her brain swells up during a migraine, creating pressure on the nerves associated with speech, sight, and movement. As Steph learns to recognize early symptoms, she starts intervention with caffeine and medicine and then moves to a dark, quiet room. By the time she's nine, she handles these episodes by herself and tells us about them later. She is brave and grown up beyond her years. After puberty, she still has occasional migraines, but the episodes disappear altogether. As these memories came back to me, I realize Steph has always been a warrior and a survivor. That provides me some comfort and hope.

I drop the kids off at their house and Colleen and I drive home. Colleen withdraws into herself and struggles as despair sets in. She walks out to the gazebo and sits in the cold rainy weather, holding our Maltese for comfort and staring out into the darkness. I try to walk her back into the house, but she asks to be alone. A crisis can create panic in the mind as if it's caught in the open and senses a violent storm approaching. A vulnerable and exposed mind seeks shelter by withdrawing into itself and the darkness. After an hour and a half, I finally coax her back into the house. I don't know what to do as I try to help her. I hold Colleen in bed, but it's not really my wife, more like her shell. I stoke her hair and gently rub her back. She finally leans into me and lets sleep quiet her mind.

Colleen feels better the next morning. She cleans the house and puts Steph's room in order so the kids can move back in after surgery. I work 12 hours catching up in my office. Keeping busy helps block out our anxiety. Mark goes to work, but struggles as everyone wants to know what's going on. He appreciates their concern and support but is reminded that we don't know what the future will bring. Steph takes care of Caden and tells us, "I am great. Well, not really great, but okay. I don't really know how I am doing. I just need to get through the day, and Caden helps a bunch with that." I send out a quick web update, and the phones begin to ring. Everyone wants to help, but there's little anyone can really do.

Our family enjoys the outdoors, allowing us an escape from busy schedules and worries. The kids drop by to fish the pond in our back yard. I show Caden how to retrieve his fishing line, but he quickly gravitates to his mother, and it seems right for her to teach him. The largemouth bass and bluegills are biting and Steph out fishes everyone, which is normal. Caden doesn't want to touch the fish but soon overcomes his fear and strokes their wet sparkling tails. His biggest excitement comes when Steph puts fish back into the water. She places the largemouth bass in the water facing the shore and then releases it. The two-pound fish flips around quickly, making a big splash in the shallow water as it swims away. Each time she does it, Caden calls us over to make sure we don't miss any of the action. His brown eyes grow big in anticipation, and he cackles and points as each fish escapes. Afterward, he reels in a fish Steph gets on her line. There is no doubt in any of our minds that he is hooked on fishing.

Nana makes roast beef with potatoes, vegetables, and biscuits for dinner. Scott joins us, and we thoroughly enjoy the meal and each other's company. After dinner, Steph and I walk the trails through our woods trying to lift each other's spirits. She confides in me that her biggest fear is dying on the table during surgery. I listen to her concerns, then tell her we have done everything we can to maximize her chances of survival. We trust the surgical team and know how well they take care of her at Mayo. Beyond that, we have no control. Any of us could die at any time. It could happen to me tomorrow in a car accident or from a heart attack. Steph hates it when I talk about my death, but she understands my point. We wipe tears from each other's eyes and agree to live our lives with as much joy as we can. We talk about how lucky we are to have each other and beautiful memories together. Even during her illness, we enjoy time together, closeness as a family, and love and support from so many people around us. We finish our walk hand in hand, reliving fun days from her childhood. The back yard sandbox, picnics at Sand Lake, and the RV trip to Yellowstone.

In bed, Colleen and I talk about the last twenty-four months. It feels like we've aged ten years. We see it in the mirror and feel it in our bodies, but agree it's a small price to pay to keep our daughter alive. We would gladly give up our remaining years for

Steph to live a full life with her family, but that's not the way these things work. She has to keep fighting for her life, and we will stay right by her side, helping any way we can.

I work all day Monday while Nana cooks meals for Scott. He will watch the house and pets while we are in Rochester. She is convinced he will starve if she doesn't fill the freezer with food. That night we pack for the trip and Caden helps by laying Lambie safely in Mommies suitcase.

chapter 33

DRIVING TO ROCHESTER, we discuss the importance of staying positive and keeping the faith. It's a mantra we keep top of mind. The fact is, everyone except Caden still quietly struggles with our demons. As we enter the hotel room, Caden runs to the bathroom and looks very disappointed. Stephanie asks what's wrong, and he tells her his markers are gone. On our last trip, Aunt Kim gave him bath crayons to play within the tub, and Caden loved drawing on the tiles. We promised he could play with them the next time we visited, so he expected them to be here waiting. Nana laughs and pulls the box of markers from her bag. Caden grins, gives Nana's leg a big hug, and asks if he can take a bath. Please? I wish all the problems in our world were solved so easily.

The next morning, Steph, Mark and I walk across the street to St Mary's Hospital for surgery. When Bill and Kim arrive to watch Caden, Colleen joins us in the waiting room as the operation begins.

I don't know what my daughter is going through, never having had a surgical procedure myself to remove a deadly disease. In more than fifty years of living, I am lucky to only experience one technically small but emotionally large surgical procedure. The one that converts a man from a station wagon to a sports car, or so I was told. Colleen and I enter the Urologist's office and sit down. I am uneasy, and it doesn't help that during my wait two men with wide, distant eyes shuffle out the door like they are walking on thin ice. Before I can bolt out the door, a smiling nurse calls my name and escorts me back. Her smile is from recognition – she was my neighbor growing up, and I visit this doctor often as part of my job. I know she works here, but it's unsettling that the nice quiet lady living across the street who used to give me cookies, is going to help turn me into a gelding. Slipping into a gown, I take in the cold room, with its stainless steel surgical table, cart loaded with torturous tools, and a massive ceiling light at its center. My anxiety grows. To my relief and then discomfort a male nurse shaves and preps me for the vasectomy.

As I lay on the surgical table, the Urologist comes in. "Hi, Mike, sorry I'm late, but we'll do this in a hurry since I am due in court." Warning bells go off in my head as he cradles my scrotum in one hand and picks up a scalpel in the other.

"What did you say?"

"Oh, some guy is suing me for malpractice." The bells are louder now as he tries to reassure me. "Don't worry, I can finish you off in a few minutes." I did not like his choice of words and offer to come back when he has more time. "No, don't be silly. Oh shit, now I really am late."

He didn't put a stick in my mouth or give me a shot of whiskey; he just starts to cut and snip and close. As it turns out, he is time efficient, thorough, and relatively gentle. A quick post-surgical summary of care and activity for the next two days, and he is gone. I never heard what happened in court that day, nor did I father another child.

Back at St. Mary's, Steph's surgery lasts an hour and a half. A tech arrives, gathers up our team, and leads us through a maze of hallways and elevators to meet with Dr. Que. Anxiety and fear grow with each step we take. As we approach the briefing room, there are nurses in the hall, enjoying a break between surgeries. I try to read their faces for signs to Steph's condition, but there is no eye contact or clues as they go about their business.

We sit and wait in the small room with eyes darting around while BDS rests heavily on our minds. Dr. Que opens the door, and even before she enters the room, says, "Everything was benign." Colleen lets out a scream and then jumps out of her chair, hugging the doctor and thanking her. After we settle down, Dr. Que reviews the surgical events for us. "We found the spot in question and removed it along with four others. Each was found to be benign. Then I felt the bottom of her liver, palpated her ovaries, and drew the small intestine out of the incision, finding it to be smooth and without nodules. Everything is great, and there is no evidence of any disease." We are excited with happy smiles plastered on our faces, as she continues. "I rarely get to share the good news about my patients, and I am so happy to be able to give you good news after both of Stephanie's surgeries. She will be in recovery for the next three hours." We are relieved as the stress melts away. Dr. Que answers our questions and then excuses herself to prepare for another surgery.

We walk out of the briefing room and notice a door leading outside to a grassy area with gardens and benches in the center of the hospital complex. The sun is shining and beckons us, so we walk out and immediately feel energized by its warmth. Colleen says it feels like God is smiling down on us. The stress is gone, and our bodies feel light from the adrenalin surge. At that moment, I feel like a child again. There is no worry. There is no fear. There is only being. We take out our phones to share the information and between calls hug each other over and over again as the great news settles in.

As Steph's bed is rolled into her room, she shouts, "Woo-Hoo, I'm still Cancer free!" We laugh and kiss and hold hands, feeling relief after a long, stressful week. Steph slips in and out of consciousness. Each time she wakes up, she plays with Caden, and he rewards her with loving kisses. I update Steph's web page to share her fantastic news and add a word of thanks. "I believe an important gift you can give in life is to help those around you. Thank you for your help, ongoing support, and prayers! It's appreciated and not taken for granted. God bless and remember to hug your kids today." Mark watches over his wife each night in the hospital. Nothing keeps them apart. Caden sleeps well, so Nana and I do too.

Steph experiences the same struggles with pain and nausea, but the staff does a great job helping her. Mayo is different from the hundreds of medical institutions I have worked with over the years. Not only does it have one of the top programs in the world for cutting edge research, but Mayo's patient care is also better and smoother, with seamless teamwork across departments. The employees are professional and skilled, but also seem genuinely happy at their jobs. I ask them what makes them so happy, and their consistent answer is they enjoy their work and the other professionals they work with. They believe they make a difference in people's lives and take pride in their jobs. They also show respect for each other no matter what their title. It's easy to understand why people come here from all over the world.

Steph is still experiencing pain but convinces the doctors to release her to our hotel. The next morning, she tells us, "My gut feels so strange like I have all this extra room inside. When I turn over in bed, my insides shift from one side to the other, like they need to be tied down. I don't like the picture that puts into my head when it happens." I ask her if she made a mistake leaving the hospital and she tells us, "Not at all. It was a long night with some pain and weird feelings, but I am so happy to be with my family and out of the hospital. Now let's get out of here and head home!"

Our patient is taking morphine but still fights pain and nausea, making it a long uncomfortable trip for her. Stephanie's recovery has plateaued over the last few days, and we hope getting her home will help, as it has with past surgeries. She improves a little at home, but cycles between pain and nausea as she continues the morphine. Nurse Nana tries things that helped in the past, but the results are inconsistent.

After two days, Steph feels worse. Her incision looks good, and there's no sign of infection, but she is increasingly moody and frustrated, crying and lashing out at everyone. Through a process of elimination, we realize she hasn't taken her antidepressants since leaving the hospital, which is causing the mood swings. Nana gets the pills, but Steph says she is too nauseated to swallow them. I know the dangers of abruptly stopping an antidepressant and become more aggressive, telling her this isn't a choice; she needs to take them now. Mark steps in and tells me to stop because I'm making things worse and increasing her frustration. This makes me angry because Steph usually listens to me, and I believe she's in danger. Not sure what to do, I leave the room to cool off.

As I think about what Mark said, my perspective slowly starts to change. Instead of being angry with Mark, I begin to feel grateful for his actions. He is trying to protect Steph just like me, but he was patient with her, while I tried to force her. His focus was on helping her, even if it made me mad. What more can I ask of my son-in-law, than to do the difficult things necessary to protect my little girl? I share this revelation with Mark and thank him for the love he has for my daughter. We hug, and then Mark rejoins Steph in their bedroom. In time he convinces her to take the antidepressant. A few hours later, she starts to feel better and begins to recover quickly. Nana replaces the morphine with Tylenol for pain and Benadryl to help Steph sleep.

In bed, I replay the conversation with Mark in my mind and smile, remembering an earlier talk we had when he asked my permission to marry Steph. I stand in my pajama bottoms brushing my teeth. Looking in the mirror's reflection, I see Mark walk into the bathroom. "Can I talk to you about something?" I turn to him and raise my index finger to communicate just a minute. His eyes are dancing around, and he seems tense.

"Um, I love Stephanie and want your permission to marry her."

I stop brushing, rinse, spit, and wipe my mouth with the towel. I smile and respond, "You realize you are asking to take one of the most important things in my life away from me?" His confused look tells me he thought we would be finished by now. "Mark, Colleen and I really like you and believe you to be a person of quality. I appreciate your thoughtfulness in asking my permission, but there are a few things I would like you to understand. Our children are the most precious things in our lives and Colleen, and I have been fully responsible for them since birth. To hand that off to someone else is a huge step. Steph is responsible for herself, but we still watch over her and provide her safety net." This talk wasn't something I had thought about or planned, it just sprung from my heart as I realized my daughter was leaving our home for another.

My thoughts, which could possibly be misunderstood as a sermon, continue for twenty minutes as I cover subjects of love, respect, putting her first, and for good measure add what I remember from the Boy Scout law: Trustworthy, Loyal, Kind, Thrifty, Brave… etc. Finishing up, I say, "Mark, I know you love my daughter and that she loves you. So many marriages don't last, and I want you both to understand the responsibility, accountability, and devotion a successful marriage demands."

With little beads of sweat on his upper lip, Mark looks me in the eye and tells me, "I understand what you are saying and promise to do my best to love and take care of her."

Smiling, I add Grandpa Bill's total reply when I asked him for Colleen's hand in marriage. "Yes, you have my blessing, but I want you to know as hard as I've tried, she's still a work in progress. Good luck!" I hug my shell-shocked son-in-law to be. He says, "Okay, thanks" and quickly walks out of the room. I look in the mirror and tell myself to start loving Mark as a member of our family. Maybe then he won't think I'm such an ass for giving him 'the big speech,' as it would later be remembered. At least he didn't ask me when I was cleaning my shotgun instead of my teeth.

I return to work while Mark stays home with Steph for a few days. Colleen takes care of everything behind the scenes, cooking, washing, and caring for Caden and Steph when Mark isn't there. Scott is back at home, so we have a full house. The kids go home for the weekend and do well. They return on Sunday telling us Steph's biggest challenge was not being able to pick up Caden, and that she tires easily. Seven days later, they move back home for good. They pack their things, and we watch them drive away with mixed feelings. We are glad Steph is feeling strong enough to be on her own but still feel the need to watch over her.

Bill and Kim visit and can't believe Steph's positive attitude is back and there are few signs of what she's been through the last few weeks. Kim keeps telling us, "Steph is amazing! I can't believe how strong she is."

A few days later, Caden gets cranky, and red spots begin to form on his skin. He hasn't received his vaccines when Steph had Chemo, because she couldn't be exposed to live virus. Caden is rescheduled to get them in a week, but now has chicken pox. Steph keeps him comfortable with advice from Nurse Nana to minimize his scratching.

It's the middle of July and Steph is officially two years cancer free! The team celebrates this milestone at a favorite restaurant. We talk about Steph overcoming the challenges of surgery and Chemo and blood clots and sepsis. We give thanks to everyone that helped us along the way to make this celebration possible. Stephanie thanks God for keeping her safe and providing what she needed, when she needed it. She tears up telling us she couldn't have done it without us and feels so lucky to be alive. It's a beautiful night filled with raw emotion, laughter, and love. We talk about the mystery woman at the Research Center who lived Steph's story forty years ago and told us not to worry, that our daughter would be fine. We recall our disappointment at not finding a leader there to take us by the hand and lead us. The table is quiet. Maybe we always had a leader with us, and perhaps the woman was His messenger.

The University of Kansas Medical Center contacts Steph to ask if they can highlight her story in their Annual Report. She is happy to agree, and an interview is completed. The two-page article begins with a picture of Steph holding Caden and then summarizes her fight under the heading: *Surviving Against All Odds*. Steph takes the opportunity to highlight the excellent care she received from Dr. Baranda and the nurses at the Cancer

Center during her chemotherapy, as well as her relief to be two years of living cancer-free. "I take every moment as it comes and make the most of every day."

chapter 34

BEFORE STEPH'S FOUR-MONTH CHECKUP we enjoy the Labor Day Weekend with family in Minnesota. Bill, Kim, Colleen, and I watch the grandkids while our children take the boat out and enjoy the lake. Kim has developed a close relationship with Caden, and he still runs to her for hugs when he sees her. This creates a short and funny debate as to which of us he likes best. It wouldn't be a family gathering without some degree of teasing.

It's a great family weekend except that none of us can completely remove the uncertainty of the Mayo appointment from our minds. In the past, we have developed a sense of security that everything will go smoothly, but then the rug was pulled out from under us and tested our resolve. We desperately want to believe, but still need the reassurance that a positive checkup provides.

Steph and Mark drive to the clinic early Tuesday morning for her tests. Steph's scarred veins are difficult to access, but after multiple tries, an IV is started. Caden, Colleen, Aunt Kim, and

I drive up late morning. Our anxiety is tempered a little since the surgeons had popped the hood and thoroughly checked out Steph's insides just four months before. Everything should be okay, right? We sit tightly together on the exam room bench and wait, trying to look brave for each other while the acid of doubt slowly eats away our positive thoughts.

Dr. Grothey comes into the room, and before he sits down, tells us everything looks great. We react to the good news with sighs of relief. The doctor reviews the test results with us and asks if we have any concerns. We mention the problems Steph has with the IV sticks, and Dr. Grothey tells us he understands and plans to do things differently. First, he wants to move the focus of Stephanie's care from the crisis of saving her life to maintaining it long term. He is concerned with the amount of radiation she has been exposed to in the last two years, so he will replace the CT scans with MRI's. Secondly, he wants us to wait four to five months for her next checkup. He tells us this is all good news and reminds us Stephanie is now beyond the two-year point when 85% of reoccurrence takes place. The odds have shifted in her favor for the first time.

Steph's face is covered with a smile at the good news, and we are relieved, but not ready for the next thing he tells us. Dr. Grothey turns to his patient and says, "I consider you cured." I can't believe what I heard. He has always been very positive, but also cautious not to overstate things. The doctor stands up, shakes our hands, and the appointment is over.

What just happened? No one says a word as we walk down the hall and enter the waiting room. I'm confused and stop our team asking, "Did anyone else hear him say that Steph was cured?" They nod yes, and we just look at each other in disbelief. Their faces tell me none of us thought we heard him correctly. Cured was something he said he would never tell us. Cured was something we didn't dream we would hear for another five years, if ever. The news begins to settle into our minds, and slowly we become a spectacle. I hug Steph and spin her around. Mark's hug lifts me off my feet as he laughs with joy. Colleen has Caden and Steph in her arms, and the love we have for each other fills the large waiting room. Our happiness is so intoxicating we are giddy. Is it really over? Can we stop worrying now? Will the fear and worry that's consumed us every day for two years really leave? "I consider you cured." Cured… what an amazing word.

We walk to the elevator, and I feel guilty about the scene we have just made. Others in the waiting room are still struggling and not receiving the good news we are. I look back and see many of them watching us and smiling. Then I realize that the individuals in that waiting room are linked to each other by circumstance, and truly happy for anyone's good news. I return their smile and say a quick prayer for them as I catch up with the team. I pray they have the faith, strength, and courage needed to fight their battles and receive the care and support they need to win them. Please fill them with hope and love.

In the car, we debrief and make calls sharing the news that the tests turned out well and Steph is doing great. As a team, we agree not to share Dr. Grothey words that Steph is cured. We are optimistic but want to let a little more time pass and hear him repeat it before we share those precious words. There have been to many surprises and complications that now make us cautious. Nonetheless, it's a joyful trip home, and each of us is recharged again. Our excitement keeps us talking all the way home about the good news. Steph's future suddenly appears bright again.

chapter 35

AUNT KIM AND COLLEEN TALK EVERY DAY, catching up on their grandkids and Steph's progress. On Halloween there is something more; Kim tells Colleen that she found a lump under her arm. They try to be positive, but both of these close friends are alarmed. A week later, Bill and Kim call to tell us an ultrasound and biopsy confirm Kim has lung cancer. CT and PET scans are scheduled to determine the extent and locations of her cancer. We are back in hell again. None of us can believe this is happening. Drawing on our experience, we know it's crucial for Aunt Kim to gather a team of medical experts and support around her as quickly as possible. They agree, and Bill has already made an appointment at the Mayo Clinic for a full assessment. We offer to join them, and they tell us they were hoping we would. Kim has been so supportive during our greatest time of need, we promise to join her for the appointments, chemo, and help any way we can.

Colleen is shattered by the news. She withdraws and becomes lost again. A lifetime of friendship and experiences with Kim flash through her memory, and then it goes dark. I don't know how to help her while I also struggle. We add more souls to our prayers.

When Colleen and I meet up with Bill and Kim at a Rochester hotel, it's easy to see from their forced smiles that they are on edge. We are always so comfortable with each other, but they seem unfamiliar, reflecting the uncertainty in their minds. Bill picked up the results of the scans yesterday, but they've waited to open them until we arrived. Seeing the fear in their eyes, we try to reassure them the unknown is often scarier than the truth. Colleen opens the envelope, reads through the medical jargon, and then summarizes the information for us. The scans show multiple tumors in each of Kim's lungs, with additional activity in her adrenal gland. Everything she reads reflects our worst fears. Although we understand the information, we aren't sure whether it leads to surgery or chemo or what, so together we write a list of questions for the next day's appointment. Later in bed, Colleen asks me to hold her. I rock her and try to comfort her, but she doesn't respond. She has run out of tears and stares out through blank eyes.

The Mayo Oncologist meets with us and lays out a plan of attack. Kim will have a battery of tests using their state-of-the-art equipment to identify the full extent of her cancer and then begin chemotherapy. The oncologist is positive, uplifting, and kind. He writes out a prescription for Kim that reads: 'Take one dose of hope five times each day.' Kim welcomes the recommendation and will soon frame and hang it in her home where she can see it every day. Right next to the plaques that read, 'I love the nights I can't remember with the friends I will never forget' and 'Lord if you can't make me skinny – please make my friends fat.'

After the appointment, we review everything the oncologist said and then discuss the lessons we learned during Steph's fight:

believe you will win, one day at a time, and focus on what you can control. Kim thinks the Mayo oncologist is a good fit and promises to follow Steph's example to win her battle. We discuss the next steps and what we can do to support them.

As we drive home, Steph calls and complains of pain in her upper GI Track. Nurse Nana listens to her symptoms and thinks it's probably reflux. Steph's been communicating with a young woman whose colon cancer spread to her stomach and esophagus. That's enough to peak Stephanie's concern. Dr. Baranda orders an upper GI, which confirms esophageal erosion from reflux. Medication is prescribed, and Steph is reassured again that no new cancer is found.

As Steph's life approaches normal again, she reaches out to her mom and me more often for advice. The team approach has served her well, and she likes to get our input. We are happy to help but are cautious not to tell the kids what to do with their lives. I try to end our suggestions by saying, "These are things to consider, but you and Mark are smart and will know what's best for you." That way, they shouldn't feel obligated or judged if they don't follow our suggestions. I treasure the relationship we have and realize it's a blessing to be close friends with both my adult children. I need to make more time for them because nothing is more rewarding.

⚘

life lesson #16

When raising children, learn when to tell them what to do and when to let them make their own decisions. First instincts are to protect them, but they need freedom of choice to learn how to make the good decisions on their own. Making bad decisions helps underscore the weight of responsibility and accountability that comes with freedom of choice. The key is to allow them to learn early from the small mistakes associated with childhood, which can be corrected easier and with less consequence. As age increases the errors can become more significant and life-altering. Help them understand the cause and effect of their actions and other choices they could make. Tell them they can decide, but they will be held responsible for that decision. Guide them to consider options, discuss potential outcomes of each, and let them make their choice. Show them that the easiest choice or the one providing immediate gratification may not be the most rewarding in the long run. If you are supportive and hold them accountable, children learn that they benefit most from the right decisions they make.

Colleen flies to Minnesota to join Kim for tests and her first chemo session at Mayo. Kim's diagnosis is Stage 4 lung cancer. Surgery is not an option based on the number and locations of the tumors. The chemotherapy session proceeds smoothly while Kim gets support from Bill, her two sons, and Colleen. I drive up to join them for the weekend, remembering how much it helps to have an extra set of hands and a shoulder to lean on. Colleen stays another week and then returns home, while Bill and their sons take Kim to her next round of therapy.

Wanting to do something special for Aunt Kim, Stephanie makes her a chemo bag. It contains peppermint gum, mints, lip balm, Benadryl, the Chicken Soup book, and other essentials. Steph fills photo pouches outside the bag with pictures of Kim's family. During chemo, Kim tells the other patients that her niece made it and survived Stage 4 Colon Cancer. Then Kim describes how Steph overcame the odds and that she is her inspiration.

chapter 36

THE NEW YEAR IS A DAY OLD as I watch Caden play with his Christmas toys. It's fascinating to watch his imagination develop. The dinosaurs from Aunt Kim are getting much of his attention. He has favorites but is quick to offer them to me, as an enticement to join in his fun. I ask him if he wants to walk the trails around our home, and he jumps up, takes my hand, and heads to the door. Caden is almost three and loves to explore outdoors. I let him lead to see what catches his eye. A rabbit runs across the trail and Caden follows it into the trees. The furball disappears, but just as quickly, the boy finds treasure. He picks up a stick and swings it around, evaluating its qualities. He shows it to me and then searches until he finds another. Comparing the two pieces of wood, he hands one to me. His thinking is simple: if he wants a stick, I will want one too. We return home an hour later, and he tells Nana about the deer we saw.

The next day Colleen and I drive to Rochester for Aunt Kim's oncology appointment. In the elevator, Colleen runs into a high school classmate, who is now a Mayo physician. "Hey Biff, it's been a while. How are you?" The surprised look and smiles on the medical staff with him, suggest they never heard this nickname before. After briefly summarizing Steph's story and our positive experience here, he tells us that the beauty of Mayo is once here, all you need to do is get on the bus and let them drive. They take care of the details and guide you through the intricacies of needed healthcare. That has been our experience, and we are thankful for the bus showing up.

After Kim completes her tests and scans, we meet with her oncologist. The scans show some tumors have shrunk by 50% and he is excited about their decline. Other tumors haven't changed at all. The doctor is positive, addresses our questions, and then reinforces the importance of Kim focusing on the things she has control over. Exercise, eating healthy, staying positive, and having faith that she will overcome her cancer.

After the appointment, we drive to Bill and Kim's home. We stay positive by focusing on the tumors that are shrinking. They are thankful for everything we do, but honestly, it just feels right to be there. We find that by helping those we love, we also help ourselves. Colleen stays in Minnesota to support her best friend while I return home for work. We have switched places with our good friends, and now it's Stephanie who calls Kim and sends her cards of support each week. She prays Kim's outcome will be as successful as her own.

Steph and Mark host her third survivor party. This celebration of life continues to be a great way to thank everyone for their ongoing support and help. Nana is still in Minnesota, helping Aunt Kim, so I take Caden for the night, which allows everyone at the party to let loose a little. The two of us play hide and seek and have a snack before bedtime. He runs away from me, giggling as I get him into his pajamas. I catch him and dump him into bed as he laughs. He hugs my neck and says, "Papa, you are my favorite." I melt a little because he has never said anything like that before. I immediately decide to change my will and leave everything to him. We cuddle, read a story, and Caden wraps his hand around my pinky finger as we drift off to sleep. The next day I share his comments with absolutely everyone I talk to including my daughter. "Yes, he really said that. No, I didn't coach him. No, he didn't mention your name, only me. Okay, ask him yourself if you don't believe me. Oh, by the way, you're out of the will."

At the end of January, we return to Minnesota for Steph's appointment and to join Aunt Kim for her chemotherapy. Everything goes smoothly for both patients. Steph gets so much strength from these checkups that it's worth the inconvenience of driving home on icy snow packed roads. Stephanie receives a written assessment of her tests a few days later. The radiology report notes a shadow seen in her lung, which starts her heart racing as panic enters her mind. She calls us, but we don't remember any discussion about a shadow at the appointment. Dr. Grothey has given Steph his cell number, so she calls him. He is not concerned about the shadow, which eases her mind. The truth is that no matter how hard Stephanie tries to be positive and have faith, there is always some degree of fear in her mind. The same is true for each member of the team, except Caden.

We celebrate Caden's third birthday with a party at the Varanka's home. They make a dinosaur cake, and we enjoy the time catching up. Teresa has undergone both surgery and chemotherapy and is doing well overall. She struggles with side effects and the worries that every cancer patient lives with, but she is strong and has the help and support of her loving family. The friendship she has with Steph continues to grow during their shared battle to survive.

Steph is excited when she's invited to join other cancer patients at the University of Kansas to create a video. It's produced by KU's Cancer Center and the American Cancer Society to promote Colon Cancer Awareness. Steph wants to do anything she can to help other patients. Over the last three years, she has been in contact with other colon cancer patients, rejoicing in their victories and devastated by their losses. She connects with them, knows their stories, and the families left behind. It reminds her how fragile life is, and she struggles to recover from each death. We want to shield Steph from the lost battles, but she insists it's essential to try and help anyone she can. If she gives them hope or brightens their day, she tells us it's worth it. A few polyps are removed at Steph's annual colonoscopy, but the doctor isn't concerned about them.

Bill, Colleen and I decide Kim needs a distraction and fly to San Francisco for a few days. We see the sights, spend time in wine country, and explore Haight/Ashbury, which was always on the news when we were teenagers in the summer of 69. Kim appreciates the escape never slows down, and no one could tell she was fighting for her life. We return relaxed and refreshed, but Colleen and I can't wait to get back to hold Caden and be with Steph and Mark. We feel the strongest when with our team.

Spring brings rain and twelve pair of Purple Martins to their white and green apartments by the pond. Caden is taking swimming lessons and growing so fast, the kids now refer to him as '*little man.*' He's also using his own rod and reel for fishing. Steph casts out his line, and he retrieves while Nana takes pictures for the fishing board. Caden is patient and so determined that he fishes for an hour straight catching three largemouth bass. Steph wonders how many three-year-olds would do that as she enjoys his excitement and ever-present smile. Everything is going well, but still anxiety creeps in, making her wonder if this could be the last time they fish together. Catching herself, she realizes, 'I have to quit thinking like that. Think positive instead of negative.' It's hard to block out anxiety after the trauma she's been through.

For years I have planned to build a tree house on our land with Scott's help. We picked a tree and basic design but have never found time in our busy schedules to make it happen. I have never built anything in a tree before and decide first to try a smaller project for Caden to enjoy. There is a large tree in our yard that is perfect. It's close to the house so we can watch him play, but far enough away to allow him some freedom.

I mention my plan to Mark, and he asks if he can help. I show him the tree, and the architect takes the idea and runs with it. Thirty minutes later, he shows me a sketch of a platform snuggled into the tree with a railing and ladder. Underneath is a complete list of materials we need to build it. Not only have I found additional help, Mark is reliving his childhood through this project just like I am. The added bonus is that he knows how to build something stable and safe for Caden to play in. That weekend we make our first trip to the lumberyard for materials.

Building the tree deck becomes a bonding experience for Mark and me. It's a great escape from our jobs and provides time together to cultivate our friendship. Mark is the boss, and I am delighted to be his unskilled labor. I love that he takes the lead and I don't have to make any decisions. He tells me where to bolt a support beam into the tree or how long to cut a board, and I feel complete freedom in the moment.

At the end of the day, we drink a beer, plan next steps, and drag out the girls to show them what we've accomplished. They tell us how wonderful, strong, and manly we are, even when they don't understand what we are talking about. Caden, on the other hand, is always excited about the project. He tries to climb the ladders and help with everything. Mark and I relax and talk of the day we will actually sit in the completed structure to enjoy our beer, and how much fun Caden will have playing in it.

Summer arrives, and I'm thankful there haven't been any emergency room visits or new health problems for our daughter. Tonight, we celebrate Steph's third anniversary of staying cancer-free. Steph gets very emotional as she thanks the team for our ironclad support and professes her love for us. She appreciates every little thing we do for her and tells us we have saved her. She doesn't acknowledge how important her own courage and positive example helped us to help her. She is our warrior and has never wavered from the difficult things she's had to fight through, always doing it with grace. By saving herself, she has saved us. We've seen some patients with similar battles refuse to fight or get surgery or have chemo. Others filled with anger and hate that overpowers their will to survive. Steph has made it easy for us to do our part. The theme of this dinner quickly becomes love.

We understand how lucky we are and how close we came to losing everything. We talk about the good and bad memories and are thankful to have lived through them together. Mixed into these deep thoughts, we laugh at the silly things we experienced along the way. Stephanie promises Colleen and me that we will never see the inside of a nursing home; instead, she will care for us in her home. I smile and ask her to put that in writing. Mark says something about keeping us in the unfinished part of their basement with occasional meals and baths until our money runs out. Laughing at ourselves always helps us find balance in our emotions.

Returning to the Mayo Clinic, we complete Steph's tests, meet with Dr. Grothey, and join Aunt Kim at chemotherapy. Some of Kim's tumors still haven't improved, so her oncologist tries new chemo drugs searching for the right combination to destroy them. Along with the distress of not seeing progress in her fight, each drug change brings with it, side effects of increased intensity. Kim has lost her hair and wears various hats, scarves, and wigs, providing new opportunities for her to make a fashion statement and display her sense of humor. She stays brave and complements Stephanie's example. "If Steph can stay positive with the nightmare she went through, so can I." Then she shares a story about Steph doing this or that, and that Kim couldn't believe how determined, brave, or strong she was. Later our families enjoy dinner together, grateful to have so much love and support in our lives.

In the fall Caden attends pre-school at Steph and Mark's church. He enjoys learning new things and interacting with other children. Labor Day weekend Stephanie and Mark purchase a Shih Tzu puppy for Caden and name her Zoey. They bring her over to meet our pets and enjoy the pool. The little black fur mop runs everywhere until exhausted; she curls into a ball and falls asleep. In the water, Caden slips on a step and hits his head on the edge of the pool, causing everyone to spring into action. He cries and has a large bump but seems to be all right. An hour later, while we eat Caden notices Zoey and asks whose dog she is. Concerned about his memory loss, we take him to the children's hospital emergency room. We wait as our concern builds. A pediatrician Colleen worked with in the past sees Caden and determines he has a slight concussion. Everything turns out fine, but we are reminded again how quickly things can change.

In September, I lose my mother to Alzheimer's disease. I feel relief knowing it's a blessing since she suffered for a long time, but she is my mom, I love her and have missed her for a long time. A lifetime of memories floods my mind, along with all the emotions that travel with them. I think about her struggles and the sacrifices she made for our family. She is a beautiful soul and in a better place.

Colleen and I have dealt with more disease and death in the last four years than all the rest of our years combined. That helps fuel my decision to retire after 34 years with my company. It has been a great career and I've learned so much about people and life from my work experience. I also keep a promise I made to myself years earlier; to go out on top. My highly skilled, hard-working sales team is currently number one in the country, and I couldn't be prouder of them.

I'm excited to start the next chapter in my life, taking some time to complete long-planned projects on our property and just catch my breath. I also want to help Aunt Kim and consolidate the journal notes of Stephanie's journey into a book for Caden.

Stephanie questions Dr. Grothey about removing her port since it must be flushed every six weeks if unused. He believes the risk of infection outweighs the benefit of easy access at this point in her recovery and supports the idea, so she has it removed.

By the end of the year, Mark and I complete our tree project. It includes the set of stairs our wives said is a must if we want them to join us. The best part of the project is the respect and friendship Mark and I develop for each other in the process.

chapter 37

CADEN IS MATURE FOR HIS AGE. Maybe it's because his mother's illness keeps him around adults much of the time or that he's adjusted to moving from hospital to hotel to home so often. He rolls with change easier than most. He is gentle and patient with other children, adults, and our pets. He is a giver and always shares his food, toys and anything he has with those around him. At the risk of sounding like every other grandparent, he is special, and I feel blessed he is a part of my life. I am proud of the way Steph and Mark raise Caden. Teaching him the importance of living life to the fullest by enjoying the everyday things around us. Taking a walk in the rain, enjoying a guy's night with Daddy, or cuddling up with Mommy at a living room campout. They reinforce the importance of kindness, giving and love. He gets an abundance of love, and we are grateful he happily gives it right back to us.

As we drive to Rochester, the roads are snow-packed and slow our progress, but we keep moving forward. I am reminded of Dr. Grothey's answer when asked why everyone is so pleasant at Mayo. "We have to be the very best to get anyone to travel to Minnesota in the winter." Growing up in South Dakota, I have ample experience driving snowy roads. We count over two hundred cars in the ditch from an overnight blizzard in Iowa and hope no one was hurt. Steph says, "I don't see any cattle, that's a good sign, isn't it, Dad?" I agree, and a memory returns.

Both cars are filled with essentials as we follow our daughter's Sable back to her college. Stephanie is excited to return after the summer break and is driving slightly over the interstate's 70 mph speed limit in light traffic. Two cars drive in front of Steph, and we trail behind her. Much of Kansas is flat, but as we drive through rolling hills, I see movement ahead in the center median that quickly disappears behind a hill. The movement materializes into a running herd of about twenty cattle, with the last two breaking out of the wide grass median toward our side of the interstate. Neither car in front of Steph reacts as the fifteen-hundred-pound animals run onto the interstate behind them and in front of Stephanie. She breaks hard as the first cow runs in front of her, then turns sharp left to miss the second. Everything moves in slow motion as Stevie Nicks on the radio is drowned out by Colleen's scream. We see the Sable go into a slide, barely missing the second cow broadside. Steph turns hard right out of the slide to avoid the median and loses control as the car changes direction. Her car slips into a 360-degree spin between the vehicles in front of her and us following. I slam on my breaks as the Sable spins across the concrete in front of our car, and then smashes the passenger side into a guardrail. The car rocks back hard as the barrier holds, saving it from plunging down a sixty-foot ravine.

Stephanie releases her seat belt and gets out to assess the damage. She is stunned but unhurt. Colleen and I are traumatized from watching our child hurl through the narrow space not occupied by beef or steel. I'm amazed how well Steph handled the car to avoid hitting the cattle. Steph is more concerned she won't have a car for school. I feel nauseous looking down the ravine and ponder what could have happened. At the bottom, I notice the fence is down and in the process of being replaced as the two cows walk through an opening a hundred yards wide. The rest of the herd trots across the empty interstate down to the pasture below. How can anyone be so stupid as to leave a fence down with cattle present? My anger falls away as I realize how lucky we are that no one has been hurt.

The Mayo Clinic's MRI equipment creates detailed images, which show a shadow not seen before. Dr. Grothey tells us not to worry about it because he believes it's only an apparition. We agree to return in three months to see if it still shows up. I ask Dr. Grothey if we can schedule future appointments in the spring and fall to skip winter driving, and he is happy to do so. BDS is still with us to various degrees, but Stephanie and Colleen worry most, leading me to believe that mothers never ever quit worrying. We return home on bad roads, but it's safer since most cars have been pulled out of the ditches.

Steph and Mark go all out for Caden's fourth birthday party, setting up games in their basement like a church bizarre and placing each of us in charge of one of them. Caden and his friends pin the tail on the donkey, fish behind the curtain for prizes, and play a half dozen other games to their delight. It's a happy day, and Steph feels lucky to be with her family to enjoy it. The truth is she has more fun than anyone else.

Colleen and I join Bill and Kim for dinner in Rochester the night before her oncology appointment. Bill brings up the trip to Europe we had planned before Steph was diagnosed with cancer. He wonders if we can do it soon. Steph is doing so well that we don't think it's a problem for us, so Bill decides to ask the oncologist if Kim can travel.

The oncologist tells us some of the tumors are still not responding. Four different chemo regimens have failed to shrink them, and today he will try a fifth combination. Bill asks about the Europe trip. Without hesitation, the doctor says it's an excellent idea and quickly adds he will alter Kim's chemo schedule so she can build up her energy for the trip. A month later, Kim visits and stays with us for a week. Her energy is depleted by the aggressive chemo cocktail, and the side effects are challenging. Kim is quieter and her mind drifts. She doesn't want to talk about what's happening to her, telling us she came here to escape. She is positive most of the time, and we enjoy reliving adventures from our years together. Like snow skiing for the first time.

Not having much money, the four of us decide to learn as we ski instead of paying for lessons. On my first run, I quickly gain speed shooting straight down the slope and don't know how to slow down or stop. I can only think of one option as I fly toward the parking lot at the bottom of the hill. Seeing a tree off to the side, I think maybe I can grab it to slow down. In my mind, this is easy, just reach over and hug the tree. It seems better than planting my face into the grill of a car. Other than breaking my thumb and looking like a complete idiot, my plan works great. My bride asks, "Why didn't you just sit down?" Yes, that would have been a much better idea if only I had thought of it. The four of us take lessons and then ski every hill in South Dakota, Minnesota, and Wisconsin. It's nothing thing like skiing mountains in Colorado, but we always have a great fun together. Colleen and Kim ski the Blue slopes while Bill and I fall down the Black.

At Steph's yearly colonoscopy, the doctor removes six polyps from the remaining inches of her colon. He stresses the importance of these annual checks to remove polyps before they become cancerous. Two months later we are back at Mayo for Steph's checkup, and for the first time, two of our team members aren't at the appointment. Caden has a cold, so Nana takes him to a bookstore while we see the doctor. Our little guy isn't that sick, but we don't want to expose patients in the waiting room who may have compromised immune systems.

The shadow from the previous MRI is gone. Dr. Grothey is pleased with Steph's progress and changes her checkups to every six months. Then he informs Steph, "If everything continues to go well, we may only have to complete three more visits." Steph answers, "I don't like changing from four to six-month checkups, let alone stopping them altogether. These visits are my check and balance system and keep me from worrying most of the time." Dr. Grothey understands and talks to her like a father, "It will be all right, and your security system isn't going anywhere. We will always be here if you need us." Mayo has become Stephanie's healing place, but who knew it would be so hard to let go of it?

We pick up Nana and Caden, and he can't wait to show us the Disney World books they purchased. Steph and Mark have decided that instead of going somewhere on their own, they want all of us to go to Orlando for their reward trip.. I remember watching the progress of the Florida theme park on Disney's 'Wonderful World of Color' as a child and thinking I would never get to visit it. When we took our children, I found it surprising and even as an adult escaped the everyday world and left inspired. Steph wants to go at the end of January to celebrate Caden's fifth birthday and her being cancer free.

In late April, Colleen and I join Bill and Kim for two weeks in Europe. We are typical tourists and enjoy the sights and food. There are no tight schedules; our only rule is to have fun. Kim is a trooper, and with the help of pain pills, we are amazed at how well she does day after day. We work in naps for her each afternoon to replenish her strength as well as our own. When the two weeks are over, we are tired and ready to return home. Kim tells us it was a trip of a lifetime, and she is so happy to have great friends to share it with.

Returning home, Bill and Kim find an envelope in the mail from Kim's oncologist. The latest tests show the tumors growing again, and they have run out of options. Two weeks later at a relative's graduation in Denver, Kim takes a turn for the worse. After a week in the hospital, Bill flies her back home.

Colleen and I visit Kim frequently for the next two months. The kids join us when they can, and everyone tries to help. Kim's extended team puts together a backyard wedding for Bill and Kim's son. It's a celebration, but Kim's illness is foremost in everyone's mind. She can attend the wedding, and when she dances with her son Ben there isn't a dry eye in the crowd.

Three weeks later we return to say our goodbyes before we lose our dear friend. Kim is surrounded by family at home and passes quietly. She has fought the disease with everything she had, but her cancer had spread too far before it was discovered. Three months earlier we were in Europe having the time of our lives, and now hers is over. We miss her every single day.

Colleen provided nursing care for her mother 24 hours before she passed away. Agnes was at peace and slept most of her last hours. She was unable to speak due to the progression of her disease, but woke up and looked past her family smiling. As Agnes gazed around at the ceiling, her expression was one of excitement and wonder. Colleen watched her mother's face, convinced she was seeing angels. It lasted a few moments before Agnes fell back to sleep and slipped away with a smile and single teardrop on her face. Colleen also helped Kim the night before she passed. At one point, Kim woke up and Colleen asked her if she was at peace and ready. Kim replied, "I'm ready to go." Kim's gaze moved past Colleen as she looked around, smiled, and said one word, "Surprise." I don't know what either woman experienced, but their last moments reflected joy and happiness. As we cope with their absence, that provides us some comfort and hope that they were moving on to a better place..

chapter 38

CADEN ENJOYS EVERYTHING ABOUT THE OUTDOORS, including helping with yard work. Nana and I are cleaning out trees behind the dam when Stephanie and Caden stop by to help. Caden is tall at four years of age and competes with us to drag out the biggest branches. His hard work pays off as he uncovers recently shed deer antlers. He's excited about his treasure and asks me if I can hang them in his bedroom. That's a great idea, but get your mom's permission first. Steph rolls her eyes at me as she tells him it's okay with her. We dump three trailer loads of wood onto the burning pile and head back to the house.

My family rides on the trailer with Max, our German Shepard, as I drive the tractor back to the barn. I notice how well Steph's damaged tree is doing. Mark and I haven't had the heart to cut it down, and now it has captured Steph's instinct to survive. A new branch has taken the lead after the top broke off in an ice storm and the tree is hearty and robust. It doesn't look like your typical oak, but it's thriving just like its namesake.

Caden starts pre-school in the fall and Steph helps out as a teachers aid for a few hours each week. Scott has been working with autistic children since finishing college. In high school, he joined a program to assist disabled students in attending classes. He enjoyed the kids, and it came naturally to him. Parents noticed and several hired Scott to help develop their kid's social skills out of school. He took them to movies and school sporting events. His love of helping others influenced his decision to major in psychology. Scott always dreamed about living in Hawaii and decides there are kids with developmental challenges everywhere, so he moves to Oahu. Colleen and I want him to live his dreams, but would have preferred they weren't so far from home. The happiness we hear during his phone calls makes us feel better, but it's hard to be separated from those you love.

The team meets with Dr. Grothey. The tests are clear, and he tells Steph she will have her last checkup with him in twelve months. Steph replies that she would rather keep seeing him. He smiles and confidently says she will be fine and he wouldn't be doing it if he didn't believe it was best for her. On the drive home, we debrief and reminisce about the challenges we've faced during the past five years. This leads to long periods of silence as we individually relive them. There were many days we were hanging by a thread. We have muscled through some and whimpered through others. Overall, they made us stronger and hopefully we learned some lessons on the way. Our moods brighten as the discussion turns to Steph's reward trip.

January starts with Steph's fifth survivor party and finishes with the team flying to Disney World. The trip is outstanding, and experiencing the park through Caden and Mark's eyes on their first visit is so much fun. Nana and I have our hands full keeping up with the kids. The parks are run smoothly, clean, and staffed with friendly cast members. There really is something magic around Disney, and most things are done incredibly well. That's not an easy task, and it reminds me of Mayo. I wonder why these places are the exception and able to do things the right way consistently. Maybe it merely boils down to the people, their vision, and commitment.

As we stand in line, my phone rings and I see it's a friend from work. I answer, and he informs me he has just been diagnosed with advanced prostate cancer, and the doctors want to operate. I leave the line and walk over to a shady bench while he shares the details. I hear in his voice the fear and uncertainty about what to do next. . Most prostate cancer patients can expect a full recovery, I tell him, but since his cancer is advanced, my advice is to seek out an institution that specializes in prostate research and treatment. This may push the odds of success even higher in his favor. He tells me I am saving his life. It's not true, but I understand. He needs someone to point out the way, and we have traveled this path before. We talk again a week later, and his research uncovered a surgeon considered one of the best for his diagnosis. The appointment is set, he has a plan in place, and his confidence has grown considerably.

Stephanie takes three pictures from our Disney trip, prints them on Valentine's Day cards, and sends them to friends. Underneath the photographs, she writes:

Live every moment – Laugh every day – Love beyond words.
Five Years Cancer Free!
Love, Mark, Steph, and Caden.

On Valentine's Day, Stephanie stops by KU's Cancer Center to visit the staff and drop off a Valentine card. Dr. Baranda isn't there, but the nurses who treated Steph are. They are always happy to see her, but today her presence lifts their spirits because they've had a challenging day. A twenty-two-year-old patient has died of her Colon Cancer. Steph thinks about unfulfilled dreams and loved ones left behind. She becomes quiet, knowing how lucky she is to be alive. Why have I been spared? Most of her medical experts have said her recovery is nothing short of a miracle. She is incredibly thankful but struggles to try to understand why one lives, and one dies.

Today one of Stephanie's dreams becomes a reality. She and Mark walk Caden into school for his first day of kindergarten. All three are filled with excitement and Caden takes to his new surroundings so quickly he doesn't notice when his parents leave. For years Steph has been haunted by thoughts of Mark doing this without her. That's all behind her now, and she's filled with joy. Two things keep running through her mind; miracles do happen, and God is GREAT!

Steph picks Caden up after school and asks him how his day went. He tells her the teacher read to them, he drew pictures, and had fun. He walked over to a boy at recess and asked him to be his friend. The boy said no. Steph's heart broke a little because Caden is sweet and friendly to everyone. As a survivor, she will experience happy times with her son as well as the challenges of parenting.

If you could control the weather, what would it be like? Would you make it 75 degrees with the sun shining every day or would you mix in some rain or snow? Do we appreciate things more when we experience their opposite? Many believe everything we experience has its purpose, even if we don't see it at first. From the doctors and hospitals that weren't a good fit, we have learned what we really needed. We wouldn't have appreciated Steph's medical dream team as much without experiencing their opposite.

We have endured many contrasts along Stephanie's journey;

the sweetness of new life to the fear of impending death; the anxiety of cancer ravishing a loved one to her becoming cancer free; fighting through the challenge of saving a loved one, only to lose another.

Zen proverb: 'Before enlightenment chopping wood carrying water. After enlightenment chopping wood carrying water.' There will always be work and challenges in life, even as we gather wisdom and perspective. It helps us to balance and appreciate the joy in our lives. The soul takes in all experiences. I believe that's one reason we are here. Enlightenment doesn't change the world; it changes the way we see and react to it.

Stephanie was committed to living and seeing Caden start school. It helped her keep going through the tough times and taught her when fighting for your life, it's critical to keep your eye on the prize. She desperately wanted to live and be her son's mom. She now needs to experience every beautiful day and help him through the days with tears. It's all part of the package she so desperately fought for.. During this fight, she never gave in or gave up. Today she has achieved her five-year goal. Stephanie is a cancer survivor. These five simple words are so gratifying. Stephanie, I love you with all my heart. Thank you for saving yourself and all of us with you.

Steph calls me a week later and tells me she is ready to help me document her story for Caden. We have discussed it often over the last two years, but emotionally she hasn't been ready until now. We begin the compilation of our journals the next day. We check the website where she posted her updates, and the counter stands at 7,630 visits. So many friends care and followed her journey.

chapter 39

CADEN IS ONE OF THE TALLEST BOYS in kindergarten and enjoys school. Taking him home afterward, I ask, "What did you learn in class today?

"We learned how to spell our names. Do you want to see me do it?" I nod yes, and he proceeds to draw block letters spelling CADEN. He is proud of his accomplishment and asks, "Do you know how to spell it or should I teach you?"

I laugh telling him, "I know how, but you teach me things every time I'm with you."

Looking puzzled, he asks, "Like what?"

"As you experience things for the first time, your excitement allows me to see them through your eyes as something new. It reminds me to slow down and enjoy life instead of taking it for granted.

After a minute pondering my comment, he asks, "That's good, isn't it?"

"Yes Caden, that's very good."

"I love you, Papa."

"I love you too, Caden." The conversation is the highlight of my day.

The team arrives at Mayo for Steph's last scheduled checkup with Dr. Grothey. Realizing this is the last time for this routine, Steph notices the little details. There is a man directing traffic at the blood draw instead of the usual lady in the blue Mayo Jacket. Each test is started as soon as she arrives like they are waiting for her. The blood test and MRI each require only one stick. Everything occurs as it did on her first Mayo visit. As the mechanics of each test proceed smoothly, her memory plays back previous visits along with their ups and downs. She wonders how many times Aunt Kim had been in the same rooms and is reminded of the necklace.

Stephanie gave Grandma Aggie a gold necklace and cross after she was diagnosed with ALS. She wore it for the remainder of her life. After Agnes's fight was over, Stephanie wore the necklace as a constant reminder of her grandmother. When Kim was diagnosed with cancer, she received the cross and chain from Steph with the following note:

Kim – I know that you are so scared right now. I understand what you are feeling. It's different being the patient. I now know what my family felt when I was diagnosed. I think it's easier being the patient because you don't have as much time to worry.

You have to fight this battle. It's okay to have down days every now and then, but you can't let it last more than one day. You can't just sit and worry, because it's not good for your immune system. You will have bumps in the road, but don't ever forget to keep fighting. Just look at your beautiful granddaughter for inspiration to live. You are strong, and you can win this battle. If you ever need someone to talk to, I am always here. Sometimes it's easier to talk to someone who has been through the same thing. Kim, I love you, and you are so special to me. You will win.

This is the necklace that I gave to Grandma Aggie. I wore it throughout chemo and want you to wear it now. When you feel down, look at the necklace, and it will help bring happy memories back to you. I love you always. Steph

Stephanie still wears the necklace each day and believes that occasionally Aggie and Kim drop by to watch over her.

After the testing is complete, Mark and his wife discuss how things have changed over the last five years. One thing that hasn't changed is her team of five, who joined Steph on every step of her journey. Technically there are six of us since Lambie is ever-present. We walk to the Italian restaurant for a celebration dinner and are seated at the same table used on our first visit. The food is excellent, but we are unsettled, and the celebration feels premature since we don't have the test results yet.

Stephanie wakes up anxious the next morning and can't shake her fear. She is scared of the unknown and begins playing 'what if.' Her mind spins as she thinks of Caden and surgery and chemo and school, and God knows what else. Emotions build and add to memories of Kim, which places our team on edge. Steph doesn't eat breakfast and is quiet until we drive into Mayo's parking garage, when her nerves overtake her and she begins to cry. Nana quietly talks to her daughter and settles her down as we walk to the appointment.

It's quiet in the exam room, and BDS sits with us while we wait. Steph tells us she's sad it's her last visit, but happy to move on with her life. Dr. Grothey walks in the door along with another physician. Mark fears something is wrong, and the second doctor is a surgical consultant. Dr. Grothey smiles and tells us. "I knew you would all be here together." He looks into Stephanie's eyes, shakes her hand, and tells her, "Everything looks good." Then he introduces his guest as a visiting physician from Canada, and we all breathe a sigh of relief.

Dr. Grothey can't believe it has been twelve months since our last visit and comments on how things have changed since our first visit. He has watched Caden grow up during our seventeen trips over the previous five years. Steph smiles and tells him, "You can measure time by the toys Caden played with in these exam rooms. From the yellow giraffe with orange spots that he cut his teeth on, to the cars he rolled on the floor, to the books we read him. There was the time he played with your stethoscope, and now he's playing games on Mark's phone."

Dr. Grothey tells Stephanie, "I am releasing you, and you don't have to come back for any more checkups."

"I don't really like that." She answers.

He laughs, telling her, "I don't really like it either." The bond that has grown between this physician and his patient is evident. The release is bittersweet and Steph's eyes well up. The doctor is nostalgic as they talk about the past events of her journey. He takes his time enjoying the moment, and we sense he isn't quite ready to let go. I think about the patients he treats that never get released and the toll it must take on him.

The good doctor talks to Steph about diet and exercise and sites a current Canadian study to support his direction. He reminds her to get a colonoscopy every year to remove new polyps because her risk of the colon cancer returning is much higher than her getting a new type of cancer. He suggests Steph take a small dose of aspirin each day, as preliminary evidence suggests it may slow polyp growth. He adds, "Eat right and exercise, and you can live another 40, 50 or 60 years." Steph asks how often she needs to get tests done in Kansas City, and he tells her she doesn't need to because she is cured. We are so used to scheduling tests, this takes us all by surprise.

I tell the doctor that we've started writing a journal to Caden about Stephanie's experience, and he will be portrayed favorably. Shunning the compliment, he stresses he was only a small part of her survival, telling us that family, ongoing support and her belief she would win her battle were the most critical factors. Dr. Grothey is positive about the writing and tells me, "So many patients need hope. They would all benefit from hearing Stephanie's story of survival."

The doctor is genuinely happy and a little reluctant to end our time together. He smiles at Stephanie and tells her, "Go out and live your life." As he rises from his chair, Steph jumps up and hugs him. She lingers, not wanting to let go. Then Nana gets a hug, and we thank him for all he has done for us. We walk out of the exam room, and Stephanie releases her emotions with a few tears. Nana holds Caden's hand and he asks, "Why is Mommy crying?" Nana tells him, "It's all right Sweetheart. Mommy is happy, and those are tears of joy."

By the time we enter the waiting room, the tears are gone, and we all wear smiles. Looking into the eyes of patients still waiting for their appointments, we are greeted by smiles from those who realize we received good news. Others are lost in worry, reminding us that everyone has a story and theirs are still playing out. I feel guilty being so happy while others still suffer and say a prayer for them as we walk to the elevators. Then I thank God over and over again for Steph's life.

Before we leave the ninth floor of the Gonda building, Steph walks over to the wall of windows that overlook Mayo's Plummer building across the street. She tells Caden, "You loved to play 'I Spy' here because you could see so many things from this high up." Nana asks him, "Do you remember seeing your first snowflakes out this window, while we waited for Mommy's appointment?" Caden nods yes and memories flood each of our minds. The first trip with an over-packed stroller to now when we hardly have anything with us. Mayo has genuinely been a healing place for us. Familiar buildings, smiling faces, piano playing in the atrium, volunteers in blue jackets, and the favorite places we ate. We are reluctant to leave and want to take one more look around, but with the fast-paced life everyone has, that isn't in the cards. Nana and I are headed to St. Paul to pick up Grandpa Bill and move him to Kansas City while Caden, Mark, and Steph drive home. We feel like we are breaking ties with an old friend and decide 'the team' will come back for a visit someday. Not something urgent or scary, just a visit to an old friend.

As we leave the building, Steph tells me, "After all that I have been through, I can't believe Dr. Grothey's advice was simply to go out and live my life. Wow!"

I ask my daughter, "If given the choice of having cancer or not, what would you choose?"

She answers without hesitation, "I would have cancer because the experience helped shape me into who I am today." The crisis has made Stephanie stronger, much like a tree gaining strength by flexing and bending with the wind. I guess what the German philosopher Friedrich Nietzsche said is true, "That what does not kill us, makes us stronger."

Stephanie has won her battle with cancer and now carries the scars to prove it. She is still hypersensitive to the cold and will live with other reminders for the rest of her life. Steph never complains and quickly tells us how lucky she is, and these reminders are just an inconvenience. She is alive and loves being a mom, wife, and daughter. She is invested in helping her son live his life to the fullest. Time is a great healer. Even the anxiety over Steph's health fades as we lose ourselves in daily life. It will never completely disappear, what parent doesn't worry, but it no longer rules our lives.

As Caden grows up, Steph even overcomes her fear of loud noises. On the fourth of July she helps her son light Black Snakes, then Smoke Bombs, and eventually Lady Fingers. When I mention it, she shares my surprise and tells me she helped Caden so he wouldn't get hurt and the fear must have just gone away. "I guess my kiddo cured me."

Last winter a deer nibbled the top off the leading branch of Caden's Sunset Maple. The tree responds by growing two branches skyward creating a double trunk. As I decide which one to remove I smile, realizing that Caden's tree is now shaped like his mother's oak in our front yard. It doesn't strike me as a coincidence, so who am I to change nature's plan.

The original Lambie still rests in Caden's room. Nana and I have the second one perched on the headboard in our bedroom. They remind us of a miracle at the start and end of each day. It turns out they accomplish what I had hoped for that day I grasped at straws; the two lambs help keep our family linked together every day.

chapter 40

STEPHANIE AND I WROTE *A Journal to Caden* for a year. The story is in journal form and a gift to Caden. The writing experience with my daughter was beautiful, emotional, and exhausting. We were surprised how much baggage we still carried around. Difficult, terrible things happened so fast, we didn't have time to process them; we just kept moving. Steph and I dealt with them together. Here are our last journal entries to Caden:

mommies journal - final entry

My angel boy, I have always believed that everything happens for a reason. As I look back over the past five years, everything in my life had a purpose. When Daddy and I found out we were expecting a baby, we felt so blessed. Little did we know what an extraordinary miracle we were given and also at the perfect time. Caden, I believe that you were brought into this world to save my life. You not only helped us find my cancer, but you helped me fight it with all I had. The first thought I had when I was told I had cancer was, do I need to make videotapes for you to remember me. As time went on, I realized that I didn't, because I was going to win this fight and see my little boy grow up. Every morning I would get up and look into your precious brown eyes and know that I had to be here to raise you.

I started living my life one day at a time, took in everything around me, and realized that getting to hold you is such a precious gift. Instead of focusing on everything happening to me, I concentrated on what was important to me. I didn't know how much time I had, but understood I needed to make every single moment count. You and Daddy and our family are everything to me. I live for the love of all of you.

Love, Mommy

✤

papa's journal - final entry

Dearest Caden. Thank you for your smiles, giggles, and unconditional love that stopped time for precious moments. They provided us relief and hope to recharge our souls before returning to your mother's fight. I can't tell you how many days you kept us moving forward.

In the end, it's the people in your life that determine your happiness. Loved ones help you survive the tough times and celebrate the good times. Live your life to the fullest, like a poster I had in college read, 'Live for Today, Plan for Tomorrow, and Party Tonight.'

Lastly, Caden, this story is not only about love, but also about hope, belief and courage. Each of us faces challenges in our lives, and some will seem impossible. Take one day at a time and do what you can to move forward. Each time you overcome a challenge, celebrate it, which will, in turn build your belief. When you believe, you create hope, and when you have hope, your courage grows. My original purpose in journaling your mother's story was to capture her spirit, in case you never had the opportunity to know her. My words cannot express how thrilled we all are that now you have found this out for yourself. You and your mother are best friends.

Everyone has a story, and now you know your mother's. I hope yours will be filled with love, joy, and people to share it with. I love you and remember, you are also my favorite!

Love, Papa

The teacher, architect, nurse, sales manager, and child, send you love, hope, and good health. Like the good doctor said, "Go out and live your life!"

✿

Postscript: 7/7/2022
Stephanie's social media entry:

Today, I celebrate 16 years of being cancer free! I am so blessed and thankful to be here today, living my life. Even through the ups and downs in life, I always take time to stop, count my blessings, and enjoy the little things that make this world a beautiful place. A huge thank you to God for allowing me to continue my journey with those I love! Thank you Mark Pfeil, Caden, Mike Schnabel, Colleen Schnabel, and Xavier

Michael. I couldn't have done it without you all. You were my TEAM, my rock, my voice of reason, my happiness and laughter, and the ones holding my hand every step. I couldn't have done this without you! Also, a huge thank you to my nurses, doctors, friends, and extended family for all your love and support during the tough times and throughout the years. I love you all! Hug your family tight tonight, and never take a minute for granted. Much love! Steph.

epilogue

I BELIEVE STEPHANIE'S STORY IS A MIRACLE, created by a power greater than us. Unfortunately, we also learned that not all stories end that way. Steph knows of five people in her high school graduating class of less than 250 who battled colorectal cancer. It was discovered in various stages and two have died. These are the ones she is aware of, there may be more.

Sometimes people do everything in their ability to fight, and it still isn't enough. I don't know why some overcome it, and others don't. What I do know is that we did everything in our power to fight Stephanie's cancer, including having faith in something greater than ourselves. I thank God every day for this miracle. I also know that if we had lost her, it would have been devastating. I don't understand how people recover from that kind of loss and defeat. A starting point may be in knowing you did everything in your power to help.

Everyone has a story and can share some overwhelming challenges experienced in their extended family. One may be more significant than another, and some are life threatening. Remember that it helps if you keep a positive attitude, take one day at a time, and believe you will overcome your challenge. It will help you grow as a person if you try to learn something from it. You may learn patience, humility, perspective, or that your faith is stronger than you thought it could be. If you expect others to understand and respect your story, it's a good practice to understand and respect theirs.

The last five years have changed each member of our team. Most of it is positive. The emotional roller coaster fused us into a closer, stronger family than we were before. I can't believe how strong our faith has been, or when things were the darkest, how we received what we needed. One of our biggest blessings was the love and support we found in our team and everyone around us. What about the other blessings that came into our lives? Finding the doctors and hospitals with the right fit, the jet and condo showing up just when we needed them, twice heading to the ER just in time to save Steph's life, and all the rest. Each of us truly believes that throughout this ordeal something bigger than ourselves provided what we needed most.. Our belief has grown from this experience.

If you are fighting a medical challenge, put together a comprehensive plan to overcome it, because action helps overcome worry. Here are some things we learned.

love
- Let people help you and love them for it.
- Gather a loving team around you to help.
- Keep those you love close to you and show them your love.

- Live your life each day and be generous with your hugs, especially with your children.
- Practice forgiveness for others as well as yourself.
- Ask for help when you need it and help others when you can.
- Reach out to survivors for their insight and learn from their experience.

disease

- Seek out medical experts that are the right fit for your illness and for you.
- Don't take the path of least resistance, do what needs to be done.
- The more aggressive or unusual the disease, the more you need the expertise from a medical center that specializes in it.
- Own your disease, take the responsibility to understand it, and become your own advocate to overcome it.
- Ask questions to understand, even if you are afraid to hear the answers. The more you know, the more likely you are to overcome it.
- Get on the Bus. Do what your experts tell you and take what they prescribe, but remember medicine is only part of the cure. Your faith, belief, hope, and support are just as important.
- Exercise and eat healthy if you can, but eat something, even if it's Cap'n Crunch.

- If everyone would exercise, eat healthily, refrain from smoking, drinking, drugs, or overeating, most of the pharmaceutical companies wouldn't be needed, and most people would feel great.

control what you can control

- Make a commitment to your team to do everything in your power to win your battle and ask them to do the same.
- Be accountable for your own positive attitude. Remind yourself to keep moving forward and never quit trying.
- Define your goals, develop a plan of attack to win your battle, and reward your achievements.
- Take one day at a time and celebrate your successes, no matter how small.
- Stay positive by finding the good in things, but realize you may not see it clearly until you look back on it with 20/20 hindsight.
- Surround yourself with positive people, pictures, and music that motivate you.
- Keep your sense of humor, enjoy funny books and movies, and laugh as often as you can.
- When you lose your cool – and you will – apologize, and make it right if you can. Then focus on doing better in the future instead of feeling guilty about the past.

faith/belief

- Believe in yourself, your plan, and a higher life force working for you.
- Have faith you will win your battle and keep your eye on the prize.
- Keep hope in your heart and never, ever give up.
- Ask for divine help and guidance when you need it. Ask God to take the wheel.
- Fight with everything you have to win and don't accept failure as an option.
- Try to be a role model and inspire others. What you give will come back to you many times over.
- Make a list of the good things in your life and give thanks every day.
- Meditate and find peace and your true self in the silence.

caregivers

- Create a nurturing environment for the patient with love, a positive attitude, and the things they enjoy (flowers, music, movies, humor, friends, and family).
- Practice patience, understanding, and acceptance with your patient.
- Place the patient first but pay attention to your own needs. Carve out personal time with exercise, meditation, walks, or a movie.
- Bring in reinforcements when needed.

acknowledgments

God, thank you for saving my daughter's life and providing solutions during the darkest time in our lives. Thank you for guiding our lives and helping in everything we do. Thank you for your love and all the blessing you shower down on us.

Colleen, thank you for a lifetime of love. You are my soul mate and the exclamation point in my life. For more than fifty years, we have shared life's joys and challenges. Nothing has been too big to handle as long as we did it together. We made our dreams come true.

Stephanie, thank you for your love, for never giving up, and for helping me document your story for Caden. I cherish the close friendship we share. We continue to be each other's confidant and sounding

board as we walk through life together. I am so
proud of you and you will always be Daddy's Girl.

Mark, thank you for being a gentle bear and adding
height to our gene pool. You have my love, respect,
and friendship. You are a great husband, dad and
son-in-law. You always do the right thing and have
made our loving family stronger. Thank you for
loving my baby girl and grandson, as you promised
you would.

Caden, thank you for sharing your love and life with
Nana and me. You are a very special part of my life
and I am proud of the way you practice your faith
each day and the compassion you show to others.
You are mature and wise beyond your years. There
seems to be nothing you don't achieve when you
put your mind to it. Dream big, take action, and
make your dreams come true.

Scott, you are the free spirit in our family. Your
minimalist life focuses on sharing love, joy, and
happiness. I am proud that you have found purpose
in helping and protecting those around you. You
have always helped others in need and done the
right thing.

We are forever indebted to all the doctors, nurses, and health-care professionals who joined in Stephanie's fight. We love you for the care and hope you provide everyone, especially those fighting for their lives. Thank you to:

Dr. Bruce Graham, Dr. Christopher Lynch, Dr. Sheri Martin, and the compassionate nurses at Shawnee Mission Medical Center who gave us our first glimpse of hope.

Dr. Teresa Varanka, for your friendship, love, and keeping us afloat in rocky waters.

Dr. Joaquina Baranda, the nurturing chemotherapy team at KU MedWest, and the great staff at The University of Kansas Medical Center for putting us on the path to recovery.

Dr. Axel Growthy, Dr. Florencia Que, and compassionate staff at The Mayo Clinic and St. Mary's Hospital. You completed our dream team and took us to the next level of hope and gratitude.

To Stephanie's special angels, we treasure you in our lives. You helped carry us through the worst days of our lives. Tommy Tullo, Kim & Bill Charron, Kristen Kief, Heather (Charron) Hedges, Pat Hansen, Bobbie Olson, and Jeanne Pfeil. Thank you to Steph and Mark's incredible neighbors and all our friends who gave so much time and effort to support her quest.

To Stan & Linda Kolb, thank you for a lifetime of friendship, laughter, and support. In addition, we thank Jack & Kathy Schnabel and Mike & Alice Charron for your generosity and support. We love you.

A very special thank you to my agent and publisher, Maryann Karinch, for believing in this story and me. You helped me take *A Journal to Caden* and transform it into *Daddy's Girl.* Thank you for taking a chance on me and guiding a first-time author through the book world maze. I love how you live your life with enthusiasm, optimism, and fearlessness. Thank you to the entire team at Armin Lear Publishing for your gentle guidance.

I am grateful to my publicist, Fauzia Burke, for your enthusiasm, guidance, and assistance in getting this book noticed in a noisy world. Your help in creating my website, arranging my events, and providing honest feedback have been invaluable.

I never dreamed that the picture I snapped of Stephanie in the backyard sandbox of our first home would find its way to a book cover. Thanks to Albatross Book Co. for their cover design and for making it compelling.

Each of our employers was incredibly supportive. Bristol Myers Squibb, Shawnee Mission Pediatrics, Olathe Public Schools, and Heofer Wysocki Architects assisted us with guidance, time off, and a jet. Thank you to the wonderful friends we worked with for all your support.

To the unnamed nurses, staff, and friends who went above and beyond anything we could wish for, you make the world a better place. Thank you from the bottom of our hearts.

about the author

MICHAEL SCHNABEL'S writing developed during thirty years of creating training, development, and motivational programs for Bristol-Myers Squibb. He learned to write presentations that taught by telling a story, flowed logically, and held his audiences' attention. His successful sales career transitioned into management, training, and development, which are the subjects of future books.

His expertise in writing *Daddy's Girl* came from experiencing the story firsthand with his family and recording it in daily journal entries.

A graduate of Northern State University, Michael lives in Overland Park, Kansas with his wife, and when not spending time with family, you can find him tending to his 26-acre tree farm. *Daddy's Girl* is his first book.

CPSIA information can be obtained
at www.ICGtesting.com
Printed in the USA
BVHW040308150323
660406BV00007B/413